AN ITALIAN
FAMILY
COOKBOOK

TONY CASILLO

AN ITALIAN
FAMILY
COOKBOOK

A Treasure Trove of Traditional Recipes and
Cooking Advice Handed Down and Enjoyed
over the Generations

CARROLL & BROWN PUBLISHERS LIMITED

For the mother of my daughters

First published in the United Kingdom by

Carroll & Brown Publishers Limited
20 Lonsdale Road
London NW6 6RD

Editor Carla Masson
Managing Art Editor Gilda Pacitti
Photography David Murray, Jules Selmes
and Karen Thomas

Text and family photographs
© Tony Casillo 2003
Illustrations and compilation
© Carroll & Brown Limited 2003

A CIP catalogue record for this book is available from
the British Library

ISBN 1 903258 42 1

10987654321

Reproduced by Colourscan
Printed and bound in India by Ajanta

CONTENTS

Dear Gina and Christina

Here is the book I promised you. When you lived with your mom and me, there was no need for it; you were regaled daily with recipes and hints. In return, you entertained us with your successes and with what was happening in your lives because I would insist on our sharing at least one meal together. It wasn't really a pain, was it? We had a lot of fun!

When you set up your own households, I resolved to write down, in one place, all the recipes that we cooked together so that you would have the formulas—not only for the family feasts, but, more important, to treat yourselves to decent, wholesome food. I know you are now busy with careers and with life, and the temptation is great to stop off at a fast-food restaurant or at the supermarket for a frozen meal. But I encourage you to resist those impulses and treat yourself better. It doesn't take any longer to make a plate of spaghetti. Remember Zia Antonietta in Naples? She worked, and for lunch she had a sandwich or occasionally a pizza from the pizzeria. But at night, no matter how late it was, she had a hot cooked meal. And remember how quickly it was prepared and how delicious it was? Do the same for yourselves. (Maybe you can try Mom's trick to motivate yourselves—you know how she would fry the garlic just before I walked in the door just to get me to cook supper!)

Along with writing down family recipes, I also set myself another task. I am one of the few in the family who actually remembers what Italy was like "in the olden days when I was young," as you so eloquently phrase it. It's Grandma Casillo, Grandma Simone, and I who still remember all those people in the funny little pictures. It would be a shame to lose even a little bit of that history, so I have included what I remember of the family stories behind the photographs, for your sakes and for those of my future grandchildren.

It's no coincidence that a lot of the photos have families around the table. You well know that our birthdays, Christmases, Easters, Thanksgivings and anniversaries are marked with a feast. We may occasionally go out to dinner on a birthday, but there is also a dinner or a lunch where the cake and the candles show up. Life moves up and down but it always moves—faster as you get older. Now and again we need to mark the passage of time by remembering not only the birthdays, anniversaries and holidays, but births, baptisms, weddings, graduations and, sadly, funerals too. Each occasion is a feast, marked by our attendance, at which we renew family bonds and celebrate ourselves and our futures. That's the way it was—and still is—at Grandma Casillo's and Grandma Simone's.

You've been in Naples, and although my grandparents were no longer there, we feasted and drank with uncles, aunts and cousins, as in days gone by. In my grandfather's time, preparation for Christmas and New Year's went on for weeks—I remember Grandma Casillo, after the war, hoarding eggs in a dresser drawer to have enough for the Easter cake. So when you think that cooking or baking a cake for a special occasion is too much to ask, ask yourself what it is you are so busy with, compared to Grandma who had six children, no running water and no washing machine!

Even though I get the credit, this book would not have been possible without your mother. I cooked and Mom presented it. I wrote it, but it was Mom who corrected it and made it legible. If I put a nice dish on the table, it was Mom who insisted on the flowers, the nice place settings, the candles and the fire in the grate. I might have made it taste good, but Mom is the one who made it elegant and an experience to cherish.

So, Gina and Christina, you have the blueprint. You have the training. Now, you have the manual. Use it and teach your future children by example.

Love
Dad

Once upon a time in America...

I come from a long line of wanderers. My father's father, Antonio, emigrated from Italy to America around 1915, where he was followed by my grandmother, Maria, and their firstborn, my Uncle Nick. My father, Francesco (Frank or Ciccio), and his brothers Pasquale (Uncle Pat) and Salvatore (Uncle Sam) and sisters Carmela, Antonietta and Maria (Aunts Carm, Tettella and Maria) were born in America, but during the Depression they returned with my grandfather to Italy. So my father, uncles and aunts had to learn Italian as a foreign language and become acclimatised to their new country.

My mother's folks, on the other hand, didn't stray far from Naples. There was my Grandfather Carmine, his wife, Maria (who died before I was born), Luigi (Zio Giggino), Anna (Zia Nina), Nunzio (Zio Nunzio), my mother (Assunta, or Grandma Casillo), Antonietta (Zia Antonietta), Ida (who died when I was little) and Giuseppe (Zio Geppino). They were, however, displaced by the Allied bombing during the war and were forced to move to a small town at the foot of Mount Vesuvius. They ended up in a little neighbourhood called Casilli, where, by some coincidence, nearly everyone was named Casillo. There my parents met, married, and produced six children, starting with me, then Carmine, Alessandro, Maria, Adriana and the last, Francesco Jr., who was born in Buffalo.

Early days in Italy

We lived in San Giuseppe Vesuviano, San Giovanni a Teduccio (a suburb of Naples), Naples itself, and Tavarnuzze, a little village outside Florence, where by another coincidence, my father was engaged in building a cemetery for the Allied war dead. The really good part about Italy at this time was that it was at least 50 years, and in places 100 years, behind the rest of the world, so I feel that I started life in Victorian times and lived through several generations.

I went to school in Italy and was a good student until I hit Latin and algebra, which caused me to quit school and take a full-time job at the age of 12 for the princely wage of 50 cents a week. It was real man stuff. At the end of the week, I ran home and handed over my wages to my mother. Occasionally, I would borrow back 5 cents to see some sword-and-sandal epic at the Cinema Vesuvio.

Wandering the streets of Naples was another pastime. The city—crumbling, smelly, theatrical, and baroque—was filled with incredible fish and vegetable markets, delicatessens, butchers, bakers, *pizzerie, rosticcerie*, drink stands, melon vendors and *baccalà* sellers. Each morning, itinerant vendors would make the rounds, announcing themselves by singing their wares. Housewives would yell down their orders and lower baskets on ropes from their tenement perches.

From Italy to America—again!

Eventually all of my uncles and aunts re-emigrated to America; our family was the last to follow, ending up in Buffalo, New York, in 1959. This time we had to learn English as a foreign language. There I resumed my school career, which took off with prizes and scholarships and so forth, eventually leading me to study mechanical engineering at Union College in Schenectady, New York. While I was still at school, I had to look after my younger siblings, cooking and caring for them, since times were tough and both parents had to work to feed and clothe the lot of us. So I got lots of practice cooking and parenting from an early age.

In Schenectady, a friend of mine had a wife who had a friend who became my blind date at a party weekend, and later my wife. That was Carol Simone. Her family was of Italian origin from Castellana Grotte, near Bari in Puglia, where, by some strange coincidence, there are a lot of people named Simone. My wife's family has lived for a half century in a village called Croton-on-Hudson, a town just north of New York City, which by another coincidence is a stone's throw from Pleasantville, New York—home of Reader's Digest, the U.S. publisher of this book. So we met in the middle, you see.

Still wandering

On Carol's side, her maternal grandfather, Natale (Christmas) and his wife, Amelia, had three daughters, Florence Rose (Grandma Flo, or Grandma Simone), Thelma (Aunt Thelma) and Antoinette (Aunt Chickie). Her paternal grandfather had a penchant for naming his children after American patriots like Theodore Roosevelt (Grandpa Theodore Simone) and George Washington (Uncle George), or Italian patriots like Pietro Mazzini (Uncle Peter), or men of letters like Dante. The girls were spared the worst of this treatment but didn't escape entirely. They were given alliterative nicknames to compensate: Vittoria Italia (Aunt Viccie), Caterina Bellina (Aunt Mimi), Gloria (Aunt GoGo) and Flora (Aunt FoFo).

Carol and I married in 1968 and moved to Connecticut, where our first daughter, Gina Carol, was born on Christmas Eve. My second job took us back to Schenectady, where our second daughter, Christina Francesca, was born. Work took the four of us to Jeannette, Pennsylvania, by way of Horseheads, New York, where we all had a great time until one day in 1977 when my boss came in and asked if I would do a little job for the company in London. (Ontario? No, England!) Being a slow worker, I am still there. But it was and is great

because, besides re-establishing our Italian roots, this move has taken us all over Europe, the Middle East, and the Far East.

In 1997, Christina, the last daughter at home, moved into her own apartment. As Gina did, she would regularly ask me how to make this or that. I said I should write it down for her. In 1998, Christina moved to San Francisco, so I said I'd better get busy writing. At the same time, I thought I'd better preserve the family photos and note down some stories before the sources for those stories disappeared, long may they live. Then Gina set a wedding date, so once again I said I'd better get busy writing. And I did, and here we are. Gina is now married to Ashley, and they have given us the wondrous gift of a grandson, Nicolas, and Christina has married Neill. Job done? Don't you believe it. We're only getting started.

Good food can be fast

My forebears, both country and city branches, worked all day. They came home to cook their evening meals; they felt entitled to one good meal a day. But they really didn't want to wait all night, so most Italian dishes are very quick to prepare. Don't cheat yourself out of good food because you think you don't have any time. Of course, there are dishes and times when a more elaborate preparation is required. Fancy cooking is for weekends and special occasions. And maybe it isn't better, only fancier. If you enjoy it, then you will take more time with it. It's only natural.

It's all in the choosing

Fresh, tasty food does not have to cost a lot. Just make sure that you are getting the freshest ingredients that can be had. Very good food can be made from humble ingredients— humble, not poor quality. The peasant, earthy cuisine, *cucina povera,* has suddenly been rediscovered by the descendants of peasants and sold in chic restaurants for a peasant's monthly wage. On a limited budget, you can still select good dishes that use economical ingredients, which can be a real treat when they are properly prepared.

Follow the seasons

The best combination of taste and economy follows the seasons. Everyone knows you have to eat corn on the cob freshly picked or the natural sugar turns to starch, but this principle holds true for any fruit, vegetable, meat, or fish.

The first product of the season is always quite pricey, but you will find that within days or weeks, the price usually drops as supplies increase. Air transport now brings us food from all over the world, wherever it is currently in season. Nonetheless the product is never as good as when it is picked fresh and eaten right away. Because they have to travel, fruits and vegetables are often picked unripe, and when they arrive, they suffer from jet lag.

Nature provides its own sell-by date—yellow parsley, flaccid cucumbers, soft aubergines, or flabby peppers are nature's way of telling you to throw them out. In Mediterranean countries fruit is sold with leaves still attached because leaves wilt long before the fruit. Courgettes, for example, are sold with the flower still attached. The flower may wilt in a few days while the fruit goes on for weeks. But what a difference in taste between a fresh courgette and one mummified on the supermarket shelf. For years I bought radicchio del Treviso that was about the size of a tennis ball from a local supermarket. Not until I saw radicchio in France the size of a cabbage did I realise that my favourite produce manager had been peeling off layers of leaves as they wilted until my mini radicchio was left.

I have an aesthetic aversion to this out-of-proper-season supply. It not only fails to mark the seasons but it also eliminates the anticipation of a treat to come. There is a cycle to the year marked by nature and signified by the varying bounties of the earth on our table. There is a progression to seasonal products that links us to the past and provides promise for the future. All of this is lost with year-round availability.

However and whatever you cook—enjoy!

Some people cook with flourishes of this and dashes of that, never looking at a recipe. Others are like research chemists in the way they dissect a recipe and use calibrated scales to measure ingredients. Whichever kind of cook you are, it doesn't matter. Bear in mind that although I have given exact measurements in this book, recipes are by nature imprecise. My philosophy is that you can't foresee all of the possible variations in the basic ingredients—after all, how big is a medium-sized onion or tomato? Discrepancies in the size and taste of various ingredients are what makes a recipe exciting and different each time you make it. It could be on the sour side and require sweetening, or be dry and need the addition of liquid. With practice you can acquire a sensitivity that will allow you to correct an unexpected situation.

This is a cookbook to restore your confidence in the kitchen. In truth, it's easy to eat well if you want to. Good cooking does not need to be complicated or expensive.

I hope you enjoy these recipes as much as my family and I have. This collection represents the dishes our family has enjoyed the most over the years.

1 APPETISERS, SALADS AND SOUPS

This selection of much-loved family recipes is designed to stimulate the appetite for the rest of the meal. The wide selection means there's something here for both everyday meals and for entertaining.

APPETISERS

PARSLEY

I much prefer to use the flat-leaf variety of parsley in dishes because it is more flavourful and stands up better to heat. The curly type is fine for garnishing.

Crostini

Crostini is a traditional dish made in Tuscan homes and offered in almost every restaurant, each of which uses a different recipe. The Tuscan custom is not to add salt to the bread dough, which can be odd on first tasting, but you can use ordinary everyday salted bread. This recipe is the one I like, and it's very nice with a glass of Chianti Riserva.

> 25g butter
>
> 280g chicken livers, cleaned and minced
>
> 2 tablespoons chopped flat-leaf parsley
>
> 2 anchovy fillets in oil, mashed with a fork
>
> 1½ teaspoons plain flour
>
> 2–3 tablespoons chicken stock or water
>
> Freshly ground black pepper
>
> 12 slices Italian bread, about 1cm thick
>
> 2 tablespoons fresh lemon juice

Melt the butter in a large frying pan over medium-high heat. Add the chicken livers and parsley and sauté until the chicken livers are just pale pink, about 5 minutes. Stir in the anchovies and flour and continue sautéing 2 minutes longer. Add the stock and pepper, to taste, reduce the heat to medium-low, and simmer 8 minutes, stirring occasionally. Meanwhile, heat the grill to high. Grill the bread 10cm from the heat until lightly toasted on both sides. Remove the frying pan from the heat and stir in the lemon juice. Spread the chicken-liver mixture on the hot toast. *Makes 12.*

VARIATION

Fried Bread Base The chicken-liver mixture also tastes good spread on bread that has been fried in olive oil. Heat 5mm olive oil in a large frying pan over medium heat until it is shimmering. Add as many bread slices as will fit in a single layer and fry until crisp on the bottom, then turn over and fry the other side until golden, about 5 minutes in total. Remove the bread from the pan and drain on paper towels. Continue frying the bread in batches until all the slices are crisp and golden, adding more oil to the pan, if necessary.

Bruschetta

I am almost embarrassed to give such a simple recipe, but simple is often best. You can also toast the bread outdoors on a barbecue, which is nice in the summertime. Incidentally, in Italian, this is pronounced brus–KET-ta.

12 slices crusty Italian bread, about 1cm thick
2 garlic cloves
Olive oil for drizzling
Salt and freshly ground black pepper

Preheat the grill to high. Grill the bread 10cm from the heat, turning once to lightly toast on both sides. Rub the garlic clove over one surface of each slice of toast. Drizzle with olive oil and season to taste. Return to the grill and continue toasting until each slice is golden. *Makes 12.*

VARIATIONS

Cheese and Tomato Topping After seasoning and before the second toasting, top each slice with a thin slice of mozzarella and a tomato slice.

Tapenade Topping Spread olive paste on one side of the toasts after the second toasting.

Anchovy Topping Place an anchovy fillet on top of each toast after the second toasting.

Tomato Flavour Toast the bread and rub with garlic, as above. Cut a tomato in half and rub on the bread. Season to taste, drizzle with oil and toast for a second time.

"As children we would toast the bread for bruschetta over an open fire in a brazier, which also happened to be the central heating system. How odd that bruschetta is now on restaurant menus."

"My mother's family was displaced by the war to a small town outside Naples at the base of Mount Vesuvius. The accommodations were what we call spartan and the supplies meagre, but that didn't keep us from having fun as my mother and Uncle Geppino demonstrate."

Little chicken

Panzanella

When I was little, if my parents wanted a snack, they would say to each other, "How about a little chicken?" Visions of plump golden birds would dance in my head, quickly to be shattered by this homely dish of bread and tomatoes. It is ironic that now I can get all the chicken I want, but the luscious tomatoes for "little chicken" are harder to come by.

8 slices day-old Italian bread, cut 4cm thick

4 tomatoes, sliced

75ml olive oil

1 tablespoon dried oregano

Salt and freshly ground black pepper

Dampen the bread with cold water and shake off any excess. Arrange the bread slices on a serving dish and top with the tomato slices. Drizzle the olive oil over, then sprinkle with the oregano. Season to taste. *Serves 4.*

Fried peppers

75ml olive oil

4 red, yellow or orange peppers, deseeded and sliced

2 garlic cloves, chopped

Salt and freshly ground black pepper

Italian bread

Heat the oil in a large frying pan over medium heat. Add the peppers and garlic and sauté until the peppers are soft, about 20 minutes. Season to taste and serve warm or at room temperature. Serve with bread to mop up the pepper juices. *Serves 4–6.*

Sweet and sour onions

100ml water, or more as needed

50ml olive oil

50ml white wine vinegar

2 tablespoons sugar

Salt

450g pickling onions, peeled and left whole

Combine the water, olive oil, vinegar, sugar and salt, to taste, in a heavy-bottomed frying pan large enough to hold the onions in a single layer. Stir to dissolve the sugar and salt. Add the onions, cover the pan, and simmer over medium heat until the onions are tender when pierced with the tip of a knife, about 25 minutes. Check occasionally to make sure the water doesn't dry out, adding extra, if necessary. Serve warm or at room temperature. *Serves 6–8.*

TONY'S TIP:
tearless peeling

Bring a saucepan of water to a boil. Immerse the onions and cook for 5 minutes. Drain. Cut off the bottom of each onion; hold the top and squeeze. The onion should come shooting out of the skin.

Grandma Flo's appetiser

This appetiser keeps for several days. It's great to accompany an antipasto of mixed cured meats and cheese or to serve with a meat sandwich or leftovers.

4 celery hearts, including leaves, finely chopped
4 red peppers, roasted, deseeded, peeled and finely chopped
50ml white wine vinegar
1 teaspoon salt

Stir all the ingredients together. Cover and chill until required. *Serves 4.*

Baked tomatoes

10 small plum or round ripe tomatoes, cut into quarters
Salt
3 tablespoons olive oil

Put the tomato wedges in a bowl, sprinkle them with salt, and allow to stand for 30 minutes. Meanwhile, preheat the oven to 170°C, gas mark 3. Stir the oil into the tomatoes, then transfer them to a roasting pan in a single layer. Roast until they are partially dry, without any liquid, but still soft and chewy, about 45 minutes. Serve warm or at room temperature. *Serves 4.*

TONY'S TIP:
blistering peppers

Peppers can be roasted under the grill or on a barbecue. Place the peppers over the fire or under the grill and allow to cook until the skin is blistered and blackened in places, while the flesh softens underneath. Keep turning the peppers to blister all over. Remove from the heat and let cool completely. Remove and discard the skin as well as the core and seeds.

TOMATOES

Plum tomatoes are becoming readily available as "vine grown"—although all tomatoes grow on vines! In my childhood, San Marzano, a variety of plum tomatoes, were the preferred type for home canning. But you can use any type of tomato when cooking—as long as they're juicy, ripe and red.

Quick asparagus

3 tablespoons olive oil

1 bunch asparagus, woody ends snapped off

Salt and freshly ground black pepper

50ml water

55g coarsely grated Parmesan

Heat the oil over medium-high heat in a frying pan large enough to hold the asparagus in a single layer. Add the asparagus and salt and pepper to taste and sauté 2 minutes, turning the spears so each side is coated in oil. Add the water and simmer, stirring frequently, until fork-tender, about 5 minutes longer. Sprinkle with the cheese. *Serves 4*.

Stuffed mushrooms

9 medium open-cup mushrooms, wiped clean

50ml sunflower oil

1 onion, finely chopped

1 garlic clove, chopped

1 anchovy fillet in oil, chopped

Salt and freshly ground black pepper

1 tablespoon chopped flat-leaf parsley

10g torn fresh white bread, soaked in water, squeezed dry

1 large egg, beaten

3 tablespoons olive oil

2 tablespoons plain dried breadcrumbs

½ lemon

Preheat the oven to 190°C, gas mark 5. Lightly grease a baking sheet; set aside. Remove the stems from eight mushrooms, keeping the cups whole. Finely chop the remaining mushroom with the stems; set aside. Heat the oil in a large frying pan over medium heat. Add the onion, garlic and anchovy and sauté until the onion is soft and the anchovy dissolves, about 5 minutes. Stir in the chopped mushrooms and salt and pepper to taste and continue sautéing 5 minutes longer. Remove the frying pan from the heat and stir in the parsley, bread and egg, stirring until well mixed. Equally divide the mixture among the eight mushrooms and spread to fill the cups. Place on the baking sheet, drizzle each with a little olive oil and dust with breadcrumbs. Bake until the mushrooms are tender, about 20 minutes. Squeeze lemon juice over and serve warm or at room temperature. *Makes 8*.

TONY'S TIP:
cooking with garlic
To peel a garlic clove quickly, place it on a flat surface and smack it with the heel of your hand or with the flat blade of a knife, and then remove the skin. Err on the side of caution when you use garlic in a dish. A whole clove is not as strong as a chopped one, which, in turn, is not as strong as a completely crushed one. And remember that as garlic cooks, it will lose some of its strength.

Aubergine purée

Crema di melanzane

This recipe is called poor man's caviar. To save time, you can mash and beat it all in an electric blender or food processor.

3 medium aubergines
3 tablespoons olive oil, plus extra for garnish
1–2 garlic cloves, crushed
2–3 tablespoons chopped flat-leaf parsley
Juice of 1 lemon
Salt and freshly ground black pepper

Preheat the grill to high. Grill the whole aubergines about 10cm from the heat, turning them often with tongs, until charred all over and very soft, about 20 minutes. Remove from the heat and set aside until cool enough to handle. Peel off the skins and use your hands to squeeze out as much juice as possible. Put the aubergines in a large bowl. Mash the aubergines with a large fork, slowly beating in 3 tablespoons olive oil until a paste forms. Beat in the garlic and parsley and add lemon juice to taste. Season with salt and pepper to taste. Transfer to a serving bowl and drizzle with a little extra oil. Serve with thinly sliced Italian bread pitta bread, or squares of focaccia for dipping. *Serves 4–6.*

"Aubergine purée is a great party dish, as nibbles to go with drinks, or as one of a group of appetisers. The Simone family gathered with cheer and food every Sunday, as well as for holidays, birthdays and anniversaries. Drink was never taken alone, but accompanied by some appetite stimulants or, in some cases, to muffle the stomach growls while waiting for dinner!"

Fried sage leaves

Frying sage leaves may sound odd because we are used to using sage as a flavouring; however, sage leaves lend themselves to frying very well and can be used as a little appetiser or as a garnish.

Sunflower oil for frying
55g plain flour
24 fresh sage leaves, rinsed and patted dry
2 medium eggs, beaten with ½ teaspoon salt

Fill a large frying pan with oil about 3mm deep and heat over high heat, until it reaches 180°C, or until a 1cm cube of bread browns in 30 seconds. Place the flour on a plate. Dip each sage leaf in flour and then in egg. Fry one side and then the other until golden brown, about 1 minute per side. Using tongs, very carefully remove each leaf from the pan (they will be brittle and can break easily) and drain on paper towels. Serve immediately, allowing 3–4 leaves per person. *Makes 24.*

VARIATIONS

Sage Leaves in Pastella Combine 55g plain flour, ½ teaspoon salt, freshly ground black pepper to taste, and 100ml water in a small bowl. Beat to a smooth batter. Dip each of the 24 sage leaves in the flour batter and fry as above until golden brown on both sides. Drain on paper towels and serve hot. *Makes 24.*

Sage Leaf Garnish Using as many dry sage leaves as you like, drop each in a large frying pan with sunflower oil heated to 180°C. Deep-fry the leaves until they are golden and crisp, 1–2 minutes. Lift out carefully because the leaves are very brittle, and drain on paper towels. Use as a garnish for soups, pasta dishes with butter, chops and roasts.

Rice balls

In Naples they have cook shops called friggitorie, *frying places. They will fry anything that doesn't move. One of my favourites is rice balls.*

250g cooked, drained and cooled arborio rice

1 large egg, beaten

3 tablespoons grated Parmesan cheese

1 tablespoon chopped flat-leaf parsley

Salt and freshly ground pepper

Dried breadcrumbs (about 100g)

100ml sunflower oil, for frying

Mix the rice, egg, Parmesan, parsley and salt and pepper to taste in a large bowl, using your hands to combine the ingredients. Shape into about twenty 6.5cm balls. Wetting your hands from time to time will reduce sticking. Roll the rice balls in the breadcrumbs until coated all over; set aside. Heat the oil in a large frying pan over medium heat. Working in batches, if necessary, to avoid overcrowding the pan, add the rice balls and fry until golden all over, about 8 minutes. Using a slotted spoon, remove from the oil and drain on paper towels. Continue until all the rice balls are fried. Serve hot. *Serves 4–6.*

VARIATION

Rice Balls with Mozzarella Slip a cube of fresh mozzarella cheese in the middle of each rice ball as you shape it, completely enclosing the cheese.

TONY'S TIP:
breadcrumbs

In Italian cooking, dried breadcrumbs are used almost universally. They are made of leftover bread, perhaps helped along in the drying process by a 30-minute stay in a slow (140°C, gas mark 1) oven. They are also unflavoured; the appropriate herbs and spices are introduced when required. I save up old bread, grind it up all at once, and store the crumbs in a lidded can ready for instant use.

◄ *Rice balls with mozzarella*

Vegetables with garlic and anchovy sauce

Bagna cauda

Raw seasonal vegetables make great appetisers. In Italy, we often ate porcini mushrooms and artichokes served raw with a little oil and salt and pepper. This recipe, which originates in Piedmont, makes use of commonly available vegetables and is a very friendly dish for a group. Serve it with Barbera, Barbaresco, Barolo or Nebbiolo, all good red wines.

2 artichokes, prepared, cooked and cooled (page 190)

2 chicory heads, separated into leaves

3 peppers, in a variety of colours, deseeded and diced

3 carrots, peeled and cut into sticks

6 celery stalks, cut into sticks

16 small mushrooms, wiped clean

225g butter, chopped

50ml olive oil

4 garlic cloves, chopped

4 anchovy fillets in oil, chopped

Salt

Arrange the artichokes, chicory, peppers, carrots, celery and mushrooms on a dish; set aside. Melt the butter with the oil in a heavy-bottomed medium saucepan over medium heat. Add the garlic and sauté until golden, 2–3 minutes. Add the anchovies and stir until they dissolve. Season to taste with salt. Pour the anchovy sauce into an earthenware bowl over a spirit lamp to keep it warm. Serve with the vegetables for dipping. *Serves 6–8.*

"In keeping with the rustic nature of this dish, choose a partially glazed or handmade ceramic bowl in which to serve the heated sauce."

Country pie

Pizza rustica

This dish is unusual in combining sweet and savoury, which under other circumstances would be unthinkable to Italians. Pizza rustica *is served as appetiser or accompaniment to predinner drinks—*aperitivi.

FOR THE PASTRY
350g plain flour
115g sugar
Salt and freshly ground black pepper
115g butter, softened
3 large eggs

FOR THE FILLING
450g ricotta cheese
4 large eggs, beaten
115g diced Neapolitan salami
55g grated Parmesan cheese
55g diced fresh mozzarella cheese, drained
25g grated provola cheese
1 tablespoon chopped flat-leaf parsley
Salt and freshly ground black pepper

Combine the flour, sugar and salt and pepper to taste in a large bowl and stir together. Add the butter and rub it into the flour. Beat two of the eggs and add to the flour mixture, beating until a smooth dough forms. Roll out onto a floured surface and knead to form an elastic ball. Cover and set aside for 30 minutes. Meanwhile, to make the filling, combine the ricotta, eggs, salami, Parmesan, mozzarella, provola, and parsley in a bowl and beat together. Season lightly with salt and generously with pepper; set aside.

Preheat the oven to 190°C, gas mark 5. Roll out two-thirds of the dough on a lightly floured surface into a 33cm circle. Use to line a 30cm pie tin and trim the edges; spoon in the filling. Roll out the remaining dough into a 30cm circle and cut into 5mm strips. Arrange the dough strips on top of the filling in a diamond pattern, crimping the ends to the dough to secure. Beat the remaining egg. Lightly brush the strips with the egg glaze. Bake until the pastry is golden brown and the filling sets, about 1 hour. Remove from the oven and let stand for 5 minutes before cutting. Serve hot or cold. *Serves 4–6.*

TONY'S TIP:
substitutes
You can use another kind of Italian salami if you can't get Napoli, just remember to peel off the casing.

Provola is a lightly smoked mozzarella. If you can't get it, a mild provolone can be substituted.

Mozzarella fritters

4 large eggs

Salt

Plain flour

115g dried breadcrumbs

**450g fresh mozzarella cheese, drained and cut
     into 5x2cm strips**

Sunflower oil, for frying

TONY'S TIP:
frying cheese

It's important to make sure
the cheese is completely
covered when it is fried;
otherwise, it will melt and
leak into the oil, which will
produce a strong smell.

Beat the eggs in a shallow bowl with a pinch of salt. Place the flour on
a plate and the breadcrumbs on another plate. One by one, dip each
cheese strip in the flour and then in the eggs, shaking off excess flour
and letting excess egg drip back into the bowl. Then dip into the
breadcrumbs, covering completely with the crumbs. Set aside the
cheese strips to dry. When you are ready to fry, heat 5mm oil in a large
frying pan over high heat until it reaches 180°C, or until a 1cm cube
of bread browns in 30 seconds. Working in batches, if necessary, to
avoid overcrowding, fry as many cheese strips as will fit in a single
layer until golden, about 3 minutes. Turn over and fry the other sides
until golden, about 3 minutes longer. Remove from the pan and drain
on paper towels. Add more oil to the pan, if necessary, and continue
until all the cheese strips are fried. *Serves 4.*

Raclette

*A crisp white wine, such as Orvieto or Frascati, would go well with
this dish.*

450g new potatoes, scrubbed and boiled

225g salami or similar cured sausage, sliced

Small pickled gherkins

450g Gruyère or raclette cheese, in one piece

Put the new potatoes, salami or sausage, and gherkins in serving dishes
on the table so diners can help themselves. (The potatoes are nicer if
served warm.) Heat the grill to high. Place the cheese on a flameproof
tray and grill 10cm from the heat until the cheese melts. As the cheese
melts, scrape it onto a plate and serve at once so diners can help
themselves. Eat the melted cheese accompanied by the potatoes,
gherkins and salami. Continue melting and serving the cheese until it
has all been used. *Serves 4.*

Fried mozzarella sandwiches

Mozzarella in carrozza

Mozzarella in carrozza *means Cinderella's coach. No, I am only joking. It means mozzarella in a carriage. Like most carriages, you can dress it up to your heart's content. You can stick in anchovies, or a slice of tomato, or whatever. For myself, just give me the plain carriage.*

> **4 large eggs**
> **Salt**
> **Plain flour**
> **450g fresh mozzarella cheese, drained and cut into 8 slices**
> **16 thin slices Italian bread**
> **Sunflower oil, for frying**

Beat the eggs in a shallow bowl with a pinch of salt. Place the flour on a plate. Sandwich a mozzarella slice between two slices of bread, and press together with your hands to make the cheese and bread adhere. Repeat until all the bread and cheese is used. Dredge the sandwiches in flour, patting on more flour, if necessary, so the sandwiches have a thick coating. Shake off the excess flour and then dip into the eggs, so the sandwich is completely covered. Let the excess drip back into the bowl; set aside. Heat 225ml oil in a large frying pan over high heat. Add as many mozzarella sandwiches as will fit in a single layer and fry until golden, 3–5 minutes on each side. Remove the sandwiches from the pan and drain on paper towels. Add more oil to the skillet, if necessary, and continue until all the sandwiches are fried. Serve hot. *Serves 4.*

Mozzarella barbecued in lemon leaves

I first tasted this dish in Amalfi. Served on a terrace, on a warm evening with the sea in view, and the bustle of holiday crowds, this dish was forever fixed in my mind as a happy one. You will have to imagine the beauty of Amalfi as you cook.

450g fresh mozzarella cheese, drained and cut into 1cm slices, at least 12 slices
24 lemon leaves

Prepare the barbecue until the coals are glowing. Sandwich each slice of mozzarella between two lemon leaves. Place on the barbecue rack and grill 10cm above the coals until the mozzarella starts to melt, 5–10 minutes. *Makes 12.*

Pecorino, salami and broad beans

Pecorino cheese is made with sheep's milk. It is very mild when young, becoming more pungent as it ages. For this recipe, a young pecorino cheese is usually preferred. My ancestors would have enjoyed this dish at the table and would have counted themselves lucky if they had had a piece of cheese or salami to take with them as they worked in the fields. The broad beans would have come straight off the plants.

225g salami, sliced
225g pecorino cheese, sliced
900g fresh young broad beans in their shells
Italian bread slices

Do nothing more than arrange the salami and cheese on a serving platter. Put the broad beans in a basket. The diners help themselves to the salami, cheese and bread. And, of course, they all shuck their own beans. *Serves 6–8.*

What's in a name?
MOZZARELLA

Most commonly sold as a cow's milk cheese, the original and more expensive mozzarella is made from the milk of the buffalo and is known as *mozzarella di bufala*. It is creamy and sweet and worth the extra cost. It has no connection whatsoever with the yellow rubber balls commonly labeled "mozzarella for pizza" and having a use-by date of two months later! Make sure the mozzarella you buy is white and is stored in water. All mozzarella is meant to be eaten fresh; it has a very subtle taste on its own and should be flavoured and/or used in conjunction with other ingredients.

"Not long after their arrival in the USA, circa 1900, the Simone family gathered in New York or Connecticut for a family portrait. Today, I can still see their features in the faces of their great-grandchildren."

Antipasto

This appetiser is such a common feature at home that I nearly forgot to include it. You don't have to cook anything; all the ingredients can be bought at an Italian deli.

TONY'S TIP:
cured meat choices
You needn't stick to the cured meats listed. *Chorizo*, *mortadella*, and cured *pancetta* are also good alternatives. And the salami can be any variety; my favorites are Neapolitan salami, *spianata* and *finocchiata*.

115g prosciutto, very thinly sliced
115g salami, thinly sliced
115g coppa, very thinly sliced
250g marinated mushrooms in oil, drained
250g marinated artichoke hearts in oil, drained
250g Sicilian-style green olives or other dressed olives
Crusty bread slices

About 1 hour before serving, remove the prosciutto, salami and coppa slices from the refrigerator and attractively arrange on a very large serving dish. Place the mushrooms, artichoke hearts, and olives in separate bowls. Serve with plenty of crusty bread slices. *Serves 4–6.*

Stuffed tomatoes

8 medium tomatoes
Sunflower oil

FOR THE FILLING
450g minced beef
55g dried breadcrumbs
1 large egg, beaten
3 tablespoons grated Parmesan cheese
2 tablespoons chopped flat-leaf parsley
1 tablespoon pine nuts
1 teaspoon salt
½ teaspoon freshly ground black pepper

Preheat the oven to 180°C, gas mark 4. Cut the tops off the tomatoes and reserve. Using a small teaspoon, carefully scoop out the seeds and core from each tomato to leave a hollow shell; set aside upside down to drain. Combine the filling ingredients and divide equally among the tomatoes, mounding it above the rims. Position the reserved tops like "hats." Put the tomatoes in an oiled roasting pan or baking dish just large enough to hold them upright in a single layer, and brush with a little oil. Bake the tomatoes for about 40 minutes, until just tender and the fillings are cooked through. Leave to cool slightly, then serve. *Makes 8.*

Liver and bacon

This simple dish is a bite to stave off the wolf while you are waiting for the main event.

6 chicken livers, cleaned and cut into bite-size pieces
Freshly ground black pepper
Fresh sage leaves (if you don't have fresh, leave them out)
6 thin slices pancetta or cured (not smoked) bacon, each cut into
  2 or 3 pieces

Preheat the oven to 200°C, gas mark 6. Season the chicken livers with pepper to taste. Put a piece of chicken liver and a small piece of sage on top of a piece of bacon. Roll up, with the bacon enclosing the sage and liver. Continue until all ingredients are used. Arrange the bacon rolls in a baking dish in a single layer, seam side down. Bake for about 10 minutes, until crisp, turning over once. *Serves 4.*

SAGE
Once established, one sage plant in your kitchen garden will supply your culinary needs all year-round. Fried on its own or used as flavouring for meat and fish, sage imparts a bass note to the dish. I always think of herbs and spices as adding notes to my cooking—garlic is the trumpet; pepper, the drums; and parsley, a clarinet!

Prosciutto with savoury pastries

In Parma they serve ham with fried dough pieces, which are easy to make. People in Parma also eat their ham accompanied by dry red fizzy wine, served in white ceramic bowls—a little odd at first but very quaint.

475g plain flour
1 sachet (7g) fast-action dried yeast
1 teaspoon salt
40g butter, melted
About 325ml milk, warmed
Sunflower oil, for deep-frying
225g prosciutto

TONY'S TIP:
cured hams

Cured ham, *prosciutto,* is made in practically all regions of Italy. There is a wide variation of dryness and saltiness. Outside Italy, the most favoured are Parma and San Daniele. Each has its own champions, but to me they are interchangeable. You can choose either when recipes call for Parma ham; just make sure that it is freshly sliced, a beautiful pink, fat all around but not much running through it.

Ask the deli person to cut the ham paper thin—you should be able to read a newspaper through it. And if your deli person is really on the ball, you should be offered the first slice to taste!

Mix the flour, yeast and salt together in a large bowl and make a well in the middle. Slowly stir in the butter and enough milk to form a soft dough. Turn out the dough onto a lightly floured surface and knead until pliable. (Don't be lazy, use elbow grease freely.) Shape the dough into a ball and place it in a bowl, cover tightly with a dish towel, and leave to rise in a warm room until it doubles in bulk. Knock back the dough and turn out onto a floured surface. Using a lightly floured rolling pin, roll out until 3mm thick. Using a 7.5cm lightly floured diamond, square or circle biscuit cutter (or all three), stamp out shapes (about 24). Re-roll the dough, if necessary, and continue stamping out shapes until all the dough is used. Place the shapes on a floured tray, cover with a dish towel, and set aside to rise again.

In a heavy-bottomed saucepan over high heat, heat the oil to 180°C, or until a 1cm cube of bread browns in 30 seconds. Working in batches, if necessary, to avoid overcrowding, add the dough shapes to the pan and fry until golden on both sides, about 3 minutes. The shapes will rise to the top. Using a slotted spoon, remove from the oil and drain on paper towels. Add more oil and reheat, if necessary, and continue until all the dough shapes are fried. Arrange slices of ham on serving plates and accompany with the pastries. *Serves 6–8.*

VARIATION

Prosciutto with Bread If you don't have time to make the savoury fritters, serve the prosciutto with fresh, buttered crusty Italian bread. It is served this way in Parma, and they should know best.

Anchovy and butter sandwiches

This is an all-time favourite of mine. With these ingredients it shouldn't taste as good as it does—bless it.

8 slices fresh French bread
8 very thin slivers unsalted butter
4 anchovy fillets in oil, cut in half lengthwise
8 parsley leaves

Spread each slice of bread with a sliver of butter. Top each with a piece of anchovy and a parsley leaf. *Makes 8.*

ANCHOVIES

Anchovies are available in cans or in glass, packed in oil or salt. Oil-packed anchovies are quite acceptable and are convenient to use straight from the can. They don't need rinsing. However, the ones packed in salt are more traditional. These need to be rinsed in several changes of water to desalt them before you use them.

Monkfish and artichokes
Pescatrice e carciofi

Italy has a very long coastline and fish is a passion at the seashore. Sea-side visitors show up in droves to sample the local fish in the summer, just when many vegetables are also in season. This dish is representative of the myriad of fish and vegetable dishes made to tickle the appetite.

6 baby artichokes
50ml olive oil
1 garlic clove, chopped
450g monkfish fillet, skinned and cut into 1cm cubes
1 tablespoon chopped flat-leaf parsley
Salt and freshly ground black pepper
100ml dry white wine
1 large tomato, deseeded and cut into 1cm cubes

Prepare the artichokes as on page 190. Slice them thinly and drop the pieces into a bowl of water into which you have squeezed the juice of a lemon, to prevent them from browning; set aside. Heat the oil in a large frying pan over medium heat. Add the garlic and sauté until golden, 2–3 minutes; remove and discard the garlic. Drain the artichokes and sauté 20 minutes, or until they begin to soften. Add the monkfish, half the parsle, and salt and pepper to taste and sauté 5 minutes. Add the wine and simmer 5 minutes longer, or until the monkfish is cooked through and flakes easily. Turn off the heat and stir in the tomato and remaining parsley. Taste and adjust the seasoning, if necessary. *Serves 4–6.*

Squid with tomatoes

450g tomatoes, deseeded and diced

100ml olive oil

2 bunches fresh basil, chopped

Freshly ground black pepper

450g squid, cleaned and cut into squares

Salt

Put the tomatoes into a bowl. Add half the oil, the basil and pepper to taste. Set aside for at least 30 minutes to marinate. When you are ready to cook, heat the remaining oil in a large frying pan over medium heat. Add the squid and salt to taste and sauté until opaque, about 2 minutes. Pour into the tomato mixture and gently stir together. Taste and adjust the seasoning. Serve while the squid is still hot. *Serves 4.*

"In Liguria, restaurants have lots of appetisers based on the local fresh seafood. Since they rely on freshness, these appetisers are often difficult to re-create. Here are some recipes that have survived the slightly aged seafood available where I live."

Prawns with garlic

100ml olive oil

4 garlic cloves, chopped

1 teaspoon chopped fresh chilli (wear gloves when handling),
   or ½ teaspoon crushed chilli flakes

8 large prawns, shelled and deveined, with the tails left on

100ml dry white wine

Salt

6 tablespoons chopped flat-leaf parsley

Crusty Italian bread

Heat the oil in a large frying pan over medium-high heat. Add the garlic and chilli and sauté until the chilli is soft, 2–3 minutes. Increase the heat to high, add the prawns and continue sautéing until the prawns are fried on both sides and start to turn pink, 3–5 minutes. Stir in the wine and salt to taste and continue sautéing for 2 minutes. Remove the pan from the heat and stir in the parsley. Serve the prawns in the sauce with plenty of bread for mopping up the sauce. I put finger bowls on the table and everyone just uses their fingers. *Serves 4.*

TONY'S TIP:
serving prawns

I prefer to use prawns with the shell and head on for the colour and exotic appearance. But some people have difficulty wielding the instruments to remove the shell at the table; others are too embarrassed to use their hands; still others are put off by the antediluvian look of the whole prawn, so it's OK to peel the prawns before cooking, but leave on the tail fans because they're so pretty.

Prawns and flageolet

50ml olive oil

1 onion, chopped

400g can flageolet beans, including the liquid

2 tablespoons chopped flat-leaf parsley

Salt and freshly ground black pepper

450g medium prawns, shelled and deveined, with tails left on

3 tablespoons lumpfish caviar

Heat the oil in a large frying pan over high heat. Add the onion and sauté until soft, 3–5 minutes. Stir in the beans, parsley and salt and pepper to taste and continue cooking until the beans are heated through. Add the prawns and continue cooking, stirring frequently, until they turn pink, about 5 minutes. Pour the prawns and beans into a serving dish and sprinkle with the lumpfish caviar. *Serves 4.*

"My maternal grandparents with some of their children in a Naples restaurant around 1930. My mother is the serious-looking baby at the table. No matter how humble the establishment, there was always a cloth on the table and the house wine was, then as now, always an acceptable choice."

Salt cod fritters

Frittelle di baccalà

You can't prepare this recipe on a whim, as the salt cod has to be prepared some days in advance. Before refrigeration, our ancestors relied on preserved fish for a lot of their protein; today, we can appreciate it for its own special taste.

450g dried salt cod pieces, soaked, rinsed
   and drained (page 156)
450g cooked potatoes, mashed
1 large egg, beaten
10g butter, melted
1 tablespoon chopped flat-leaf parsley
Salt and freshly ground black pepper
115g dried breadcrumbs
Sunflower oil, for deep frying
Lemon wedges (optional)

To cook the salt cod, bring a heavy-bottomed medium saucepan of water to a boil over high heat. Add the salt cod, reduce the heat to low, and simmer until tender, about 30 minutes. Drain well and set aside to cool. When cool enough to handle, remove any skin and bones, then flake the fish.

Combine the salt-cod flakes, mashed potatoes, egg, butter, parsley and salt and pepper in a large bowl, taking care how much salt you add because the cod is already salty. Beat together until a smooth paste forms. Cover and chill for at least 1 hour. Just before you are ready to fry, place the breadcrumbs into a shallow dish. Heat the oil for deep-frying in a large, heavy-bottomed pan over high heat until it reaches 180°C, or until a 1cm cube of bread browns in 30 seconds. Shape the salt-cod mixture into 2.5cm balls (about 30). Roll the balls in the breadcrumbs so they are coated all over. Working in batches, if necessary, to avoid overcrowding, fry the balls until golden all over, about 6 minutes. Drain well on paper towels. Continue until all the salt-cod mixture has been fried. Serve hot with a wedge of lemon for squeezing over or just for looks. *Serves 4–6.*

What's in a name? BACCALÀ

Otherwise known as salt cod, this is whole gutted fish or fillets that are soaked in brine or layered with dry salt, then dried. In the old days, *baccalà* was the means by which poor people, who didn't have access to fresh fish, could maintain the prohibition on eating meat on Fridays and the vigils of feast days. Today, *baccalà* is available from delis or specialist shops. Before cooking, *baccalà* must be soaked to reconstitute it and to remove the excess salt.

SALADS

TONY'S TIP:
ideas for salads

Green salad There are many different kinds of lettuce, so experiment a little. A bit of bitter greens adds dimension to any salad. Try escarole, both curly and smooth, radicchio, endive, and whenever possible, add a few leaves of rocket .

Mixed salad At other times, you may feel like a salad extravaganza. Try using lettuce, tomatoes, celery, grated carrots, onion, radishes, spring onions, cooked broccoli, and green beans.

Flavour in salads Whether you are making a green or mixed salad, turn it into something special with some herbs. Try adding chives, cress, watercress, parsley, fennel or even a couple of basil leaves.

TONY'S TIP:
drying lettuce
Recipes usually tell you to dry lettuce leaves. Too much water from the washing dilutes the dressing. Some of you no doubt have a salad spinner; but if not, a few minutes in a colander and a few shakes should do the trick.

Grandma Simone's Caesar salad

This anchovy and lettuce salad is the family version of the famous salad created in 1924 at Caesar's Place in Tijuana, Mexico, by Italian immigrant and restaurant owner, Caesar Cardini. Anyway, Grandma's is better.

> 1 garlic clove, cut in half
>
> 4 slices Italian bread, toasted
>
> 1 head romaine lettuce, rinsed and dried
>
> 3 tablespoons grated Parmesan cheese
>
> **FOR THE DRESSING**
>
> 3 anchovy fillets in oil, chopped
>
> 50ml olive oil
>
> 1 tablespoon white wine vinegar
>
> Juice of ½ lemon

Rub one garlic half gently over the toasted bread. Cut the bread into bite-size pieces; set aside. Rub the remaining garlic around the inside of a large salad bowl. To make the dressing, mash the anchovies in the bowl with a fork. Beat in the olive oil, vinegar and lemon juice. Break the lettuce into individual leaves and add to the bowl with the dressing. Toss the leaves until coated. Sprinkle the Parmesan and toasted garlic croutons over. *Serves 4.*

Rocket and Parmesan

225g rocket, washed and dried

25g pine nuts

50ml olive oil

115g Parmesan cheese in one piece

Freshly ground black pepper

Toss the rocket with the pine nuts in a large salad bowl. Add the olive oil and toss again. Equally divide the salad among four serving plates. Using a potato peeler, "peel" off thin slivers of cheese, letting the slivers fall over the salads. Grind the pepper over the salads and serve. *Serves 4.*

Summer tomato salad

900g tomatoes, cut into wedges

2 onions, thinly sliced

2 green peppers, deseeded and thinly sliced

6 fresh basil leaves

1 tablespoon dried oregano

100ml sunflower oil

Salt and freshly ground black pepper

Italian bread

Combine the tomatoes, onions, peppers, basil leaves and oregano. Pour the oil over, season to taste, and gently toss together. Cover and chill for at least 2 hours. Serve with plenty of Italian bread. *Serves 4–6.*

VARIATION

Tomato and Spring Onion Salad Replace the onions in the above recipe with a bunch of spring onions, washed and trimmed. Cut them into thin slices (including the green part) and combine with the other ingredients, omitting the black pepper and replacing the basil with the leaves of two bunches of flat-leaf parsley.

What's in a name?
ROCKET

In Britain, it's called rocket; in Italy, it's *rucola*; in America, it's arugula. There are several varieties with different degrees of pungency.

There is uncertainty about why *rucola* came to be called arugula in America. On Italian radio I heard two DJs saying that an immigrant was asked what that green stuff was and he answered "A rugola!" meaning "the *rucola*." (Kind of like Tahiti, which, when it was first discovered, was called Otahiti because when a native was asked what the name of the place was, he answered, "Oh, Tahiti," meaning "It is Tahiti." Don't believe me? Look at an old map.)

"One of our favourite holiday destinations was the island of Ischia, situated in the bay of Naples. It is part of the group of islands in that area including Procida and Capri, where great dishes like *insalata Caprese* were invented."

Tomato, mozzarella and basil salad

Insalata Caprese

This dish wholly depends on the goodness of its ingredients. In the sunny south of Italy, there are two things that are constantly excellent and readily available—mozzarella and tomatoes. If you don't have delicious ripe tomatoes and fresh mozzarella, don't even think about making this dish.

450g fresh mozzarella cheese, drained and sliced
4 ripe tomatoes, sliced
Salt and freshly ground black pepper
Olive oil
Fresh basil leaves

Attractively overlap the mozzarella and tomato slices on one large serving dish or four individual salad plates. Sprinkle with salt and pepper, then drizzle with olive oil to taste. Garnish with fresh basil leaves. *Serves 4.*

Mushroom salad

450g white mushrooms, wiped clean
75ml olive oil
Juice of ½ lemon
Salt and freshly ground black pepper
1 teaspoon finely chopped flat-leaf parsley
55g Parmesan cheese in one piece

Thinly slice the mushrooms lengthwise. Arrange the mushrooms attractively on a serving dish. Combine the olive oil, lemon juice, and salt and pepper to taste in a screwtop jar. Secure the lid and shake. Pour the dressing over the mushrooms so as much of the surface as possible is covered. Sprinkle with parsley. Using a vegetable peeler, "peel" thin slices of Parmesan, letting the slivers fall over the mushrooms. *Serves 4–6.*

Salad with poached egg and hot bacon

2 heads escarole, rinsed and dried
100ml olive oil
50ml fresh lemon juice
115g thick-cut cured (not smoked) bacon, about
  6mm thick
2 tablespoons white wine vinegar
4 large eggs
Freshly ground black pepper
Italian or French bread

Tear the escarole into a large salad bowl. Add all but 2 tablespoons of the olive oil and all the lemon juice and toss. Equally divide the salad among four salad plates; set aside. Using a sharp knife, cut the bacon into 1cm cubes. Heat the remaining 2 tablespoons oil in a medium frying pan over medium heat. Add the bacon and cook through, but do not allow it to crisp, about 5 minutes; set aside and keep warm.

Meanwhile, heat 2.5cm water with the vinegar in a large frying pan over medium heat, until the bubbles barely break the surface. One at a time, break the eggs into a small shallow bowl, then slip them into the water. Spoon the hot water over the eggs, and continue simmering until the whites are set and the yolks are still runny with a pale "film," 3–5 minutes. Spoon the bacon and hot fat equally over the four salads. Using a slotted spoon, remove the eggs from the water one at a time and let the water drip off. Top each salad with an egg and grind black pepper over. Serve, accompanied by the bread. *Serves 4.*

What's in a name?
PANCETTA/BACON?
The word *pancetta* is frequently used as if it were something exotic. *Pancetta* literally means "little belly" and stands for bacon—except that it is not smoked and not so heavily cured with nitrates as bacon is.

Hot goat's cheese salad

2 heads escarole, rinsed and dried

100ml olive oil

50ml fresh lemon juice

2 large eggs

55g fine plain dried breadcrumbs

4 whole goat's cheeses, about 55g each

Sunflower oil, for frying

Freshly ground black pepper

Tear the escarole into a large bowl. Add the olive oil and lemon juice and toss so all the escarole leaves are coated. Equally divide the salad among four salad plates; set aside. Into a small, shallow bowl, break the eggs and beat them with a fork. Place the breadcrumbs on a plate. Working with one goat's cheese at a time, dip it first in the eggs and then in the breadcrumbs, patting them on all over. In a large frying pan over medium-high heat, heat 5mm sunflower oil until it reaches 180°C, or until a 1cm cube of bread browns in 30 seconds. Add the goat's cheeses and fry until golden brown, about 5 minutes on each side. Using a fish slice, remove the cheeses from the pan and drain well on paper towels. Top each plate of escarole leaves with a fried cheese and grind black pepper over. *Serves 4.*

TONY'S TIP:
frying goat's cheese
When frying the goat's cheeses, try not to puncture them, so that the coating remains whole and no cheese runs out to burn and smell up your kitchen or, indeed, the whole house.

Aunt Thelma's salad dressing

225ml olive oil

100ml white wine vinegar

2 tablespoons sugar

1½ teaspoons salt

1 teaspoon paprika

Heaped ½ teaspoon mustard powder

¼ garlic clove, crushed

Put all the ingredients in a jar with a screwtop lid, secure the lid, and shake until blended. This will keep for about a week in the refrigerator. *Makes about 350ml.*

"Grandma Florence Simone and her sister, Aunt Thelma, inherited their love of cooking from their Apulian grandmother."

TONY'S TIP:
dressing for dinner

You can prepare the dressing ahead of time, but don't add it to the salad until you are ready to serve. If you add it too soon, the lettuce will wilt. There are some nice wilted leaf salads, but you don't need to make one unintentionally.

Tony's Italian dressing

True Italian salad dressing is, of course, only oil and vinegar poured directly onto the salad leaves.

100ml olive oil

50ml white wine vinegar

1 garlic clove, cut in half

½ teaspoon mustard powder

½ teaspoon salt

Put all the ingredients in a jar with a screwtop lid, secure the lid, and shake until blended. This will keep for about a week in the refrigerator. *Makes 150ml.*

VARIATIONS

Cheese Dressing Crumble 55g blue cheese, such as Roquefort or gorgonzola, into the dressing before shaking. However, you may want to reserve a little cheese to sprinkle over the top of the salad just before serving.

Lemon Dressing Use lemon juice instead of the vinegar. This is especially good on a salad that accompanies fried or baked fish.

Pasta and bean soup

Pasta e fagioli

100ml sunflower oil

2 small onions, chopped, or 2 garlic cloves, chopped, or both

900g canned beans, such as cannellini or borlotti

4 tablespoons chopped flat-leaf parsley

Salt and freshly ground black pepper

1.35 litres water, or more as needed

175g small soup pasta, such as tubettini, ditalini, pennette,
  or broken spaghetti

Heat the oil in a large, heavy-bottomed saucepan over medium heat. Add the onions, or garlic, or both and sauté until the onions are golden, 5–8 minutes, or the garlic is golden, 2–3 minutes. Stir in the beans with their juice, the parsley and salt and pepper to taste. Using a wooden spoon, crush about a quarter of the beans against the side of the saucepan. Stir in the water and slowly bring to a boil, stirring occasionally. Add the pasta, reduce the heat to medium, and simmer until the pasta is tender, about 10 minutes. Stir in extra water if the soup is too thick for your taste. Taste and adjust the seasoning, if necessary. *Serves 4–6.*

VARIATIONS

Pasta and Potato Soup Replace the cans of beans with 2 peeled and cubed medium potatoes. When the onions are golden, stir in the potatoes and sauté 10 minutes. Add the water, parsley and seasonings as above, and simmer until the potatoes can be pierced easily with a fork. Mash about a quarter of the potatoes against the side of the saucepan with the spoon. Add the pasta and continue cooking as above.

Red Pasta and Bean Soup Add 1 or 2 chopped and deseeded tomatoes or 2 tablespoons passata or tomato purée with the onions and continue with the recipe as above.

Pasta and Ham Soup You can add another dimension to your soup by adding chopped ham or bacon, when frying the onions.

TONY'S TIP:
using pasta in soup
You can use any kind of pasta you like in your soup. If you choose long pasta, such as spaghetti, break it up into 2.5cm lengths before using—this will give you something to do while waiting for the water to boil. You can also mix different types of pasta, thus getting rid of all those bits and pieces that you have been saving.

TONY'S TIP:
spicy serving trick
My father's trick for a spicy flavour was to put two slices of raw onion in the bottom of each bowl and then ladle the hot soup over. When you try this, keep a handkerchief handy—I did warn you.

Tony's ribollita

100ml olive oil

2 large leeks, rinsed and chopped

3 garlic cloves, chopped

1 large onion, chopped

1 large carrot, chopped

1 large celery stalk, chopped

1 small fresh chilli, deseeded and chopped
(wear gloves when handling; optional)

500g dried cannellini beans, soaked overnight and drained

1 ham bone

Water

Salt and freshly ground black pepper

Pinch fresh thyme or rosemary

4–6 slices Italian bread, toasted

85g grated Parmesan cheese

Heat half the oil in a large, heavy-bottomed saucepan over medium heat. Add the leeks, 1 garlic clove, onion, carrot, celery and chilli and sauté until the onion is soft, about 5 minutes. Add the beans and the ham bone. Pour in enough water to cover and bring to a boil. Reduce the heat and simmer, covered, until the beans are tender, about 2 hours, topping up the water, if necessary. When the beans are tender, remove and discard the ham bone. Using a wooden spoon, crush one-third of the beans against the side of the saucepan and add salt and pepper to taste. (At this point, the soup can be left to cool, then covered and chilled for up to 3 days in the refrigerator.)

Just before serving, heat the remaining oil in a medium frying pan over medium heat. Add the remaining 2 garlic cloves and thyme or rosemary leaves and sauté until the garlic is golden, 2–3 minutes. Remove the pan from the heat. Using a slotted spoon, remove and discard the garlic. Reheat the soup until piping hot. Pour half the garlic-flavoured oil into the soup. Taste and adjust the seasoning. Put a slice of bread in the bottom of each soup bowl and sprinkle with half the cheese. Ladle the soup into the bowls. Pour the remaining oil over each bowl of soup, then sprinkle with the remaining cheese. *Serves 4–6.*

VARIATION
Ligurian Minestrone Prepare as for ribollita, but stir in some pesto just before serving.

What's in a name?
RIBOLLITA

Ribollita means "boiled twice"; this suggests that you can make a huge pot of this soup and keep reheating it.

TONY'S TIP:
canned beans

For those who haven't planned ahead and don't want to start with dried beans, use two cans of cooked beans (drained and rinsed), and you won't have to boil the soup for 2 hours.

A FAMILY OF VEGETABLE SOUPS

These are first-aid dishes, for when you get home, want something hot and have nothing in the fridge. All you need is some pasta and vegetables. Basically, these are peasant dishes, even though you may have been ploughing the word processor rather than the fields. Now, fancy restaurants call them *cucina povera,* which means "poor cuisine," and charge a peasant's yearly wages for it!

Here is my basic formula for vegetable soup, so you can make your own creations. The theory is that there should be at least one item from each group. There is no law that says you can't use two or three from each food group. I like to have a potato in the soup even if I am using pasta or rice. Tomato, as well as herbs, go very well. But I am giving you the minimum requirements, so you are not restricted by your ingredients.

Fat: oil, margarine, butter or bacon
Flavour 1: garlic, onion, celery or carrot
Flavour 2: parsley, tomato, spoonful of tomato purée, oregano or basil
Starch: potato, any kind of pasta, rice or barley
Legumes: beans (cannellini, borlotti, flageolet, broad), chickpeas or lentils
Greens: lettuce, escarole, chicory, spinach, Swiss chard, kale, cabbage, spring greens, radish tops or celery leaves

Clean-the-larder soup

50ml olive or sunflower oil
1 medium onion, chopped
1 medium tomato, chopped
1 medium potato, peeled and cubed
Handful spaghetti, broken up
Handful penne
400g can borlotti beans, drained and rinsed
1 handful salad greens
1 litre water, or more as needed
Salt and freshly ground black pepper

Heat the oil in a large, heavy-bottomed saucepan over high heat. Add the onion and sauté until soft, about 5 minutes. Stir in the remaining ingredients and bring to a boil. Reduce the heat, cover, and simmer until the potato is tender and the pasta is firm-tender, about 30 minutes. Add more water, if necessary. *Serves 4.*

Clean-the-fridge soup

50ml olive or sunflower oil

55g bacon, diced

1 medium onion, chopped

1 medium celery stalk, chopped

1 medium carrot, chopped

**400g can cannellini beans, drained
   and rinsed**

Handful of white or brown long-grain rice

75g shredded Savoy cabbage

1 litre water

Salt and freshly ground black pepper

Heat the oil in a large, heavy-bottomed saucepan
over high heat. Add the bacon, onion, celery and
carrot and sauté until the onion is soft, about
5 minutes. Stir in the remaining ingredients and
bring to a boil. Reduce the heat, cover, and simmer
until the rice is tender, about 30 minutes. *Serves 4.*

Carrot soup

This soup is easy to make and looks elegant when finished. Garnish each plate with a sprig of parsley.

225ml water

9 carrots, peeled and shredded

30g butter

1 small onion, chopped

1 tablespoon plain flour

1½ teaspoons salt

Freshly ground black pepper

700ml milk

75ml single cream

Bring a medium saucepan of salted water to a boil over high heat. Add the carrots and boil until very tender, about 10 minutes. Meanwhile, melt the butter in a large, heavy-bottomed saucepan over medium heat. Add the onion and sauté until soft, about 5 minutes. Stir in the flour, salt, and pepper to taste and cook for 2 minutes, stirring. Remove the saucepan from the heat and slowly stir in the milk until blended and smooth. Place the pan over low heat and simmer, stirring constantly, until the mixture is thick, about 5 minutes. Stir in the carrots, their cooking liquid, and the cream. Taste and adjust the seasoning, if necessary. *Serves 4–6.*

VARIATIONS

Creamed Carrot Soup Prepare the soup as above, but do not stir in the cream. Ladle the soup into a food processor or blender and process until smooth. Add the cream and taste and adjust the seasoning, if necessary.

Fried Onion Garnish Heat 2 tablespoons sunflower oil in a small frying pan over medium heat. Add 1 small chopped onion and sauté until brown and begining to crisp, about 15 minutes. Remove from the pan and drain on paper towels. Sprinkle a few over each serving.

Courgette soup

50ml olive oil

900g courgettes, sliced into 3mm-thick rounds

2 garlic cloves, chopped

450ml chicken stock

Salt and freshly ground black pepper

100ml double cream

25g grated Parmesan cheese

3 tablespoons chopped fresh basil

3 tablespoons chopped flat-leaf parsley

Whole basil leaves

Heat the oil in a large, heavy-bottomed saucepan over medium heat. Add the courgettes and garlic and sauté until golden, about 30 minutes. Stir in the stock with salt and pepper to taste, and bring to a boil. Ladle the soup into a food processor or blender and process until blended. Return to the saucepan over medium heat and stir in the cream, cheese, basil and parsley, stirring until the cheese melts; do not boil. Taste and adjust the seasoning, if necessary. Ladle the soup into bowls, add a few basil leaves, and coarsely grind pepper over each. *Serves 4–6.*

GARNISH VARIATIONS

For a really elegant touch, top each bowl with a fried courgette flower. For each serving, deep-fry one medium flower, including about 2cm of the stem, about 4 minutes; drain and float in each bowl.

Alternatively, you can use fried courgette slices for garnish. Heat 2 tablespoons sunflower oil in a small frying pan over medium-high heat. Add 12–18 thin courgette slices and fry until golden brown on each side, 5–7 minutes. Drain on paper towels. Add 2 or 3 slices to each bowl with a leaf of fresh basil or parsley.

Neapolitan minestrone

I have never seen this minestrone in any book, so I guess it must be a family invention because my grandpa used to make it in Naples. It is a very hearty dish. Of course, he always started with dried beans, which you can too, if you want. One of its special treats for us as kids was that no matter how carefully it was cooked, a burnt crust always seemed to form at the bottom of the pan. We kids fought for the privilege of scraping and eating the burnt bottom pieces.

50ml olive oil

1 garlic clove, chopped

1 medium celery stalk, chopped

1 head escarole, rinsed and chopped

2 medium potatoes, peeled and cubed

900g canned cannellini beans, drained and rinsed

2 tablespoons tomato purée

Salt and freshly ground black pepper

1.8 litres water, or more as needed

100g long-grain white or brown rice

Heat the oil in a large, heavy-bottomed saucepan over medium heat. Add the garlic, celery and escarole and sauté until the garlic is golden, 2–3 minutes. Add the potatoes, beans, tomato purée and salt and pepper to taste. Stir in the water and bring to a boil. Reduce the heat, cover, and simmer until the potatoes are tender, 30–40 minutes, topping up the water, if necessary. Stir in the rice, return to a boil, and boil until the rice is tender, about 30 minutes. Taste and adjust the seasoning, if necessary. *Serves 4–6.*

"My great uncle (the one with the hat on) had a clever dog who helped him cultivate the fields with his paws. But the dog always stopped when the church bell tolled at noon, indicating time for lunch, which may well have been minestrone left over from the night before."

Stuffed lettuce soup

Signor Valerio on top of Castelnuovo Magra served this soup. This dish is worth all the trouble needed to make it and for an extra-special taste, make the chicken stock from scratch, following the recipe on page 55.

1 large egg

1 boneless, skinless chicken breast, cooked and finely minced

25g dried breadcrumbs

2 tablespoons grated Parmesan cheese

1 teaspoon chopped flat-leaf parsley

1 teaspoon chopped fresh thyme

Salt

½ teaspoon freshly ground white pepper

1 head romaine lettuce, using the outer and middle 8 leaves,
   rinsed and patted dry

1.8 litres chicken stock

Crack the egg into a medium bowl. Stir in the chicken, breadcrumbs, cheese, parsley, thyme, salt to taste, and pepper, stirring to form a smooth paste; set aside. Bring about 5cm water to a boil in a heavy-bottomed saucepan. Add the lettuce leaves and cover. Cook until the leaves just wilt, about 5 minutes. Drain and cool. From each leaf remove the central rib and cut into four approximately square pieces. Discard any pieces that are torn. Working with one lettuce piece at a time, put 1 mounded teaspoon of the chicken mixture on the leaf. Turn up the bottom of the leaf to enclose the filling, then fold in each side. Roll up to completely enclose the filling; set aside. Continue until all the filling and all the lettuce leaves are used.

When you are ready to serve, bring the chicken stock to a boil in a large, heavy-bottomed saucepan over high heat. Reduce the heat to medium-low, carefully add the lettuce rolls to the pan, and simmer until they are heated through, about 15 minutes; do not boil or they may fall apart. Taste and adjust the seasoning, if necessary. Ladle the soup into bowls, including 4–6 lettuce rolls in each. *Serves 4–6.*

TONY'S TIP:
advance preparation
To save yourself time, you can prepare the lettuce rolls in advance. Just cover and chill the lettuce rolls after you've made them—they will keep for up to one day in the refrigerator.

Onion soup

50g butter
6 medium onions, thinly sliced
1 teaspoon sugar
1.35 litres beef stock
Salt and freshly ground black pepper
4 slices Italian bread, toasted
25g grated Parmesan cheese
Parsley sprigs (optional)

Melt the butter in a large, heavy-bottomed saucepan over medium heat. Stir in the onions and sugar and sauté until the onions are brown, about 10 minutes. Stir in the stock and bring to a boil. Reduce the heat, cover, and simmer 1 hour. Add salt and pepper to taste. To serve, put a slice of bread in the bottom of each bowl, ladle the hot soup over, and sprinkle the cheese over each. A little sprig of parsley for garnish is a good idea. *Serves 4.*

TONY'S TIP:
extra things to do

For a more interesting version of Grandma Flo's red soup, add some of the following ingredients.

Pastina Bring the strained broth to a boil, add a handful of pastina, and cook until tender, about 10 minutes.

Vegetables Bring the strained broth to a boil, add a peeled and diced potato and a chopped celery stalk to the broth, and cook until tender, about 30 minutes.

Meat Dice some of the cooked meat and add it to the strained soup.

Barley Add a cup of cooked barley to the broth before serving.

Grandma Flo's red soup

1.3kg beef bones and beef chuck
2 large celery stalks, chopped
2 medium carrots, chopped
1 medium onion, chopped
1 small can cream of tomato soup, or 55g tomato purée
Salt and freshly ground black pepper
Water

Combine the beef bones and meat, celery, carrots, onion, soup and salt and pepper to taste in a large saucepan. Pour in enough water to cover and bring to a boil, skimming the surface as necessary. Reduce the heat to low, cover, and simmer until the meat is tender, 1½–2 hours. Strain the soup through a colander set over a large bowl in the sink. Remove and reserve the beef chunks, but discard the other solid ingredients. Using a large metal spoon, skim any fat from the surface of the broth. Return the broth to the washed saucepan over medium-high heat and heat through. *Serves 4–6.*

Chicken soup

When my daughters were small, they had a book called My Grandma
Puts Chicken Feet in Her Soup. *My grandma put in not only the feet
but also the head, the gizzards and the unformed eggs!*

1 chicken, about 900g

3 litres water

Salt

1 large celery stalk, broken in half

1 medium onion, peeled but left whole

1 medium carrot, peeled and broken in half

3 sprigs parsley, stems bruised

Combine the chicken, water and salt to taste in a large saucepan or
stockpot. Bring to a boil very slowly over low heat. Add the remaining
ingredients and increase the heat to medium. Cover and simmer until
the chicken is very tender and almost falling from the bones, about
3 hours. Strain the soup through a colander set over a large bowl in
the sink. Remove and reserve the chicken pieces if you are serving it
in the broth, but discard the other solid ingredients. Using a large
metal spoon, skim any fat from the surface of the soup. Return the
broth to the washed saucepan over medium-high heat and reheat.
Serves 6.

VARIATIONS

Clear Soup Beat 2 egg whites in a bowl, and then beat in a few
tablespoons of the strained broth. Pour this mixture into the
remaining broth in the saucepan over high heat and stir vigorously.
Bring to a boil, stirring constantly. You should see tiny flecks of egg
forming. Remove the saucepan from the heat, cover, and let stand
for 10 minutes. Strain the soup through the colander lined with
wet muslin or paper towels set over a bowl in the sink. You should
now have a perfectly clear, sparkling broth.

Italian Soup (*Stracciatella*) Beat 2 large eggs in a bowl with
2 tablespoons grated Parmesan cheese. Bring the strained broth to
a rolling boil over high heat. Beat a couple of tablespoons of the
broth into the eggs. Stir the eggs into the boiling broth.

Soup Extras Add a handful of any of the following: cooked egg
noodles; cooked peas and Parmesan; cooked rice or barley; cooked
tortellini or tiny pastina.

"Three generations at
the table is a usual
occurrence in Italy.
Everyday meals start
with pasta or soup and,
of course, the wine is
always on the table."

2 PASTA, GRAINS AND PIZZA

Here you will find dishes that are favourites not only of my own family, but of many of my friends as well. In addition to being served before a meat or fish course, as Italians do, many of these recipes can be prepared as main courses or as substantial snacks.

PASTA SAUCES

"Now as we dip into sauces for pasta, let me ask you to be open-minded and adventurous. In America, whenever anyone learned of our Italian extraction, the first question was, 'How do you make your spaghetti sauce?' And then they proceeded with stories of how their grandma would simmer the sauce for hours and hours. One time, to answer the eternal question, we had a spaghetti party, when we served nothing but spaghetti with a choice of six different sauces. Sauce for pasta goes all the way from pesto, where the sauce is not cooked at all, to *ragù*, which has to be cooked for hours."

Chopped tomato sauce

Making tomato sauce for your pasta is very easy. A basic sauce can be made from chopped canned tomatoes, tomato passata, or tomato purée—each sauce with its particular texture and uses. And once you have mastered the basic recipe, there are many variations that can be made by adding more ingredients—you can vary it to your taste. If you make your own sauce rather than buying it, you'll know for sure that it's been made from wholesome and simple ingredients. Just look at the ingredients of ready-bottled sauces—it seems they require various chemicals to make them work! And, of course, keeping a few cans of tomato in your cupboard, along with dried pasta, means that you will be able to whip up a decent meal in record time.

50ml sunflower oil
1 medium onion, chopped, or 1 garlic clove, chopped, or both
2x400g cans chopped tomatoes
8 fresh basil leaves
Salt and freshly ground black pepper

Heat the oil in a large, heavy-bottomed saucepan over medium heat. Add the onions or garlic and sauté until the onions are soft and golden, but not brown, about 7 minutes, or the garlic is golden, 2–3 minutes. Stir in the chopped tomatoes, half the basil, and salt and pepper to taste. Reduce the heat to low and simmer, uncovered, about 10 minutes. If the sauce becomes too thick, add a little water. Taste and adjust the seasoning, if necessary. Stir in the remaining basil just before serving. *Serves 4.*

VARIATIONS

Tomato Passata Sauce Make the sauce as above, except instead of chopped tomatoes add a 680g jar of passata. Simmer 20 minutes instead of 10. This sauce has a thicker consistency than the one above and can be used for both long and short pasta. *Serves 4.*

Tomato Purée Sauce Make the sauce as above, except instead of chopped tomatoes add 350g tomato purée dissolved in 225ml water. Simmer 30 minutes. You may need to add more water to get a thick cream-like consistency. This sauce has the thickest consistency and is ideal for short pasta like penne and rigatoni. *Serves 4.*

MORE VARIATIONS

All the following will dress 500g pasta, cooked and drained, and will serve 4 people.

Mushroom Sauce Prepare **Chopped Tomato Sauce** or **Tomato Passata Sauce**; set aside. Heat 50ml sunflower oil in a medium frying pan over medium heat. Add 225g sliced white mushrooms and salt and freshly ground black pepper to taste and sauté until the mushrooms brown and the liquid evaporates, about 10 minutes. Add to the tomato sauce and reheat.

Courgette Sauce Prepare **Chopped Tomato Sauce** or **Tomato Passata Sauce**; set aside. Heat 50ml sunflower oil in a medium frying pan over medium heat. Add 225g sliced courgettes with salt and freshly ground black pepper to taste and sauté until the courgettes soften and brown, about 10 minutes. Add to the tomato sauce and reheat. Serve with grated Parmesan cheese.

Ricotta Sauce Prepare **Tomato Passata Sauce**. Put 225g ricotta cheese and 25g grated Parmesan cheese in a large bowl; mix with a fork. Gradually add the sauce a spoonful or two at a time, until the mixture is pink and has the consistency of very thick cream; you might not need all the sauce. Combine with hot, drained pasta and any remaining sauce. Add a few fresh basil leaves just before serving. This sauce is recommended with short pasta.

Cream Sauce Prepare **Tomato Passata Sauce**. During the last 2 minutes of cooking, remove the pan from the heat and stir in 50ml double cream. Dress the pasta with this sauce and 25g grated Parmesan cheese.

Grandma's Sauce Prepare **Tomato Purée Sauce**, but do not dissolve the tomato purée in the water. Add the tomato purée to the sautéed onions and/or garlic as above, and continue sautéing 15 minutes. Now add the water and simmer 10 minutes longer.

Sauce with Pork Remove the bone from one pork chop and cut the meat into 1cm cubes. Using the **Tomato Purée Sauce** recipe, sauté the pork with the onions or garlic, until the pork is brown, about 10 minutes. Then add the tomato purée and continue with the recipe.

CANNED TOMATOES
When you buy canned tomatoes, choose those that are either whole—which can be easily chopped in the pan with a fork and knife—chopped, or chopped with juice. Avoid tomatoes packed with flavouring ingredients such as basil and oregano because you will want to control the flavouring yourself.

TONY'S TIP:
using tomato sauce
These sauces are not exclusively for pasta. I've also used this sauce as an ingredient in some of my other pasta and vegetable dishes, such as **Christina's All-Time Favourite Gnocchi** (page 82) and **Aubergine Parmesan** (page 177).

Fresh tomato sauce

This sauce and its variations all use fresh tomatoes, but only vine-ripened tomatoes will give you the flavour you need. This version is family style because we don't go through the trouble of removing tomato skins and seeds.

50ml olive oil
1 medium onion, chopped, or 2 garlic cloves, chopped, or both
900g juicy, vine-ripened tomatoes, cut into eighths
6 fresh basil leaves
Salt and freshly ground black pepper

Heat the oil in a large, heavy-bottomed saucepan over medium heat. Add the onions or garlic, and sauté until the onions are golden, but not brown, about 7 minutes, or the garlic is golden, 2–3 minutes. Add the tomatoes, half the basil, and salt and pepper to taste. Reduce the heat to medium-low and cook, uncovered, until the tomatoes are soft and tender, but not reduced to a paste, about 10 minutes. Taste and adjust the seasoning, if necessary. Stir in the remaining basil just before serving. *Serves 4–6.*

VARIATIONS

Elegant Sauce Make this sauce when you are having guests for dinner, and you don't want to give them pasta with messes of tomato skins—they're indigestible. You really have to like the people to go through this trouble! Prepare the sauce as above, except use peeled and deseeded tomatoes.

Extra Elegant Sauce This variation is for really important people coming to dinner. It is also great if you have a lot of fresh tomatoes that you would like to preserve. Cook the tomatoes until they are very soft and break up, about 20 minutes. Remove the pan from the heat and leave the tomatoes to cool. Using a wooden spoon, press the sauce through a sieve placed over a large bowl, pressing until only the seeds and skins are left; discard. Use the tomato purée instead of the tomatoes to make the sauce as above. You also can freeze the tomato purée for up to 1 month to use in sauces, soups and casseroles.

TONY'S TIP:
peeling and deseeding

Core the tomatoes and cut an "X" in the bottoms. Place in a bowl and cover with boiling water. After about 30 seconds, drain the hot water and replace with cold water. The skin should now peel off easily. Cut the tomatoes in half and, holding each half over a bowl, squeeze out the seeds.

TONY'S TIP:
perfect pasta sauce

Let the onions become soft and golden before adding the tomatoes; adding the tomatoes to the uncooked onions fixes the acidity into the sauce. Cook onions quickly so that they don't stew. For the same reason, don't cover the sauce while it simmers.

Bolognese sauce

Ragù

This recipe is my version of the classic sauce, which, if I may say so myself, knocks the socks off of what is usually served. It's excellent with fresh tagliatelle. It's a hearty dish, so if you're serving it as an appetiser rather than a main course, give small portions.

75g butter

2½ tablespoons olive oil

140g pancetta or cured (not smoked) bacon, finely chopped

1 medium onion, finely chopped

1 medium carrot, finely chopped

1 medium celery stalk, finely chopped

175g minced pork

175g minced beef

55g sausage meat, preferably Italian, casing removed if necessary

150ml dry white wine

325ml chicken stock

3 tablespoons tomato purée

Salt and freshly ground black pepper

50ml single cream

Melt half the butter with the oil in a large, heavy-bottomed saucepan over medium heat. Add the bacon, onions, carrot and celery, and sauté until the vegetables are soft, about 5 minutes. Stir in the pork, beef, and sausage meat and continue sautéing until all are brown and crumbly, about 15 minutes. Reduce the heat to low, add the wine, 50ml stock, the tomato purée and salt and pepper to taste. Cover and simmer for about 1½ hours, stirring frequently, and gradually adding more stock as it is absorbed until it has all been used. The sauce should be a thick gruel at this point. Stir in the cream and then the remaining butter. Taste and adjust the seasoning, if necessary. *Serves 6.*

"Carol and I once took a car trip through Bruges, Aix-la-Chapelle, Heidelberg, and Zurich. We drove over the Alps but never saw them because of the clouds and rain. Fed up with rain and wind for four days, we headed south and never stopped until we reached Bologna. All of a sudden, it was balmy and pleasant. It was evening. We sat under the stars and had *tagliatelle alla Bolognese* and Lambrusco. We had reached heaven."

Pesto

One of the nicest pasta sauces ever. It is known as pesto alla Genovese, *but all Liguria makes it. In fact, the whole world makes it. Make it fresh when the basil is plentiful. When it isn't, don't bother. And never be tempted to buy pre-made sauce in a sealed jar. If you like garlic, you can add another clove. If you really like cheese, you can increase the quantity, but you may need to compensate with a little more oil.*

100g fresh basil, rinsed and dried

2 garlic cloves

25g grated Parmesan cheese

25g grated pecorino cheese

3 tablespoons pine nuts, toasted

Pinch of salt

¼ teaspoon freshly ground black pepper

225ml olive oil

Combine all the ingredients, except the oil, in a food processor or blender. With the motor running, slowly add the oil through the feed tube until a thick and creamy sauce forms. This sauce will keep in the refrigerator for 3–4 days. *Serves 4–6.*

TONY'S TIP:

other uses for pesto

Use on pasta like spaghetti, linguine, trenette, and so on. Also, add to soups just before serving.

Sauce marinara

50ml olive oil

1 medium onion, chopped, or 3 garlic cloves, chopped, or both

3 anchovy fillets in oil

2x400g cans whole tomatoes

75g coarsely chopped kalamata or Gaeta olives

3 tablespoons capers, rinsed

3 bunches fresh basil, chopped

Salt and freshly ground black pepper

Heat the oil in a large, heavy-bottomed saucepan over medium heat. Add the onion or garli, and the anchovies, and sauté until the onion is soft and golden but not brown, about 7 minutes, or the garlic is golden, 2–3 minutes. Add the tomatoes, olives, capers, half the basil, and salt and pepper to taste. Reduce the heat to medium and cook, uncovered, until the tomatoes are soft and tender, but not reduced to a paste, about 10 minutes. Taste and adjust the seasoning, if necessary. Stir in the remaining basil before serving with spaghetti or linguine. *Serves 4–6.*

Fake bottarga sauce with spaghetti

This is a popular dish in Sardinia, which is where I tried it for the very first time.

500g spaghetti

50ml olive oil

3 garlic cloves, crushed

6 anchovy fillets in oil, chopped (optional)

1 small fresh chilli, deseeded and chopped (wear gloves when handling), or freshly ground black pepper

115g dried breadcrumbs

50g butter, cubed

2 tablespoons chopped flat-leaf parsley

Bring a large saucepan of salted water to the boil. Add the pasta, stir, and continue boiling until the pasta is firm-tender, according to the package directions. Meanwhile, heat the oil in a large frying pan over medium heat. Add the garlic, anchovies, if using, and chilli, if using, and sauté until the anchovies dissolve, about 5 minutes. (If you don't like anchovies, omitting them will still give a very flavourful sauce.) Stir in the breadcrumbs and fry, stirring occasionally, until crisp and golden, about 10 minutes. Add pepper to taste, if you haven't used the chilli. Drain the pasta, reserving a few tablespoons of the cooking water. Put the pasta in a large bowl and stir in the butter, stirring until it melts. If the pasta gets too dry, add 1–2 tablespoons of the reserved cooking water. Equally divide the pasta among individual plates, top with the breadcrumb and anchovy mixture, and sprinkle with parsley. *Serves 4–6.*

SPAGHETTI DISHES

What's in a name? BOTTARGA

Bottarga is dried, salted, and pressed fish eggs. They are grated over pasta after it is seasoned with oil or butter. Just in case your supermarket happens to be out of bottarga, the recipe to the left will do in a pinch. The breadcrumbs used in this recipe resemble grated bottarga.

Spaghetti with mussels

If you live near a place that sells fresh shellfish, try cherrystone clams, cockles, or baby clams instead of the mussels.

1.3kg live mussels, scrubbed and rinsed
50ml olive oil
3 garlic cloves, chopped
Salt
500g spaghetti or linguine
Freshly ground black pepper
Handful chopped flat-leaf parsley

TONY'S TIP:
cooked to perfection

The key to cooking pasta is using sufficient boiling water. Use 3–4 litres per 500g of pasta, even more for large pasta like rigatoni and lasagne. Bring the water to a boil, add 1–2 teaspoons salt and the pasta, and stir. No need to add any oil, as some suggest.

When the water boils again, turn the heat down so there's a gentle rolling boil. Stir the pasta from time to time as it cooks. Fresh pasta will take about 3–5 minutes to cook. For dried pasta, follow the recommended cooking time on the package. About 2 or 3 minutes before the end of cooking time, take a piece out and taste it. Try to stop cooking the pasta when it is slightly underdone, or *al dente,* as the heat will go on cooking it after draining. Drain the pasta in a colander. Dress and serve the pasta immediately.

Pick over the mussels and discard any with cracked shells, or open ones that do not close when tapped firmly. Place in a large, heavy-bottomed saucepan or stockpot, with a tight-fitting lid, over high heat. Cover tightly and cook, shaking the pot frequently, just until all mussels open, about 5 minutes. Remove from the heat and leave to cool, discarding any mussels that are not open. Reserve any liquid that has accumulated in the bottom of the pot. Remove all but 8–12 mussels from their shells; discard the shells. Coarsely chop about one-third of the shelled mussels; set aside the shelled and unshelled mussels. Line a small sieve with a piece of wet muslin or paper towels and set it over a bowl. Strain the reserved cooking liquid to eliminate any sand.

Heat the oil in a large frying pan over medium heat. Add the garlic and sauté until golden, 2–3 minutes. Reduce the heat to low, stir in the chopped mussels and cooking liquid, and simmer until the liquid reduces by half. Add the remaining shelled and unshelled mussels and continue simmering for 3 minutes. Meanwhile, bring a large saucepan of salted water to a boil. Add the pasta, stir, and continue boiling until the pasta is firm-tender, according to the package directions. Drain the pasta, then return it to the saucepan over low heat. Add the mussel sauce and toss so the pasta is coated with the sauce and the mussels are distributed throughout. Continue simmering until the sauce turns from watery to a light gravy consistency. Turn off the heat and add a generous grinding of pepper and the parsley. *Serves 4–6.*

"Living in Naples, my family was always close to the sea. On Sundays, my grandmother and the family would visit the fish market for lunchtime fare. Clams and other shellfish would usually be served raw but might appear again in the pasta."

Spaghetti with clams, Syracusa style

1kg raw baby clams, rinsed
50ml olive oil
2 garlic cloves, chopped
Freshly ground black pepper
Salt
3 tablespoons chopped flat-leaf parsley
500g spaghetti

Pick over the clams and discard any with cracked shells, or open ones that do not close when tapped firmly. Place in a large, heavy-bottomed saucepan or stockpot, with a tight-fitting lid, over high heat. Cover tightly and cook, shaking the pot frequently, just until the clams open, 5–8 minutes. Discard any clams that are not open. Line a small sieve with wet muslin or paper towels and set it over a bowl. Strain the clams; set the clams and cooking liquid aside separately.

Heat the oil in a large frying pan over medium heat. Add the garlic and sauté until golden, 2–3 minutes. Add the reserved cooking liquid from the clams and let it simmer until reduced by one-third. Stir in the reserved clams and a good grinding of pepper, then simmer for 3 minutes. Meanwhile, bring a large saucepan of salted water to a boil. Add the spaghetti, stir, and continue boiling until the spaghetti is firm-tender, or according to the package directions. Drain the spaghetti. Add the spaghetti to the clam sauce and simmer, stirring, until the sauce begins to thicken, about 3 minutes. *Serves 4–6.*

VARIATION

Spaghetti with Canned Clams Cook the garlic in oil as above. Add 450g canned clams and their liquid and 1 large deseeded and chopped tomato. Simmer 5 minutes. When you are ready to serve, stir in 1 large deseeded tomato, cut into wedges, and sprinkle over some fresh basil leaves.

Spaghetti with garlic and oil
Spaghetti aglio e olio

When there is really nothing else in the house to make a meal, surely there is enough to prepare this dish. But take care. If you are going to spend any time socialising after this dish, make sure that your companions have some, too.

500g spaghetti
50ml olive oil
4–6 garlic cloves, chopped
1 small fresh chilli, deseeded and chopped
    (wear gloves when handling; optional)
2 tablespoons chopped flat-leaf parsley
Freshly ground black pepper
Grated Parmesan cheese (optional)

Bring a large saucepan of salted water to a boil. Add the spaghetti, stir, and continue boiling until the pasta is firm-tender, according to the package directions. Meanwhile, heat the oil in a large frying pan over medium heat. Add the garlic and sauté until golden, 2–3 minutes. If you use chilli, add it now. Drain the spaghetti. Stir the spaghetti into the garlic and oil in the pan over medium heat and continue stirring 1 minute, then turn off the heat. Stir in the parsley. Grind in some black pepper and serve with Parmesan for sprinkling over, if you like. *Serves 4–6.*

VARIATIONS

Colourful and Spicy If you can find mild fresh chilli peppers, such as wax or New Mexico chillies, deseed and slice them (wear gloves when handling). Add them to the frying pan with the garlic and sauté. This will make for a very pretty dish.

Garlic Mania When you stir the drained pasta into the sauce, add half a garlic clove pressed through a garlic press. Don't cook or you will lose the zing.

Fish Mania Add 6 anchovy fillets in oil to the garlic and sauté until they dissolve.

TONY'S TIP:
eating spaghetti

If you cut up your spaghetti and then eat it with a spoon, or if you make a mess of trying to roll it on a fork, don't despair—here's how to do it the Italian way. Take a soup spoon in your left hand and a fork in your right hand (or vice versa if you are a lefty!)

Lesson 1 Rake up three strands of spaghetti on the fork, shift the spoon under it, and wind it in the spoon.

Lesson 2 If you have mastered lesson one, perform the same operation of picking up three strands, but this time without the spoon—use the rim of the plate instead.

Lesson 3 Now try the winding in the middle of the pasta—but only three strands! Following these steps you will become an expert spaghetti eater—indistinguishable from the natives in five meals.

TONY'S TIP:
cooking bacon

When cooked, bacon first becomes translucent and soft and gradually turns opaque and ultimately brittle as cooking continues. We don't want crispy bacon in these recipes, so initial cooking is to translucency, then additional liquid is added to keep the bacon soft.

Spaghetti Roman style
Spaghetti all'amatriciana

- 50ml olive oil
- 2 small onions, thinly sliced
- 175g pancetta or cured (not smoked) bacon, cut into thin matchstick strips
- 150ml dry white wine
- 675g canned chopped tomatoes
- Salt and freshly ground black pepper
- 500g spaghetti
- 115g grated mature pecorino cheese

Heat the oil in a large, heavy-bottomed saucepan over medium heat. Add the onions and sauté until soft, about 5 minutes. Add the bacon and continue sautéing until translucent, about 10 minutes. Add the wine and cook until it evaporates by half. Stir in the tomatoes and leave to bubble 15 minutes. Season with the salt and pepper to taste. Meanwhile, bring a large saucepan of salted water to a boil. Add the spaghetti, stir, and continue boiling until the pasta is firm-tender, according to the package directions. Drain the spaghetti. Stir the spaghetti into the sauce and add the cheese. Taste and adjust the seasoning, if necessary. *Serves 4–6.*

Pasta alla carbonara

500g pasta, such as rigatoni, spaghetti, or linguine

50ml olive oil

175g pancetta or cured (not smoked) bacon, finely chopped

2 garlic cloves, crushed

5 large eggs

55g grated Parmesan cheese

55g grated mature pecorino cheese

Freshly ground black pepper

Bring a large saucepan of salted water to a boil. Add the pasta, stir, and continue boiling until the pasta is firm-tender, according to the package directions. Meanwhile, heat the oil in a large frying pan over medium heat. Add the bacon and garlic and sauté until the bacon is translucent, 5–8 minutes. In another large frying pan, beat the eggs with the cheeses and pepper to taste. Drain the pasta; immediately add it to the pan with the eggs. Add the bacon and oil, put the pan over low heat, and cook, stirring, until the eggs are creamy. Do not increase the heat or the eggs will set and the dish will be too dry. *Serves 4–6.*

Rigatoni à la vodka

55g butter

**1 small fresh chilli, deseeded and chopped
(wear gloves when handling)**

125ml vodka

600g passata

Salt

150ml double cream

55g grated Parmesan cheese

500g rigatoni or penne rigate

Melt the butter in a large, heavy-bottomed saucepan over medium heat. Add the chilli and vodka and simmer 2 minutes. Stir in the passata and salt to taste, reduce the heat, and simmer 20 minutes, uncovered, stirring occasionally. Stir the cream and cheese into the sauce and heat through; do not boil. Meanwhile, bring a large saucepan of salted water to a boil. Add the rigatoni, stir, and continue boiling until the pasta is firm-tender, according to the package directions. Drain the pasta well, shaking off the liquid. Stir into the sauce. *Serves 4–6.*

MORE PASTA DISHES

TONY'S TIP:
adding parmesan

I use about 1 heaped tablespoon of Parmesan per serving and stir it into the pasta and sauce before I serve. Then I put additional Parmesan in a bowl for guests to help themselves.

Grated Parmesan cheese is served with pasta and soups with vegetable or meat sauces, but never with fish or shellfish dishes.

MAKING PASTA

If you live near a specialty shop that makes pasta with good flour and eggs, you are lucky. After all, most Italians still buy their pasta fresh from specialty shops. Don't be tempted by the supermarket variety—it is full of additives. Stick to dried pasta if you buy it from a supermarket. However, for the best flavour, and fun, make your own fresh pasta.

Durum wheat is a type of hard wheat, traditionally grown in Southern Italy, where a lot of the pasta is made. It is held to give a better flavour to pasta and bread than other types of wheat, so you can try it. However, plain flour will also give a satisfactory result.

Fresh pasta dough

This basic recipe can be used to make almost any flat pasta shape, such as tagliatelle, linguine, trenette, lasagne, pappardelle or canneloni. You can also use this recipe for making filled pasta such as ravioli, tortellini or cappelletti.

> **About 115g durum wheat or plain**
> **flour per serving**
> **1 large egg per serving**

Put one half of the flour in a large bowl and make a well in the middle. Break the eggs into the well and gradually mix the flour into the eggs, until the dough becomes too stiff to stir with a wooden spoon. Turn out onto a floured surface and knead, working in the rest of the flour, until a smooth, elastic dough forms. Use your whole body weight, not just your wrists when you knead. If the dough is sticky or lumpy, knead in a little extra flour. The longer you knead, the better the pasta. You want an elastic, homogeneous dough. Shape the dough into a ball, cover with a dish towel, and leave to rest for 15 minutes.

Shaping pasta by hand
Break off the dough into manageable pieces, no bigger than a tennis ball. Using a lightly floured rolling pin, roll each piece of dough into a rectangle,

twice as long as it is wide, until the dough is of the desired thickness. (Thickness is a matter of personal taste—for thin pasta, it should be just under 1mm thick (equalling setting 6 on a pasta machine); for medium it should be 1.5mm thick (setting 5); and for thick, 2mm thick (setting 4). Set aside and leave to dry, uncovered, for at least 30 minutes.

Starting with the short edge, roll the pasta sheet into a spiral cylinder. Using a sharp knife, slice the pasta—thin slices for linguine (3mm); wider slices for tagliatelle (5mm); wider yet for pappardelle (3cm); widest for lasagne (7.5–10cm). Unroll the slices, lightly dust with flour, and set aside until required. You can keep these noodles in the open for 2–3 hours; any more than that, you need to put them in an airtight container.

Using a pasta machine

Cut a slice from the dough ball, flatten it with your hand, and flour generously. Put your machine on setting 1, the widest gap in the roller, and dust the rollers with flour. Feed the dough through. Dust the dough with more flour, increase the setting to 2, and feed the sheet of dough through again. Repeat, gradually increasing the settings until the dough reaches the desired thickness. Repeat with the remaining dough until it has all been rolled out. Set aside and let the pasta sheets dry, uncovered, for at least half an hour. Using the cutting edge of the machine, and working with one sheet of dough at a time, lightly dust the dough and rollers with flour, and feed it through to cut it to the desired width. If it doesn't cut cleanly, let the dough dry for another 30 minutes before cutting it. Lightly flour the surface, loosely pile the cut pasta on it, and leave to rest until required.

Freezing fresh pasta

Fresh pasta can be frozen for up to 4 weeks, and then used directly from the freezer. The only problem with freezing fresh pasta is that frozen pasta is very brittle. So, if you end up with pastina, use it in soups.

Tagliatelle with artichokes

50ml olive oil

85g pancetta or cured (not smoked) bacon, finely chopped

1 large onion, chopped

6 medium artichokes, cleaned (following the method on
page 190) and thinly sliced

675ml chicken stock or water

Salt

500g tagliatelle

2 small tomatoes, seeded and diced

Grated Parmesan cheese

"My daughters always ask: How is it possible that you can make a quick and perfectly acceptable pasta dish from the dregs of the refrigerator? My wife says: Tony, you've got to write down the recipes for the meals you invent. So, in this section, I have mixed in some inventions with traditional pasta recipes."

Heat the oil in a large frying pan over medium heat. Add the bacon and onion and sauté until the bacon is translucent and the onion soft, 5–8 minutes. Add the artichokes and continue to sauté for 5 minutes. Stir in the stock or water and salt to taste. Reduce the heat to low and simmer until the artichokes are tender, about 20 minutes. Meanwhile, bring a large saucepan of salted water to a boil. Add the tagliatelle, stir, and continue boiling until the tagliatelle is firm-tender, according to the package directions. Drain the tagliatelle, shaking off the liquid. Stir the tagliatelle into the sauce and add the tomatoes. Taste and adjust the seasoning, if necessary. Serve with Parmesan for sprinkling over. *Serves 6.*

VARIATIONS

Artichokes Neapolitan After the artichokes have cooked for 15 minutes, stir in 115g chopped, pitted kalamata olives and 2 tablespoons rinsed capers.

Artichokes and Cream When the artichokes are tender, pour 100ml single cream into the pan and warm through. Do not boil.

Tagliatelle with Broccoli Cook the bacon and onions as above and stir in the stock or water and salt to taste. Replace the artichokes with 450g broccoli, chopped into florets and bite-size pieces. Simmer until tender, about 10 minutes.

Vegetarian Tagliatelle with Artichokes Omit the bacon.

Tagliatelle with asparagus and prawns

This dish is a study in freshness and light. Use thin noodles. If you have fresh pasta, it's even better. Make the noodles extra wide and cut them up into odd pieces—the Italian name for these is stracci, *meaning rags.*

50ml olive oil

1 medium onion, chopped

675g asparagus spears, trimmed and cut into
   1cm pieces

450ml chicken or vegetable stock or water

Salt

500g medium or large raw prawns, shelled and deveined

500g tagliatelle, or linguine, trenette, or pappardelle

2 small tomatoes, deseeded and diced

Freshly ground black pepper

Heat the oil in a large frying pan over medium heat. Add the onion and sauté until soft, about 5 minutes. Add the asparagus, stock or water, and salt to taste. Reduce the heat to low and simmer until the asparagus is very soft and some of it appears to be "melting," 20–25 minutes. Add the prawns and continue cooking, uncovered, until they turn pink and curl, 3–5 minutes. Meanwhile, bring a large saucepan of salted water to a boil. Add the tagliatelle, stir, and continue boiling until the tagliatelle is firm-tender, according to the package directions. Drain the tagliatelle, shaking off the liquid. Stir the tagliatelle into the sauce and add the tomatoes. Season to taste with pepper. *Serves 4–6.*

What's in a name?

ACINI DI PEPE Peppercorns

BUCATINI
   Ones with little holes

CAPPELLETTI Little hats

CONCHIGLIE Shells

FARFALLE Butterflies

FETTUCCINE Little ribbons

LINGUINE Little tongues

LUMACHELLE Little snails

ORECCHIETTE Little ears

PENNE Feathers

RIGATONI
   The ones with lines on them

SPAGHETTI Little strings

TAGLIATELLE
   Little cut-up ones

TUBETTINI Little tubes

"Grandma Casillo, Uncle Nunzio, and Maria walking home from shopping for pasta in San Giuseppe Vesuviano in 1956."

Creamy mushroom and sausage pasta
Paglia e fieno

Paglia e fieno *means straw and hay, and in this recipe, two kinds of coloured pasta are used—plain egg noodles and spinach (green) noodles in equal parts. Watch the consistency; the pasta has a tendency to dry, so don't let it drain too long. The pasta should be wet and the sauce creamy, but you don't want the pasta to swim in it. If necessary, add a few tablespoons hot water and stir.*

55g butter
1 garlic clove, crushed
500g white mushrooms, wiped clean and sliced
Salt
250g sausage meat, casings removed if necessary
225ml single cream
250g fresh egg pasta
250g fresh spinach pasta
85g grated Parmesan cheese

Melt half the butter in a large frying pan over medium heat. Add the garlic and sauté until golden, 2–3 minutes. Remove and discard the garlic, then add the mushrooms and salt to taste and sauté until the mushrooms are brown and the liquid evaporates, about 10 minutes. Meanwhile, melt the remaining butter in a small saucepan over medium heat. Stir in the sausage meat and fry, stirring occasionally, until brown and crumbly, about 10 minutes. Heat the cream in a small saucepan over medium heat; do not boil. Bring a large saucepan of salted water to a boil. Add both pastas, stir, and continue boiling until the pasta is firm-tender, according to the package directions. Drain the pasta and transfer to a serving dish. Add the mushrooms, sausage meat, cream and Parmesan and mix together. *Serves 4–6.*

VARIATION
Mushroom-Free Creamy Pasta If you don't have any mushrooms, sauté ½ chopped onion and 2 chopped bacon slices in the garlic-flavoured butter until the onion is soft, about 5 minutes, and add 75g shelled fresh or frozen peas. Continue with the recipe as above.

Vegetable pasta

Pull out this recipe when…you don't want to go out…you don't want to fuss…you don't have anything in the fridge…you want some comfort food…and you want to make it quickly.

15g dried porcini mushrooms

Water

500g spaghetti, linguine, tagliatelle, or other long noodles

50ml olive oil

2 garlic cloves, sliced

1 small fresh chilli, deseeded and chopped (wear gloves
   when handling)

1 medium tomato, chopped

100ml single cream

3 tablespoons chopped fresh basil, parsley or oregano,
   or 1 tablespoon dried oregano

Salt

Grated Parmesan cheese

About 20 minutes before you plan to cook, put the mushrooms in a small, heatproof bowl, pour over enough boiling water to cover, and set aside until soft, about 20 minutes. Line a small sieve with wet muslin or paper towels and set it over a bowl. Strain the mushrooms, reserving the soaking water; set the mushrooms and liquid aside separately. Bring a large saucepan of salted water to a boil. Add the pasta, stir, and continue boiling until the pasta is firm-tender, according to the package directions.

Meanwhile, heat the oil in a large frying pan over medium heat. Add the garlic and chilli and sauté until the garlic is golden, 2–3 minutes. Stir in the tomato and reserved mushrooms and continue sautéing 5 minutes. Stir in the strained mushroom soaking liquid, reduce the heat, and simmer until most of the liquid evaporates, stirring occasionally. Stir in the cream, herbs and salt to taste and warm through; do not boil. Drain the pasta and transfer to a serving dish. Add the sauce and mix well. Serve with the cheese. *Serves 4–6.*

VARIATION
Vegetable Pasta with Fresh Mushrooms You can substitute fresh mushrooms for the dried porcini. Before you add the tomato, sauté 100g sliced mushrooms until they brown and the liquid evaporates, about 10 minutes. Continue as above.

TONY'S TIP:
consistency
To get the right consistency, cook the pasta until it is slightly underdone, then add the pasta to the sauce as it heats. Stir and watch the sauce thicken and stick to the pasta, but don't leave it too long since you don't want to overcook the pasta.

TONY'S TIP:
substitutes
If you don't have a fresh tomato, use one from a can.

If you don't have canned tomatoes, use a teaspoon of purée.

If you don't have purée, skip the tomatoes and double the cream.

If you don't have any garlic, use onion.

If you don't have any spaghetti, use any other pasta. But for a real treat, use egg pasta—fresh or dried.

If you don't have cream, then use 100ml milk and 25g butter.

If you don't have any milk, cream or butter, triple the amount of tomato.

Seduction linguine

I made up this recipe one summer afternoon when the local supermarket could only supply a few prawns and even fewer scallops. But it turned out all right. Dry white wine, sunny afternoon, the lawn already mowed, and children away...

50ml olive oil

2 garlic cloves, cut in half

2 medium yellow peppers, deseeded and sliced

5–7 tablespoons plain flour

12 large raw prawns, shelled and deveined

12 scallops

50ml brandy

2 medium tomatoes, peeled, seeded, and diced

500g linguine

50ml single cream

Salt and freshly ground black pepper

2 tablespoons chopped flat-leaf parsley or fresh basil

Heat the oil in a large frying pan over medium heat. Add the garlic and sauté until golden, 2–3 minutes; remove and discard the garlic. Add the peppers to the pan and sauté until tender, about 5 minutes; remove and set aside. Reduce the heat to medium-low. Put the flour on a plate. Lightly dredge the prawns and scallops in the flour. Add the prawns to the frying pan and sauté until they turn pink and curl, 3–5 minutes; remove and set aside. Add the scallops to the pan and fry until just opaque, about 1½ minutes on each side; remove and set aside. Increase the heat to high. Add the brandy to the pan and boil until reduced by half. Stir in the tomatoes and a couple of tablespoons water and leave the sauce to boil a couple of minutes longer.

Meanwhile, bring a large saucepan of salted water to a boil. Add the linguine, stir, and continue boiling until the linguine is firm-tender, according to the package directions. Reduce the heat under the sauce to low. Return the peppers, prawns and scallops to the sauce and warm through gently. Stir in the cream and take off the heat. Season to taste with salt and pepper. Drain the linguine, shaking off the liquid. Stir into the sauce and sprinkle with the parsley or basil. *Serves 4–6.*

"My Uncle Geppino and Aunt Maria in Rome on their honeymoon trip."

Penne with prawns

If made with fresh, not freshly thawed prawns, this dish will bring tears to your eyes, which is, in our family, the highest culinary accolade we can bestow—higher than any stars. This dish is often found in Liguria, where the prawns jump straight from the sea into the nets and from the nets into your pot.

50ml olive oil

1 garlic clove, chopped

1 small fresh chilli, deseeded and chopped
   (wear gloves when handling)

500g prawns, shelled and deveined

100ml dry white wine

2 tablespoons passata

2 tablespoons chopped flat-leaf parsley

Salt and freshly ground black pepper

100ml double cream

500g penne rigate

Heat the oil in a large, heavy-bottomed saucepan over medium heat. Add the garlic and chilli and sauté until the garlic is golden, 2–3 minutes. Add the prawns and continue sautéing until they turn pink and curl, 3–5 minutes. Add the wine, reduce the heat, and simmer 5 minutes, uncovered. Transfer about one-third of the prawns to a blender or food processor and process until a coarse paste forms. Return the paste to the pan, along with the passata, parsley and salt and pepper to taste and simmer 10 minutes longer, again uncovered.

Meanwhile, bring a large saucepan of salted water to a boil. Add the penne, stir, and continue boiling until the penne is firm-tender, according to the package directions. Drain the penne. Stir the cream into the sauce, then remove the saucepan from the heat. Stir in the penne. *Serves 4–6.*

TONY'S TIP:
heat control

How much chilli to use? Well, how hot is the pepper and how spicy do you like your food? Err on the side of caution, then you can always add more later.

Fusilli with olives

Fusilli alla Sorrentina

Fusilli are a thick spaghetti that has been twisted into a spiral. An alternative would be mafalde, which are those ribbons with the ruffled edges. Both hold a lot of sauce, which will add to the tastiness of this dish.

100ml olive oil
500g tomatoes, peeled, deseeded, and diced
140g black olives, such as Gaeta or kalamata
2 garlic cloves, chopped
1½ teaspoons dried oregano
50g loosely packed chopped fresh basil
500g fusilli
115g shredded caciotta or mozzarella cheese
55g grated Parmesan cheese

Combine the oil, tomatoes, olives, garlic, oregano and basil in a large, heavy-bottomed saucepan over medium-high heat. Stir together and fry 10 minutes, stirring occasionally; set aside.

Meanwhile, bring a large saucepan of salted water to a boil. Add the fusilli, stir, and continue boiling until the fusilli is firm-tender, according to the package directions. Drain the fusilli, shaking off the liquid. Return the pan of sauce to medium heat and reheat. Stir the pasta into the sauce with the cheeses, stirring until the cheeses melt. *Serves 6.*

TONY'S TIP:
olives and capers

I always choose kalamata or Greek olives, or Gaeta. Don't use those ugly things called black olives that come in a can and have lost their pits. If the olives aren't pitted, don't panic. Lay each on a cutting board and hit it with the heel of your hand or with the flat of a knife, if you are dainty. The olive will split and the pit will pop out.

You can buy two kinds of capers—one packed in vinegar, the other in salt. The salted ones are preferable to avoid the vinegar where it isn't wanted. You can soak the salted ones in water or use them directly, remembering to cut back on the salt in the recipe to compensate.

Lasagne

Many lasagne al forno *recipes include béchamel sauce, but we are watching our weight, aren't we? Like heck! This version is lighter and fresher than most.*

    2 tablespoons olive oil
    250g minced beef
    250g minced pork
    1 medium onion, chopped
    400g can chopped tomatoes or passata
    225g tomato purée, dissolved in 125ml water
    1 garlic clove, chopped
    2 teaspoons chopped flat-leaf parsley or chopped fresh basil
    1 teaspoon sugar
    ½ teaspoon freshly ground black pepper
    ½ teaspoon dried oregano
    Salt
    225g lasagne
    450g ricotta cheese
    170g shredded mozzarella cheese
    115g grated Parmesan cheese

Heat the oil in a large, heavy-bottomed saucepan over medium heat. Add the beef, pork and onion and sauté until the meat and onion are brown, about 10 minutes. Stir in the tomatoes or passata, the tomato purée, garlic, parsley or basil, sugar, pepper, oregano and 2 teaspoons salt. Reduce the heat to medium-low and simmer, about 30 minutes, uncovered and stirring often.

Meanwhile, bring a large saucepan of salted water to a boil. Add the lasagne sheets, stir, and continue boiling until the sheets are almost, but not quite, cooked, about 10 minutes or according to the package directions. Drain the pasta well, shaking off the liquid. Heat the oven to 180°C, gas mark 4. Spread a layer of sauce over the bottom of a 18x28cm baking dish. Add a single layer of lasagne. Top with another layer of sauce, a layer of ricotta, a layer of mozzarella, and a layer of Parmesan. Repeat these layers until all the ingredients are used, finishing with a layer of sauce. Bake for 40–50 minutes, until the sauce is bubbling and the cheese has melted through. Remove from the oven and let stand for 15 minutes before cutting into squares to serve. *Serves 6–8.*

What's in a name?
LASAGNE
Strictly speaking, lasagne is a type of wide noodle. More correctly this recipe is *lasagne al forno*, baked lasagne, because lasagne can also be used in other pasta recipes.

GNOCCHI

TONY'S TIP:
keeping gnocchi

Over-cooking flour or potato gnocchi or letting them stand in the water or in the colander prepares them for the glue factory, not the table. You can freeze gnocchi quite easily, and they will keep for up to 3 months. I spread them in a single layer on a tray and pop them into the freezer. Once they are frozen, I bag them.

Flour gnocchi

400g plain flour, plus extra for sprinkling
225ml boiling water

Put the flour in a large bowl. Make a well and add the water. Stir with a spoon for about 5 minutes to make a dough. Sprinkle about 2 tablespoons of flour onto a flat surface. Turn out the dough and knead until you obtain an elastic ball—it should take about 10 minutes. Sprinkle more flour, as needed, onto the surface to keep the dough from sticking. Knead with the flour and lots of elbow grease for another 10 minutes, until you end up with a uniform, elastic dough. Cover and let it rest for 15 minutes.

Cut off a slice and, with a rolling pin, roll it flat to about 1cm thick. Cut into 1cm-long ribbons. Then cut the ribbons into 1cm cubes. Repeat until the dough is used up. Dry on a floured surface until you are ready to finish. You can roll a little indentation in each cube by placing the tip of your finger on top and rolling it toward you to make a shell shape. This is an extra nicety and it will also hold more sauce. You may prefer to give the gnocchi a ridge pattern by rolling the dough piece on the back of the tines of a fork instead of a flat surface.

Bring a saucepan of salted water to a rolling boil. Add the gnocchi. When they float to the surface, they are done. It takes 2–5 minutes, that's all. Drain, garnish, and serve immediately. *Serves 2.*

Gnocchi with tomato sauce and mozzarella ▶

Potato gnocchi

Potato gnocchi are much lighter than flour gnocchi and are generally preferred, although they are a little more trouble to prepare. To keep their lightness, a minimum amount of flour is necessary. This means no extra water, so drain well and leave the potatoes to cool completely before using them. It is worth making a big batch—you don't want to make these too often, do you?

1kg floury potatoes, scrubbed
250g plain flour (at most)

Bring a large saucepan of water to a rolling boil over high heat. Add the potatoes and boil until tender, about 25 minutes. Drain well, shaking off any liquid, and leave to cool; then peel and cut into cubes. Put the potato cubes into a large bowl and, using a potato masher or large fork, mash the potatoes into a smooth paste. Gradually add small amounts of flour and knead until the dough forms an elastic ball. Continue kneading with a lot of elbow grease until the dough is uniformly elastic. Cover the dough with a dish towel and leave to rest for 15 minutes. Shape as for flour gnocchi (page 80).

Bring a saucepan of salted water to a rolling boil. Add the gnocchi and cook 2–5 minutes. When they float to the surface, they are done. Drain, garnish, and serve immediately. *Serves 4–6.*

VARIATIONS

Gnocchi and Tomato Sauce In a large, warm serving bowl, combine the cooked gnocchi with hot **Tomato Passata Sauce** (page 58) and 25g grated Parmesan cheese.

Christina's All-time Favourite Gnocchi In the rinsed saucepan, combine the cooked gnocchi with hot **Tomato Passata Sauce** (page 58), 225g shredded fresh mozzarella cheese, and 25g grated Parmesan cheese. The cheese should melt as it is stirred in, but if not, return the saucepan to the heat for a minute and continue stirring.

Other Sauce Combinations Gnocchi can be served with almost any pasta sauce. It can be a hearty dish, like **Christina's All-Time Favourite Gnocchi** (above), or a delicate one, when dressed with a vegetable sauce or with **Pesto** (page 62).

"I've given you an abbreviated version of gnocchi making of my own invention. When I was little, children were drafted to make gnocchi. That was before the passage of child labour laws— in the far-distant mists of time! In any case, in my family it was a ritual and a tradition, so it was OK. What we had to do was to shape the dough into long sausages about 1cm in diameter, then cut each sausage into 1cm lengths, then roll each piece into a shell shape. And we didn't have a companionable cup of coffee or glass of wine either."

Orecchiette with broccoli

Make either the **Flour Gnocchi** *(page 80) or the* **Potato Gnocchi** *(opposite), but stop when you have those cute little cubes of dough—actually they look more like pillows, don't they? Hold each little piece of dough in your palm and press your thumb in the middle of the dough to form a "little hat." Actually orecchiette means "little ears," but either way, do you get the sense of the shape?*

50ml olive oil

3 garlic cloves, chopped

1 small fresh chilli, deseeded and sliced
  (wear gloves when handling)

6 anchovy fillets in oil

500g broccoli, sprouting broccoli or broccoli rabe
  cut into florets

225ml chicken stock or water

500g orecchiette

55g grated Parmesan cheese

Salt

Heat the oil in a large frying pan over medium heat. Add the garlic and chilli and sauté until the garlic is golden, 2–3 minutes. Add the anchovies and continue sautéing until they dissolve, about 3 minutes. Add the broccoli and sauté 3 minutes. Stir in the stock or water and salt to taste, increase the heat to medium-high, and boil until the broccoli is soft, about 5 minutes longer.

Meanwhile, bring a large saucepan of salted water to a rolling boil. Add the orecchiette, stir, and continue boiling until the orecchiette is fork-tender, about 10 minutes. Drain the orecchiette, shaking off the liquid. Stir the orecchiette into the sauce and add half the Parmesan. Taste and adjust the seasoning, if necessary. Serve with the remaining Parmesan to sprinkle over. *Serves 4–6.*

"Great Grandma Vittoria Simone would make orecchiette with broccoli—a classic country dish from Puglia—in Croton-on-Hudson. The family came from Castellana in the province of Bari. At least it was called Castellana until a huge system of caves was discovered not too long ago. Now it calls itself Castellana Grotte, and is famous for making wedding dressses."

POLENTA

TONY'S TIP:
a smooth mix
Prevent lumps by pouring the polenta slowly into the boiling water and stirring constantly. If lumps form, just keep stirring; you'll wear them away. (Or add some raisins and hope that no one will notice!)

Basic polenta

In the olden days, before my time, polenta took hours to make. Today you can buy pre-cooked polenta. It takes 5–7 minutes to cook. There are also some super-fast-cooking polentas, so check the package for directions if you are not sure.

> **1.5 litres water**
> **½ teaspoon salt**
> **200g quick–cooking polenta**
> **75g butter**
> **6 heaped tablespoons grated Parmesan cheese**

Bring the water and salt to a rolling boil in a large, heavy-bottomed saucepan over high heat. Slowly add the polenta. If you add it like a "fine rain," it minimises the amount of lumps that form. Stirring constantly should get rid of any lumps.

This polenta needs to be flavoured. One easy way is to stir in 6 heaped tablespoons grated Parmesan cheese and 75g butter.

You also can serve polenta with any hearty sauce that you use with pasta. **Mushroom Sauce** (page 59), **Bolognese Sauce** (page 61), and **Pesto** (page 62) are all good with it. I also like to serve polenta with the sauce left over from a beef casserole. Or, try **Sautéed Mushrooms** (page 195).

VARIATIONS

Grilled Polenta Cook the polenta as described in the basic recipe. Using a wet metal spatula, spread the hot polenta out on a flat surface until 1cm thick; leave to cool completely. Meanwhile, heat the grill to high. Using a sharp knife, cut the polenta into triangles. Working in batches, if necessary, depending on the size of your grill pan, brush the triangles with oil, then transfer to the rack. Grill 10cm from the heat until golden, about 5 minutes. Turn the polenta triangles over, brush with oil again, and continue grilling until golden. Continue until all the polenta is grilled. These are excellent served with stews and casseroles.

Fried Polenta Cook polenta as described in the basic recipe. Spread and cool the hot polenta as above, then cut into 7.5x0.5cm strips. Heat 100ml sunflower oil in a large frying pan over high heat. Working in batches, if necessary, to avoid overcrowding the pan, fry the polenta strips on both sides until golden, about 8 minutes. Drain well on paper towels. Continue until all the polenta strips are fried.

Special Fried Polenta Heat 50ml sunflower oil in a medium saucepan over medium heat. Add 2 chopped garlic cloves and 175g cubed or sliced prosciutto, salami or cured bacon, and sauté until the garlic is soft, 2–3 minutes. Stir in 3 tablespoons finely chopped fresh rosemary leaves and 150g grated Parmesan cheese until blended. Stir the above mixture into the hot polenta. Shape and fry as above.

TONY'S TIP:
special effects
If you really want to impress, cut round polenta slices with a glass before frying. (Of course you can do heart shaped on St. Valentine's Day, fir shaped at Christmas, and so on.) Serve this polenta with roast chicken or lamb. You can fry the scraps and feed them to the kids.

RICE DISHES

ARBORIO RICE

Incredible as it may seem to some people, Italy is a rice-growing country. The rice paddies are mostly found in the North, so the northern cooking relies more on rice than pasta. Of the many varieties of rice grown and used, arborio is perhaps best known. For Italian recipes, it is best to use arborio rice or a similar variety, such as carnaroli.

Rice cake

Torta di riso

400g arborio rice
225g frozen, chopped spinach
50ml sunflower oil
1 onion, chopped
3 large eggs, lightly beaten
25g grated Parmesan cheese
¼ teaspoon ground nutmeg
Salt and freshly ground black pepper

FOR THE SAUCE (optional)
25g butter
1½ tablespoons plain flour
325ml milk
3 tablespoons grated Parmesan cheese
Salt and freshly ground black pepper

Grease and flour a 23cm pie dish; set aside. Bring a large saucepan of salted water to a rolling boil over high heat. Add the rice and continue boiling until almost tender, about 12 minutes. Stir in the spinach and drain; set aside. Meanwhile, heat the oven to 200°C, gas mark 6. Preheat the oil in a large frying pan over medium heat. Add the onion and sauté until soft, about 5 minutes. Stir in the rice and spinach mixture, the eggs, Parmesan, nutmeg and salt and pepper to taste. Spoon the rice-and-spinach mixture into the prepared dish and smooth the surface. Bake about 20 minutes, until the top is golden.

Meanwhile, if you are serving the rice tart hot, make the sauce. Melt the butter in a medium saucepan over medium heat. Add the flour to make a thick paste and cook, stirring, for 2 minutes. Slowly stir in the milk until a smooth, thin sauce forms. Simmer 6 minutes, stirring frequently. Stir in the cheese and salt and pepper to taste. Cut the tart into wedges. Serve with the sauce if the wedges are hot, or without sauce if cool. *Serves 4–6.*

Rice with nuts

This makes a very attractive dish on a buffet or at the dinner table. Hazelnuts or cashews also work very well.

- **400g long-grain rice**
- **150g butter, melted**
- **3 tablespoons sunflower oil**
- **70g each almonds and pistachios, crushed**
- **50g pine nuts**
- **1 tablespoon finely chopped parsley**

Lightly butter the inside of a ring mould (with a capacity of at least 1.8 litres); set aside. Bring a large saucepan of salted water to a rolling boil over high heat. Add the rice and continue boiling until tender, according to the package directions. Drain well, transfer to a large bowl, and stir in the butter; set aside. Meanwhile, heat the oil in a large frying pan over medium heat. Add the crushed nuts and pine nuts and sauté until golden, about 3 minutes. Immediately pour the nuts into the bottom of the mould. Spoon in the rice mixture, cover with aluminum foil, and keep warm until required. To serve, place a warm serving dish over the top of the mould and, using oven gloves, invert the rice onto the dish, giving a firm shake halfway over. Lift off the mould. Sprinkle with the chopped parsley. *Serves 6–8.*

TONY'S TIP:
washing rice

Basmati, jasmine and other long-grain rice benefit from being rinsed or soaked in water prior to cooking to remove excess starch. Soaking also speeds up the cooking time by increasing the moisture content of the grains. Place the rice in a large bowl, cover with cold water, and stir with your fingers. The water will become cloudy. Let the rice settle, then gently tip the bowl so the water drains away. Repeat 2 or 3 times until the water runs clear. Then drain through a sieve.

RISOTTO

To make a fragrant, creamy risotto is not difficult, but it requires time and stirring, patience and stirring, and some more patience and stirring! Once the basic risotto is mastered, it's easy to add more ingredients.

Basic risotto

50ml sunflower oil
1 medium onion, chopped
400g arborio or carnaroli rice
About 1.35 litres stock or water, simmering
25g butter
3 tablespoons grated Parmesan cheese

Heat the oil in a large, heavy-bottomed saucepan over medium heat. Add the onion and sauté until golden, about 5 minutes. Add the rice and stir for 2 minutes. Add about 100ml stock or water and stir until the liquid is absorbed. Continue adding liquid, 100ml at a time and stirring constantly, until the rice is tender and has a creamy consistency, about 25 minutes. Turn off the heat and stir in the butter and cheese. Leave to rest for 5 minutes before serving. *Serves 6.*

VARIATIONS

Mushroom Risotto Melt 50g butter in a medium frying pan over medium heat. Add 225g sliced white mushrooms and sauté until the mushrooms brown and the liquid evaporates, about 10 minutes. Stir into the rice at the end of cooking. Turn off the heat and stir in the cheese (but no more butter). Leave to rest for 5 minutes before serving.

Pumpkin Risotto Add 250g raw, diced pumpkin and a pinch of chopped fresh basil to the onions when you fry them. Continue with the recipe as above.

Courgette Risotto Sauté 225g sliced courgettes in a separate saucepan. Add to the rice at the end of cooking.

Risotto alla Milanese

Traditionally, this dish is served with **Osso Buco** *(page 126). It's also good on its own. It's hard to find beef marrow and if you leave it out, no one will know. I only put it in to stay with tradition.*

½ teaspoon powdered saffron
About 1.35 litres chicken or vegetable stock or water, simmering
50ml sunflower oil
1 medium onion, chopped
55g raw beef marrow, sliced
600g arborio or carnaroli rice
25g butter
6 tablespoons grated Parmesan cheese

Dissolve the saffron in the simmering stock; set aside over low heat. Heat the oil in a large, heavy-bottomed saucepan over medium heat. Add the onions and marrow and sauté until the onion is golden, about 5 minutes. Add the rice and stir 2 minutes. Add about 100ml stock or water and stir until the liquid is absorbed. Continue adding liquid, 100ml at a time, and stirring constantly, until the rice is tender and has a creamy consistency, about 25 minutes. Turn off the heat and stir in the butter and cheese. Leave to rest for 5 minutes before serving. *Serves 6.*

TONY'S TIP:
taking stock

Stock is a great asset in improving risotto dishes. But how do you get it? Leftover chicken soup is one. Boiling leftover turkey or chicken is another. You can even buy stock in tubs or cartons in the chilled section. Last, you can buy bouillon cubes or powder—but stick to chicken or vegetable for making risotto since beef stock is too strong.

Buttery pea risotto

Risi e bisi

50ml sunflower oil

1 medium onion, chopped

600g arborio or carnaroli rice

About 1.35ml stock or water, simmering

6 lettuce leaves, any kind, finely shredded

170g frozen peas

50g butter

6 tablespoons grated Parmesan cheese

Prepare the risotto as on page 89, using the oil, onion, rice and stock or water, and sautéing the lettuce leaves with the onions. Meanwhile, combine the peas, a quarter of the butter, and enough water to cover the peas by about 5mm in a separate saucepan over high heat. You want enough water so some is left at the end. Bring to a boil and cook until the peas are tender, about 10 minutes. When the risotto is tender and creamy, turn off the heat and stir in the peas with their cooking liquid, the remaining butter, and the cheese. Leave to rest for 5 minutes before serving. *Serves 6.*

What's in a name?
RISI E BISI
Risi e bisi is Venetian dialect for rice and peas.

"Besides school and play, our time as children in Italy included doing chores for the adults. One of these was shelling peas and beans. This had to be done because they came fresh from the farmer. But the pile to be shelled never seemed to shrink, and the minute pile of shelled peas never seemed to grow."

PIZZA

Pizza is perhaps the most ubiquitous Italian dish—it is found absolutely everywhere and in the most remarkable variety. If you make it at home, you will get a better result than most commercial pizza makers.

Basic pizza dough

1 sachet (7g) easy-blend dried yeast
1 cup warm (40–45°C) water
400g plain flour, plus more as needed
1 teaspoon salt
1 teaspoon sugar
2 teaspoons olive oil
1 CD of Italian music, preferably Neapolitan

Stir the yeast into the water and set aside until foamy, about 10 minutes. Meanwhile, stir 225g flour, the salt and the sugar together in a large bowl and make a well in the middle. Add the olive oil and yeast mixture to the well and stir to mix the flour into the liquid. Gradually work in the remaining flour until a smooth dough forms. Turn on the Italian music. Turn out the dough onto a lightly floured surface and knead until the dough is smooth and elastic. Place the dough in a greased bowl. Cover tightly with clingfilm and let stand in a warm, draft-free place until it doubles in bulk, which can take 45 minutes to several hours, depending on the room temperature. Meanwhile, preheat the oven to 200°C, gas mark 6, and assemble the ingredients for the topping (following pages). Knock back the dough and knead lightly for about 30 seconds. Divide the dough in half and roll each half into a ball. Working with one ball at a time, roll it into a 40cm circle, 5mm thick. Place on a lightly floured baking tray, add the topping, and bake until the crust is golden and crisp, about 20 minutes. Assemble and bake the other pizza. *Each pizza makes 4–6 slices.*

Fast-Action Dried Yeast This type of yeast does not need to be activated in warm water before it is used. If you are using this type of yeast, stir it into the flour before any liquid is added, then continue with the recipe as above.

Pizza Margherita

Margherita was a Queen of Italy, who took a trip to Naples, the capital of pizza. There, Neapolitan chefs created Pizza Margherita in the patriotic colours of red, white and green.

50ml olive oil, plus a little extra for drizzling
1 garlic clove
400g can chopped tomatoes
115g tomato purée, dissolved in 150ml water
3 tablespoons dried basil or 1 teaspoon dried oregano
1 teaspoon salt
25g grated Parmesan cheese
225g fresh mozzarella cheese, drained and shredded
Fresh basil leaves

Prepare and shape the **Basic Pizza Dough** as on page 92. While the dough is rising, prepare the topping. Heat the oil in a large, heavy-bottomed saucepan over medium heat. Add the garlic and sauté until golden, 2–3 minutes. Add the tomatoes, tomato purée, half the basil or all the oregano, and salt. Simmer 10 minutes, stirring occasionally.

Preheat the oven to 200°C, gas mark 6. Equally divide the sauce between the two pizza bases and spread within 5mm of the edges. Sprinkle with the Parmesan and drizzle with a little olive oil. Bake until the bottom of the crust is a golden colour, about 20 minutes. Lift a corner of the pizza to check that it is done, then sprinkle the mozzarella over the pizza, and return it to the oven until the cheese melts, about 5 minutes longer. Top with basil just before serving. Bake one pizza at a time unless you have a very large oven. *Makes 2 pizzas, each of which makes 4–6 slices.*

VARIATION
Aubergine Topping Thinly slice 1 medium aubergine lengthwise (or a large one if you really like aubergine). Heat 50ml olive oil in a large frying pan over medium heat. Add the aubergine slices and fry on both sides until lightly browned, about 10 minutes. Add to the tomato-sauce–topped pizzas just before baking. Bake as above. Add the mozzarella and basil as above.

"No one makes pizza like they make it in Naples—the world capital of pizza—and few people know their secret. What is a Neapolitan pizza like? It is round and thin; after baking, the dough is still soft and pliable but parts have blistered black. It is very lightly loaded with sauce and cheese, yet it is juicy and flavourful. Other parts of Italy make nice pizzas, but never quite like these."

"In Naples almost nobody makes pizza at home. My aunts, who worked in the family's shoe-making shop, would often send to the corner pizzeria for lunch. And they would always drink beer with it."

White pizza

Pizza in bianco

Basic Pizza Dough (page 92)
450g ricotta cheese
450g sliced cooked broccoli florets
Freshly ground white pepper
Olive oil for drizzling
225g fresh mozzarella cheese, drained and shredded
25g grated Parmesan cheese

Prepare and shape the **Basic Pizza Dough** as directed on page 92. Preheat the oven to 200°C, gas mark 6. Roll out the dough and place on lightly floured baking trays. Spread the ricotta cheese over the pizza bases and arrange the broccoli on top. Grind the pepper over the tops and drizzle with a small amount of olive oil. Bake until the bottom of the crust is golden—check by lifting a corner—about 20 minutes. Sprinkle the mozzarella and Parmesan over the pizzas and return them to the oven until the cheeses melt, about 5 minutes longer. *Makes 2 pizzas, each of which makes 4–6 slices.*

TONY'S TIP:
leftover dough
If you have pizza dough left over from your pizza making, try out **Grandma Simone's Honey Buns** (page 241) for a simple dessert.

Focaccia

In northern Italy, particularly in Liguria and Tuscany, focaccia is a staple food. You can buy it everywhere, and it is placed on the tables of most restaurants. Focaccia is often used to make delicious sandwiches. The real thing bears no resemblance to what is generally sold in supermarkets. I am giving you this recipe so you can taste something like the real thing. It takes a bit of work, but it is worth it.

> **2 sachets (7g each) easy blend dried yeast**
> **450ml warm (40–45°C) water**
> **450g plain flour**
> **1 teaspoon salt**
> **100ml olive oil**
> **Coarse sea salt**

Stir the yeast into half the warm water and set aside until foamy, about 10 minutes. Meanwhile, stir half the flour and salt together in a large bowl and make a well in the middle. Add 50ml olive oil, the yeast mixture, and the remaining water to the well and stir to mix the flour into the liquid. Gradually work in the remaining flour until a smooth dough forms. Turn out the dough onto a lightly floured surface and knead until the dough is smooth and elastic.

Place the dough in a bowl. Cover tightly with clingfilm and let stand in a warm, draft-free place until it doubles in bulk, which can take 45 minutes to several hours, depending on how warm the room is.

Lightly grease two baking sheets. Knock back the dough and knead lightly for about 30 seconds. Divide the dough in half and roll out each half until about 1cm thick. Place each half on a baking sheet and brush generously with the remaining olive oil. Sprinkle with sea salt and use your fingers to make indentations all over. Leave to rise for 30 minutes. Preheat the oven to 200°C, gas mark 6. Bake until golden, about 20 minutes, switching the baking sheets halfway through. Leave to cool, then cut into 7.5x2.5cm strips. *Makes 2 focaccias.*

VARIATIONS

Focaccia rosmarino Sprinkle rosemary needles over the surfaces with the salt, just before you make the indentations.

Focaccia pinoli Sprinkle the surfaces with 3 tablespoons pine nuts, just before you make the indentations.

Focaccia alla cipolla Sprinkle the surfaces with 1 finely sliced medium onion per focaccia, just before you make the indentations.

Focaccia all' oliva Sprinkle the surfaces with 35g sliced black or green olives, just before you make the indentations.

3 COURSES FROM THE LAND

Poultry and eggs, beef, veal, pork

and lamb, form the basis of the

mostly main course dishes found

in this chapter.

OMELETTES

TONY'S TIP:
flipping omelettes
If a flick of the wrist won't do
it for you, use a spatula on
small omelettes. On large
omelettes, slide a flat plate
about half way under the
omelette and use it to turn
over or fold the omelette. If
you still have problems, stick
the omelette under a
medium-hot grill to finish it.
Flipping Type 2 omelettes (see
opposite page) gets to be
more difficult. It's usually
easier to finish the top under
the grill. Heat the grill and
place the frying pan on a rack
10cm from the heat and cook
about 2 minutes or until set.

Basic omelette

3 large eggs
3 half eggshells filled with water or milk
Salt and freshly ground black pepper
15g butter

Beat the eggs, water or milk, and salt and pepper to taste together in
a medium bowl. Heat a 20cm omelette or frying pan over medium
heat. Add 10g butter and melt until it sizzles, tilting the pan so the
bottom is covered. Pour the eggs into the pan, shaking the pan
occasionally so the omelette doesn't stick. As the bottom of the
omelette sets, use a metal spatula to lift the edge so the uncooked egg
mixture flows underneath. Continue shaking the pan until you can
feel the omelette sliding around freely. When the omelette is set, but
still slightly moist on the surface, increase the heat to brown the
bottom. To fold the omelette, tilt the pan away from you and use a
spatula to lift the edge of the omelette and fold it in half. Slide the
omelette onto a plate. Rub the remaining butter over the omelette
until it melts. *Serves 2.*

TYPES OF OMELETTE

Having mastered the basic omelette, variety will add spice. You can show off with your omelette even if it is a last-minute thought. Here are flavouring suggestions for the three types of omelettes.

TYPE 1 OMELETTES

Extra ingredients should be beaten with the eggs before cooking the omelette.

Herb Add 2 tablespoons chopped fresh herbs, mixed or individual. Try parsley or tarragon.

Gina's Chive and Cream Cheese Add 2 tablespoons cream cheese and 1 tablespoon snipped fresh chives.

Ricotta Add 2 tablespoons strained ricotta cheese.

TYPE 2 OMELETTES

Extra ingredients are cooked in the skillet before the beaten eggs are added.

Courgette Heat 2 tablespoons sunflower oil in the frying pan over medium heat. Add 1 small courgette, sliced, and ½ onion, sliced, and sauté until soft, about 10 minutes.

Western Heat 2 tablespoons sunflower oil in the frying pan over medium heat. Add 1 green pepper, deseeded and sliced, and ½ small onion, sliced, and sauté until soft, about 5 minutes.

TYPE 3 OMELETTES

Extra ingredients are added during the final moments of cooking, just before the omelette is folded to enclose the filling.

Cheese Add 55g any grated cheese (except blue). Fold and finish cooking the omelette over low until the cheese melts.

Mushroom Spoon 100g sautéed portobella mushrooms on the set omelette.

Ham Add very thinly sliced cooked ham, or, if thicker, sauté ham cubes before adding them.

Omelette with tomato sauce

FOR THE SAUCE

2 tablespoons olive oil

1 small onion, chopped, or 1 garlic clove, chopped, or both

450g fresh tomatoes, roughly chopped and seeded, or
   400g can chopped tomatoes

1 tablespoon chopped fresh basil

Salt and freshly ground black pepper

3 basil leaves

FOR THE OMELETTE

3 large eggs

3 half eggshells filled with water or milk

Salt and freshly ground black pepper

1 tablespoon butter

To make the sauce Heat the oil in a large, heavy-bottomed saucepan over medium heat. Add the onions, or garlic, or both, and sauté until the onions are soft and golden, but not brown, about 7 minutes, or the garlic is golden, 2–3 minutes. Add the tomatoes, half the basil, and salt and pepper to taste. Reduce the heat to medium and cook until the tomatoes are soft and tender, but not reduced to a paste, about 10 minutes. Taste and adjust the seasoning, if necessary. Stir in the remaining basil just before serving.

Meanwhile, prepare and cook the **Basic Omelette** (page 100) and fold it in half. Slide the omelette onto a plate and spoon the sauce around it. Garnish with the basil leaves. *Serves 2.*

VARIATION

Eggs with Tomato Sauce Prepare the sauce above; you can use 1 teaspoon dried oregano instead of the basil, but do use a herb. When the sauce is done, drop 3 large eggs out of their shells into the saucepan. Season with salt and pepper, cover, and cook over low heat until the egg white is set and the yolk is warm. Serve on or with toasted buttered Italian bread.

"Pellegrino Artusi is one of the luminaries of Italian cookery writing. His great and well regarded *Science in the kitchen and the art of eating well* is still being translated and printed more than a hundred years after initial publication! Anyway, he tells the story of a priest who was very inquisitive and stuck his nose in absolutely everything. However, he did it so kindly and was so well regarded, many of his parishioners called him Don Pomodoro, Father Tomato. Because, like the tomato, you found him in practically everything!"

Carol's Mediterranean chicken

2 teaspoons paprika

1 chicken, about 1.3kg, cut into 8 pieces

3 tablespoons olive oil

1 small onion, chopped

2 cloves garlic, chopped

4-5 bacon rashers, diced

Small piece dried chilli

100g button mushrooms, sliced

3 red peppers, chopped

400g can whole plum tomatoes

1 teaspoon dried oregano

12 kalamata olives, pitted

Salt and freshly ground black pepper

Rub the paprika on the chicken pieces; set aside. Over medium heat, heat the oil in a deep roasting pan large enough to hold the chicken pieces in a single layer. Add the onion, garlic, bacon, chilli and chicken pieces to the pan and sauté until golden all over, about 20 minutes. Drain off all but 2 tablespoons of fat and discard. Add the mushrooms to the pan and sauté about 5 minutes.

Meanwhile, preheat the oven to 190°C, gas mark 5. Place the peppers in a heatproof bowl and pour over enough boiling water to cover; let stand 10 minutes, then drain well. Stir the peppers, tomatoes and their juice, oregano, olives and salt and pepper to taste into the pan. Give it all a good stir and transfer to the oven. Bake about 30 minutes, until the chicken is tender and the juices run clear. *Serves 4–6.*

"Carol and her brother Tom in 1952 working up an appetite in Croton-on-Hudson, New York. Carol's mischievousness as a child is the stuff of family legends. You wouldn't credit the tales by looking at the photo."

Chicken Marengo

*This dish was supposedly served to Napoleon after the Battle of
Marengo. However, I suspect that it has been embellished over the years.*

50ml olive oil

1 chicken, about 1.3kg, cut into 8 pieces

100ml dry white wine

**4 large ripe tomatoes, chopped, or a 400g can
chopped tomatoes**

1 clove garlic, chopped

Salt and freshly ground black pepper

4 bread slices

4 large eggs

2 tablespoons chopped flat-leaf parsley

Heat the oil in a large frying pan. Brown the chicken pieces all over,
about 10 minutes. Pour off all but 2 tablespoons of the oil and reserve
it. To the chicken add the wine, tomatoes, garlic and salt and pepper to
taste. Cover and simmer until the chicken is cooked through and the
juices run clear, about 25 minutes longer.

In another large frying pan, heat the reserved oil over medium heat.
Add the bread slices and fry them until golden, about 3 minutes. Using
tongs or a fork, flip the slices over and continue frying until golden on
the other side, about 3 minutes longer. Drain on paper towels and cut
into triangles; set aside and keep warm.

Break the eggs into the oil remaining in the frying pan and fry sunny
side up, about 5 minutes. Serve the chicken in its sauce with the eggs
and toast, and sprinkled with parsley. *Serves 4.*

VARIATION

Prawn garnish This is an unusual addition in that Italians won't
happily mix chicken, prawns and eggs in normal circumstances.
However it does suggest inventiveness in the use of available
ingredients. Bring a small saucepan of salted water to boil, then add
four large shelled deveined prawns. Cook for five minutes, drain
and add to the chicken as garnish.

Oven-fried chicken

1 large egg

225ml milk

55g plain flour

1 teaspoon salt

½ teaspoon freshly ground black pepper

1 teaspoon chopped flat-leaf parsley

1 teaspoon chopped fresh rosemary

Grated zest of 1 lemon

1 chicken, 1-1.3kg, cut into pieces

50g butter

50ml olive oil

Preheat the oven to 200°C, gas mark 6. Beat the egg in a small, shallow bowl with the milk. Place the flour on a plate and stir in the salt, pepper, parsley, rosemary and lemon zest. One by one, dip each piece of chicken in the egg and milk mixture, letting the excess drip back into the bowl, then roll it in the seasoned flour. Shake off the excess. Melt the butter with the olive oil until sizzling in a roasting pan large enough to hold all the chicken pieces in a single layer in the oven. Add the chicken pieces and spoon the hot oil over them. Roast for 40–50 minutes, turning the pieces over several times, until the skins are golden and the juices run clear when each piece is pierced with the tip of a knife. *Serves 4.*

Pan-fried chicken

2 tablespoons olive oil

1 chicken, 1.3-1.8kg pounds, cut into pieces

3 cloves garlic, chopped

2 sprigs fresh rosemary, leaves chopped,
    or 2 teaspoons dried rosemary

100ml dry white wine

Salt and freshly ground black pepper

Heat the oil in a large frying pan with a tight-fitting lid over medium heat. Working in batches, if necessary, to avoid overcrowding the pan, add the chicken pieces and brown all over. Remove the chicken and set aside. Add the garlic and rosemary to the frying pan and sauté until the garlic is golden, about 2 minutes. Return the chicken to the pan. Add the wine and salt and pepper to taste and let the wine bubble for 1 minute. Reduce the heat to low, cover, and cook until the chicken is cooked through, and the juices run clear when the chicken is pierced with the tip of a knife, about 40 minutes. If the pan becomes dry, stir in 1–2 tablespoons water. Transfer the chicken to a serving dish and cover loosely with foil to keep hot. Meanwhile, skim the fat and boil the juices until reduced by half. Pour over the chicken to serve. *Serves 4–6.*

VARIATION

Oven-Baked Chicken Preheat the oven to 180°C, gas mark 4. Brown the chicken in a lidded frying pan or sauté pan, with ovensafe handle, or flameproof casserole dish. Follow the recipe above until the wine has reduced. Cover the pan or casserole tightly and bake in the oven for about 45 minutes, until the chicken is cooked through and the juices run clear when each piece is pierced with the tip of a knife. Reduce the pan juices as above.

Uncle Tony's chicken

1 chicken, 1–1.3kg, cut into pieces
225g dried breadcrumbs
115g grated Parmesan cheese
2 tablespoons dried oregano
1 tablespoon paprika
1 teaspoon freshly ground black pepper
22ml milk
225ml sunflower oil

Bring a large, heavy-bottomed saucepan of salted water to a boil. Add the chicken pieces and parboil 20 minutes; drain well and set aside to cool. Meanwhile, combine the breadcrumbs, cheese, oregano, paprika and pepper in a shallow bowl. Put the milk in another shallow bowl. One by one, dip each piece of chicken in the milk, letting the excess drip back into the bowl, and then roll it in the breadcrumb mixture. Shake off the excess and set aside for 20 minutes. Heat the oil in a large frying pan over medium heat. Working in batches, if necessary, to avoid overcrowding, fry the chicken pieces, turning over several times, until the pieces are golden and the juices run clear when each piece is pierced with the tip of a knife, about 15 minutes. Drain well on paper towels. Keep warm in a low (140°C, gas mark 1) oven until all the chicken pieces are fried. *Serves 4.*

VARIATION

Quicker Method Don't parboil the chicken. Coat the pieces as above and roast them in a single layer in a roasting pan in an oven preheated to 200°C, gas mark 6. Roast for 40–50 minutes, until the chicken is crisp and the juices run clear when each piece is pierced with the tip of a knife.

"These rambunctious children spread on top of me at a picnic in 1962 are my siblings. As far back as that, this chicken recipe was a family favourite, but it wasn't until many decades later, when my niece and nephew were as old as their mother is in the picture, that they gave me the credit for the dish."

"The story goes that my grandma didn't like to see my father going to school. She would ask him to stay home, and she would make him a little chicken. Seventy years ago, a little chicken was a huge bribe. Normally, one chicken was divided among 15 people. So now, occasionally, when my wife kisses me good-bye as I go out the door, she says, 'Why don't you stay home? I'll make you a little chicken!'"

Roast chicken with rosemary

3 cloves garlic, cut in half
4 sprigs fresh rosemary
Salt and freshly ground black pepper
1 chicken, 1.3–1.8kg
2 tablespoons sunflower oil

Preheat the oven to 190°C, gas mark 5. Place the garlic, the leaves of 1 sprig rosemary, and salt and pepper to taste in the chicken's cavity. Rub 1 tablespoon oil all over the chicken, then sprinkle with the leaves of another sprig of rosemary and season with salt and pepper to taste. Weigh the chicken and calculate the roasting time at 20 minutes per 450g.

Pour the remaining oil into a roasting pan. Place the chicken in the pan. Roast, basting every 15 minutes, until cooked through, when the juices run clear when pierced with the tip of a knife or the internal temperature reaches 80°C on a meat thermometer. Transfer the chicken to a serving dish, cover loosely with foil, and leave to rest for 15 minutes before carving. Garnish with the remaining sprigs of rosemary. Meanwhile, pour the pan juices into a small, heavy-bottomed saucepan and place over high heat. Skim the fat and boil the juices until reduced by half. Serve with the chicken. *Serves 4.*

ROSEMARY
Besides garlic, there is no other herb which is so evocative of sunny skies and deep blue sea as rosemary. This herb is wonderful flavouring for beef, chicken, pork, veal, as well as soups. Strip the stems of their leaves and use to thread vegetables or tender cuts of meat for grilling.

Roast stuffed chicken

You can just throw a chicken into the oven, or you can do this to make a delicious family meal.

FOR THE STUFFING

50ml sunflower oil

1 medium onion, chopped

1 medium carrot, chopped

1 medium stalk celery, chopped

130g cubed day-old Italian bread

1 small bunch fresh herbs, such as parsley,
    rosemary, or sage, chopped

Salt and freshly ground black pepper

1 chicken, 1.3–1.8kg

Olive oil

Salt and freshly ground black pepper

To make the stuffing Heat the oil in a large frying pan over medium heat. Add the onion and sauté until soft, about 5 minutes. Stir in the carrot and celery and continue sautéing until soft, about 5 minutes longer. Add the bread cubes and herbs and season with salt and pepper to taste.

Preheat the oven to 190°C, gas mark 5. Stuff the chicken in its cavity and the neck. Truss the bird, tying the drumsticks around the "nose" and the wing tips under the shoulders. Rub all over with oil and season with salt and pepper to taste. Weigh the chicken and calculate the roasting time at 20 minutes per 450g plus 20–30 minutes extra for the stuffing. Place the chicken in a roasting pan. Roast until the skin is crisp and golden, the juices run clear when pierced with the tip of a knife and the internal temperature reaches 80°C on a meat thermometer. Transfer the chicken to a serving dish, cover loosely with foil, and leave to rest for 15 minutes before carving. There should be enough juices in the pan to make gravy (page 117). *Serves 4–6.*

"Zia Nina is scalding pieces of chicken in boiling water preparatory to removing its feathers. In the village where the family lived, chickens were bought from neighbouring farmers and the most they would do for you was wring the necks. You had to do the plucking yourself."

Chicken cacciatore

All over Italy, chicken cacciatore—chicken hunter's style—is made, but each cook makes it in a slightly different way. If you don't like anchovies, leave them out (although I promise you won't taste them when this dish is done). If you don't like olives, leave those out as well. Or, maybe you'd like to make Grandma Flo's version (opposite page), which has a red sauce.

"When my family lived in Florence, the wind would whistle through some tall laurel trees at the back of the house overlooking the Tuscan hills. I can't hear the wind whistling without being reminded of laurel. Nor can I smell bay leaves without remembering those sunny, windy afternoons in Tuscany."

50ml olive oil
1 medium onion, chopped
1 stalk celery, chopped
1 clove garlic, chopped
1 small chicken, about 1kg, cut into 4 pieces
100ml dry white wine
100ml water
10 kalamata, Gaeta or similar black olives, pitted and halved
2 anchovy fillets in oil, chopped
2 bay leaves
Salt and freshly ground black pepper
1–2 tablespoons water (optional)

Heat the oil in a large frying pan over medium heat. Add the onion, celery and garlic and sauté until the onion is soft, about 5 minutes. Add the chicken pieces and brown all over. Pour in the wine, stir, and let it bubble until it evaporates. Stir in the water, olives, anchovies and bay leaves. Season with salt and pepper to taste. Simmer, covered, about 25 minutes. Uncover and continue cooking until the chicken is cooked through, the juices run clear when pierced with the tip of a knife, and a thick sauce has formed, about 20 minutes longer. If the sauce becomes too dry, stir in the water. Remove the bay leaves before serving. *Serves 4.*

Grandma Flo's chicken cacciatore

3 tablespoons olive oil

1 clove garlic, chopped

1 small chicken, about 1kg, cut into 4 pieces

**400g can chopped or whole plum tomatoes
     or 325ml passata**

2 tablespoons red wine vinegar

Salt and freshly ground black pepper

Heat the oil in a large frying pan over medium heat. Add the garlic and chicken pieces and fry until the chicken is brown all over. Stir in the tomatoes or passata, vinegar and salt and pepper to taste. Cover and simmer, stirring occasionally, until the chicken is cooked through, the juices run clear when pierced with the tip of a knife, and a sauce forms, about 40 minutes. *Serves 4.*

"My grandfather takes aim with his cane, making him a *cacciatore* (hunter). I have this romantic dream that hunters carry with them the necessary ingredients to make this favourite dish once they return to camp. In the United States, however, *cacciatore* means with tomato, peppers and onions. Surely no hunter would carry those in his pocket."

TURKEY

"I always liked turkey, but as a newly married couple, Carol and I found it difficult to deal with the enormous amount of meat one turkey provided. Our solution was to get together with another couple. With great anticipation, the other fellow and I awaited the turkey cooked by Carol and Lynn. It was our wives' first quantity cooking experience. Dinner was wonderful—except for the strange stuffing that popped out when we carved the bird. It was the giblets, cooked and still in their paper wrapper. Turkey gizzards *al cartoccio.*"

Roast stuffed turkey

FOR THE STUFFING
2 tablespoons sunflower oil
1 large onion, finely chopped
6 stalks celery, finely chopped
2 medium carrots, finely chopped
400g cubed day-old Italian bread (1cm cubes)
1 medium apple or pear, grated
1 tablespoon fennel seeds, crushed
Small bunch fresh herbs, such as parsley, rosemary,
    or sage, chopped
Salt
Freshly ground black pepper

1 oven-ready turkey, 4.5–6.5kg, giblets removed
Salt and freshly ground black pepper
Sunflower oil
Basic Good Gravy (page 117)

To make the stuffing Heat the oil in a large frying pan over medium heat. Add the onion and sauté until soft, about 5 minutes. Stir in the celery, carrots, bread cubes, apple or pear, fennel seeds, herbs and salt and pepper to taste; set aside to cool completely.

Preheat the oven to 230°C, gas mark 8. In a roasting pan large enough to hold the turkey, place a sheet of aluminum foil large enough to wrap around the turkey. If you don't have a large enough sheet of foil, put two sheets side by side, folding the edges together to make the foil leakproof. Rinse the turkey inside and out and pat dry. Season inside with salt. Loosely spoon the stuffing into the main cavity and neck. To truss, tuck the fatty end portion of the tail up and tie the end of the drumsticks around the "nose." Tuck the wing tips under the shoulders. Rub all over with oil and season with salt and pepper. Weigh the stuffed turkey and calculate the roasting time at 10 minutes per 450g. Put it in the roasting pan. Fold the foil up around the turkey and seal the edges. Roast, checking for doneness during the last hour. Peel back the foil for the final 15 iminutes so the skin browns. Continue roasting until the juices run clear when the thigh joint is pierced with the tip of a knife, and the internal temperature in this joint reaches 80°C on a meat thermometer. Transfer the turkey to a serving dish and leave to rest for at least 15 minutes before carving. Meanwhile, make the gravy, adding any juices from the serving dish. *Serves 10–14.*

STUFFING VARIATIONS

This is good basic stuffing, but you can add other ingredients for a special occasion. Don't, however, add too many extra ingredients or the turkey will get confused:

Grapes, cut in half and seeded
Parboiled peeled and chopped
    chestnuts
Handful of cranberries
Fried Italian pork sausage meat
Chopped dates or other dried fruit

"Turkey was seldom cooked in Italy. We happily learned new ways in America, enthusiastically joining in Thanksgiving celebrations, right from our first days in the New World."

TONY'S TIP:
using up the leftovers

We actually look forward to turkey leftovers; sandwiches are the first line of defence using Grandma Flo's **Antipasto** (page 30) as a condiment. And when you think that the turkey is done and gone, there is still the carcass, which will make you a very tasty soup.

DRY WHITE WINE

White wine is often used to flavour poultry and fish dishes. Don't buy "cooking wine." Buy a decent bottle because most recipes use only a glass or two at the most, and you will have the pleasure of finishing the bottle.

Pot-roasted quail

These small birds are a bit of a nuisance in that they are almost never properly cleaned. Take a few minutes to pluck out the last few feathers on the ankles, wings and backs.

FOR THE MARINADE
150ml dry white wine
2 sprigs fresh rosemary, leaves chopped
Freshly ground black pepper

8 oven-ready quail, thawed if frozen
2 tablespoons olive oil
75g diced sliced pancetta or cured (not smoked) bacon
Special Fried Polenta (page 85)

To make the marinade Combine the wine, rosemary and a generous amount of pepper in a large, non-metallic bowl. Add the quail and roll them around so they are coated. Cover with clingfilm and marinate in the fridge for at least 4 hours, but ideally overnight.

When you are ready to cook, preheat the oven to 180°C, gas mark 4. Heat the oil in a large flameproof casserole dish over medium heat. Add the bacon and sauté 5 minutes. Remove the quail from the marinade and pat dry. Increase the heat under the casserole to high, add the quail in a single layer, and brown all sides. Pour in the marinade and bring to a boil. Roast in the casserole, uncovered, for about 25 minutes, until the quail are fork-tender and the sauce has a good pouring consistency. If the sauce is too thin, remove the quail and boil until reduced; if it is too thick, stir in a few tablespoons wine. Meanwhile, prepare the polenta and cut it into squares, each large enough to hold a quail, rather than triangles. Fry the polenta, as in the recipe. To serve, place two polenta squares on each plate and top each with a quail. Spoon the sauce over. *Serves 4.*

VARIATION
Poussins If your local butcher or supermarket happens to be out of quail, you can prepare these small birds using the above recipes. One bird will be enough for each diner.

Pheasant in red wine sauce

Pheasant in red wine sauce is a hearty and elegant dish for a special occasion. You can substitute chicken in a pinch, but it doesn't stand up to the symphony of flavours that the recipe prescribes.

3 tablespoons olive oil

75g diced pancetta or cured
  (not smoked) bacon

2 oven-ready pheasants, quartered

1 medium onion, chopped

1 clove garlic, chopped

1 medium carrot, chopped

1 stalk celery, chopped

450ml dry red wine, or more as needed

50ml gin

2 sprigs fresh rosemary

2 bay leaves

2 cloves

Salt and freshly ground black pepper

Special Fried Polenta (page 85)

"My uncles and aunts in about 1936 on a restaurant terrace in Naples. Lengthy car journeys were and continue to be made to sample the particular delicacies of an area or a specific restaurant's most famous dish."

Heat the oil in a large flameproof casserole over medium heat. Add the bacon and sauté for 5 minutes. Increase the heat to high, and, working in batches, if necessary, to prevent overcrowding, brown the pheasant pieces in a single layer; remove and set aside. Reduce the heat under the casserole to medium. Add the onion and garlic and sauté until the onion is soft, about 5 minutes. Add the carrot and celery and sauté for 5 minutes longer. Stir in the wine, gin, rosemary, bay leaves, cloves and salt and pepper to taste and bring to a boil. Reduce the heat, return the pheasant pieces, and simmer, covered, until tender, about 40 minutes. If the sauce is too thick, stir in a few more tablespoons wine. Meanwhile, prepare the polenta and cut it into squares, each large enough to hold a pheasant piece, rather than triangles. Fry the polenta, as in the recipe. To serve, place two polenta squares on each plate and top each with a piece of pheasant. Spoon the sauce over. *Serves 4.*

BEEF

"When Carol and I were young and unschooled and newly married, we gave our first dinner party for six people and prepared rib roast. Not knowing any better, we bought one rib per person and a spare in case anyone was hungry. This turned into a ten-kilo roast, and we didn't go hungry for weeks. We were heartily sick of roast beef long before we'd seen the last of the beef."

Roast beef

The bigger the roast, the better the results. Many different cuts of beef suitable for roasting are available, but I think the rib roast with the bone in is the best.

> **1 bone-in rib roast, 2.2–3.6kg**
> **2 tablespoons sunflower oil or 25g butter, at room temperature**
> **Freshly ground black pepper**
> **50ml water or red wine**

Preheat the oven to 230°C, gas mark 8. Rub the meat all over with oil or butter and dust with pepper. Calculate the approximate roasting time at 15–20 minutes per 450g for medium-rare, 25 minutes per 450g for medium, and 30 minutes per 450g for well done. Put the beef on a rack in a roasting pan and roast for 15 minutes. Reduce the temperature to 170°C, gas mark 3, and add the water or wine to the pan. Continue roasting, basting occasionally with the water or wine, until the internal temperature on a meat thermometer reaches 50–55°C for medium-rare, 60–65°C for medium, and 80–85°C for well done. Leave to rest 15 minutes before carving. *Serves 4–6.*

TONY'S TIP:
carving the roast
Ideally, a roast should be sliced horizontally across the grain. This may be difficult for a thin roast, so slice it diagonally across the grain, with the knife held as flat as possible.

Basic good gravy

The key to lump-free gravy is to add the liquid slowly and to stir it until it is incorporated into the flour and butter before adding more. If you do get lumps and you can't crush them with a spoon, strain the gravy through a sieve.

25g butter or margarine
2 tablespoons plain flour
225ml warm liquid (see Liquid for Gravy below)
Salt and freshly ground black pepper

Melt the butter or margarine in a medium, heavy-bottomed saucepan over low heat. Stir in the flour and cook 2 minutes. Slowly pour in the liquid, stirring constantly to avoid lumps. Continue cooking, letting it bubble gently 5 minutes longer. Season with salt and pepper to taste. *Serves 4–6.*

VARIATIONS

French-Style Combine the flour with softened butter in a small bowl, stirring until a smooth paste forms. The mixture of equal amounts of butter and flour kneaded together is called *beurre manié* in French cooking, and is a useful way to thicken liquids at the end of cooking. To use, bring the liquid to a rolling boil and whisk in small pieces of *beurre manié*. As the butter melts, the flour is distributed throughout the liquid, thickening it. Cook for a couple of minutes.

Saucier To each 225ml of liquid, add 10g butter. Bring the liquid to a brisk boil. Add the butter and continue boiling 5–6 minutes.

Liquid for Gravy Whether you roast chicken, beef or pork, you will end up with liquid and fat in the roasting pan. You want to use this as the basis for your gravy, after you spoon off and discard the fat floating on the surface. If the roast has been in the oven for a long time, the liquid at the bottom of the pan will be too thick to pour. In this case, stir in a little water, scraping up all the sediment and juices from the bottom—you want to recover every bit of flavour. You need to do this over low heat if the pan has cooled down. If any of these sources of liquids are unavailable, use clear chicken soup, broth or bouillon powder. It's worth paying a little extra for high-quality chicken or vegetable stock or bouillon because cheaper brands can be overly salty.

TONY'S TIP:
separating fat
There are three ways to separate the fat from the pan juices. First, let the juices sit so the fat rises to the top. The tedious way is to skim the fat, using a large metal spoon. Or, pour the pan juices into a bowl, leave to cool, and then put in the refrigerator. As the fat cools, it will solidify and set on the surface, so it can easily be lifted off. The quickest way is to buy a special jug, called a fat separator, that lets you pour liquid juices from the bottom of the cup while the fat remains behind. There are few kitchen gadgets that I like, but this is one that I do. You may wish to get one.

Pot roast

If you're lucky to have any meat left over, pot roast makes a great sandwich on wholemeal bread with mayonnaise and a thin slice of raw onion, salt, and pepper.

> "Carmine, my Neapolitan cousin, believes in using onions to flavour meat and garlic to flavour fish. It's a good rule but there are still lots of exceptions."

3 tablespoons olive oil
2 medium onions, sliced
1.3kg topside or top rump, tied and basting fat removed
2 bay leaves
Salt and freshly ground black pepper
Water
15g butter
1 tablespoon plain flour

Heat the oil in a large flameproof casserole dish or heavy-based saucepan over medium heat. Add the onions and sauté until soft, about 5 minutes. Add the beef and brown all over. Add the bay leaves, salt and pepper to taste, and enough water to cover the beef by about 4cm. Cover and simmer, turning the beef over occasionally, until the beef is fork-tender, about 2 hours. Meanwhile, mix the butter and flour together to make a *beurre manié* (see p117). Transfer the beef to a serving dish, cover loosely with foil, and leave to rest while you make the gravy before carving. Bring the cooking liquid to a rolling boil. Drop small pieces of the *beurre manié* into the liquid, whisking constantly. Continue simmering, about 2 minutes. Taste and adjust the seasoning, if necessary. Remove and discard the bay leaves before serving with the sliced beef. *Serves 4–6.*

Grandma's beef stew

3 tablespoons olive oil

1 medium onion, sliced

900g stewing beef, such as chuck, cubed

2 teaspoons plain flour

1 bay leaf

Salt and freshly ground black pepper

225ml water, or more as needed

3 medium potatoes, peeled and diced

3 medium carrots, diced

225g green beans, topped and tailed

Heat the oil in a large flameproof casserole dish or heavy-based saucepan over medium heat. Add the onion and sauté until soft, about 5 minutes. Add the beef and fry until brown on all sides. Sprinkle with the flour, add the bay leaf and season with salt and pepper to taste. Stir in the water. Cover tightly and simmer 2 hours. Stir in the potatoes, carrots, and green beans, adding more water, if necessary. Cover the pan and continue simmering 30 minutes longer. Remove the bay leaf before serving. *Serves 4–6.*

"Carol's grandmother presided over the Sunday lunch table, which all her children attended—even after they were married. Regrettably, I never met her, but I feel I got to know her through the many dishes still cooked by her family."

Chargrilled steak

Bistecca alla Fiorentina

"The first time we had Fiorentina was at a restaurant called Certosa, across from the abbey just south of Florence. The steak was roasted over a great big charcoal fire. Carol and I and our two young girls went for dinner. I thought we would try *bistecca alla Fiorentina*. I ordered one for myself, one for Carol, and one for the daughters to share. The waiter looked at me funny; he had heard that Americans were big meat eaters, but this surpassed all his imaginings. Very diplomatically he suggested we try one and share it. We thought it strange to share a steak but when in Florence... . And, of course, one was too much for all of us."

It is difficult outside of Italy to get this steak right because the proper meat is not available. It is made from a young Chiana that is not quite an adult, but no longer a child. Buy a steak that is 2.5–5cm thick. You have to make this for at least a couple because the cooking method doesn't work for a thin single serving piece. For more people, buy a thicker steak or two or more 2.5cm thick steaks. Never get anything thinner.

It is my contention that the best wine to serve with a dish is wine made in the same region as the dish. Bistecca alla Fiorentina comes from Tuscany and therefore a good Chianti will suit it very well. If your budget stretches that far, go ahead and have a Chianti Riserva.

1 T-bone steak, at least 2.5cm thick, about 900g
Salt

Light a barbecue and leave until the coals are glowing. Position the rack 7.5cm above the coals. Grill the steak 5 minutes on one side, turn it over, and continue grilling 5 minutes longer. Raise the rack to about 12.5cm above the coals and continue grilling, turning over once, approximately 5 minutes for rare, 7 minutes for medium, and 10 minutes for well done. However, I tell you, it isn't worthwhile doing it well done. The steak should be a shell of well-done flesh with a rare centre. Salt before slicing. Slice diagonally into 1cm thick slices. Since this kind of steak has a tender portion and a firmer portion, distribute the slices so each person gets a little of each. *Serves 2–4.*

Steak and barbecued vegetables

Tagliata alla Ceparana

This dish was first served to me on a wooden board in a restaurant in Ceparana. It was autumn with pouring rain, but the texture and colour of this dish lit up the table.

1 medium tomato, thickly sliced

1 medium onion, thickly sliced

1 medium head radicchio

1 medium fennel bulb, quartered

Olive oil

1 T-bone steak, at least 2.5cm thick, about 900g

Salt

Light a barbecue and leave until the coals are glowing. Lightly brush all the vegetable pieces with olive oil. Put the vegetable slices on the rack and grill, turning them over once, until tender and lightly charred. Remove and keep warm in a low (140°C, gas mark 1) oven. Position the rack 7.5cm above the coals. Grill the steak 5 minutes on one side, turn over, and continue grilling 5 minutes longer. Raise the rack to about 12.5cm above the coals and continue grilling, turning over once, 5 minutes for rare, 7 minutes for medium, and 10 minutes for well done. Slice the steak 5mm thick or less. Arrange the vegetables and the steak on a platter. Salt before serving. *Serves 4.*

VARIATIONS

Grilled To cook indoors, heat the grill to high. Grill the vegetables for about 10 minutes, turning once. Remove and keep warm. Grill the steak, turning once, until done as desired.

Tagliata with Mushrooms Serve the sliced steak with about some **Sautéed Mushrooms** (page 195). If you can get porcini mushrooms, this would be the cherry on top.

Tagliata with Artichokes Serve the steak with the **Sautéed Artichokes** (page 189).

Tagliata with Rocket Serve the sliced steak on a serving dish lined with rocket.

What's in a name?
TAGLIATA

Tagliata means cut or sliced. This is an elegant way of serving steak, whether for two or a whole crowd. It adds colour, taste, and flair to an otherwise boring slab of meat. In a crowd, it permits diners to eat to their desire rather than being pressured to eat what is put in front of them.

Beef with tomatoes

Bistecca alla pizzaiola

50ml olive oil

4 cloves garlic, chopped

4–6 slices beef steak, rump or sirloin, cut 5-10mm thick,
about 900g

900g fresh tomatoes or 2x400g cans chopped tomatoes

2 teaspoons dried oregano

Salt and freshly ground black pepper

500g spaghetti

Grated Parmesan cheese

Heat the oil in a large frying pan over medium heat. Add the garlic and sauté until soft, 2–3 minutes. Add the beef and fry until brown all over and only half cooked, about 2 minutes each side. Remove and set aside. Add the tomatoes, oregano and salt and pepper to taste to the pan and simmer, uncovered, until the tomatoes are soft, about 15 minutes. Return the beef slices to the pan and cook until done to your liking—5 minutes for medium and 10 minutes for well done.

Meanwhile, bring a large saucepan of salted water to a boil. Add the spaghetti, stir, and continue boiling until firm-tender, according to the package directions. Drain well. Serve the spaghetti dressed with the tomato sauce, with Parmesan cheese on the side for those who like it, and serve the beef as a second course. *Serves 4–6.*

"When unexpected guests fly in, beef with tomatoes is a quick two-dish meal to make them happy. This canvas prop from the early 1930s was as close to flying as my uncles and aunt ever came. *Bistecca alla pizzaiola* was a popular dish at the time. As an alternative to pasta, it was sometimes served with mashed potatoes."

Meatballs for a crowd

Ziti con polpette

- 50ml olive oil
- 1 large onion, chopped
- 450g minced beef
- 450g minced pork
- 115g dry breadcrumbs
- 70g sultanas
- 55g grated Parmesan cheese, plus extra to serve
- 25g pine nuts
- 1 tablespoon chopped flat-leaf parsley
- Salt and freshly ground black pepper
- 2x400g cans chopped tomatoes
- 225g tomato purée, dissolved in 1 litre water
- 1 teaspoon dried oregano
- Sprig of basil
- 500g ziti or penne

Preheat the oven to 190°C, gas mark 5. Heat the oil in a large flameproof casserole over medium heat. Add the onion and sauté until soft, about 5 minutes. Meanwhile, in a large bowl, combine the beef, pork, breadcrumbs, sultanas, cheese, pine nuts, parsley, and salt and pepper to taste. Add half the soft onions when they are cool enough to handle and work everything together with your hands until well blended. Wet your hands with water and form 40 meatballs, each 2.5–4cm in diameter. (Keeping your hands wet will prevent the mixture from sticking.) Arrange the meatballs on one or two baking sheets and bake about 20 minutes, until brown all over.

Add the tomatoes and their juice, the tomato purée, oregano, basil and salt and pepper to taste to the onions remaining in the casserole. Bring to a boil, stirring, then lower the heat and simmer, partially covered, 30 minutes. Add the meatballs, stir, cover the pot, and continue simmering 30 minutes.

Meanwhile, bring a large saucepan of salted water to a boil. Add the pasta, stir, and continue boiling until the ziti is firm-tender, according to the package directions. Drain the pasta. Remove the meatballs from the sauce and toss the ziti with the sauce. Serve the ziti as a first course with extra Parmesan cheese sprinkled over. Serve the meatballs as a second course. *Serves 6–8.*

TONY'S TIP:
no breadcrumbs?
If you don't have any dry breadcrumbs, soak an equal amount of finely torn fresh bread in milk for 10 minutes, then squeeze dry and add to the other ingredients.

TONY'S TIP:
using other pasta
As an alternative to ziti, you can use penne or rigatoni, but never, never spaghetti.

FEEDING THE FAMILY

This meatloaf recipe is Christina's set piece for a family meal. Meatloaf has humble origins and is still considered a "homey" dish. But done this way, it is transformed into an elegant and sophisticated meal. In Italian, it's known as polpettone, *which literally means "huge meatball."*

Christina's meatloaf

25g butter or margarine

2 cloves garlic, chopped

1 small onion, chopped

1 stalk celery, diced

450g lean minced beef

450g lean minced pork

2 large eggs, beaten

50g fine, fresh homemade breadcrumbs

2 tablespoons Worcestershire sauce

50ml tomato ketchup

6 tablespoons chopped flat-leaf parsley

2 tablespoons chopped fresh basil

½ teaspoon fresh or dried thyme

½ teaspoon salt

½ teaspoon freshly ground black pepper

2 large eggs, hard-boiled and shelled

6 bacon rashers

Preheat the oven to 180°C, gas mark 4. Melt the butter or margarine in a large frying pan over low heat. Add the garlic, onion and celery and sauté until soft and golden, 8–10 minutes. Remove from the heat and leave to cool slightly. Combine the beef, pork, beaten eggs, breadcrumbs, Worcestershire sauce, ketchup, herbs, salt and pepper in a bowl. Add the vegetables and use your hands to mix together lightly. Form half the mixture into an oval loaf and place in a shallow roasting pan or baking dish. Embed the hard-boiled eggs on top and then add the remaining mixture to cover and shape flat. Arrange the bacon slices over the top. Bake for 1¼ hours, basting occasionally with the juices and bacon fat in the pan. Remove from the oven and drain off the fat. Let the meatloaf stand for 10 minutes before serving. *Serves 6–8.*

VEAL

What's in a name?
OSSO BUCO

Osso buco describes the type of bone used in this recipe. It literally means the bone with a hole in it, that is, the shin bone.

Osso Buco

I once tried to do osso buco with beef shin, which is more readily available, but it doesn't work as well. I recommend veal if you can get it. The traditional accompaniment is **Risotto alla Milanese** *(page 90).*

4–6 veal hind shanks, sawed into 4cm slices by the butcher
Plain flour
50g butter
50ml olive oil
4 cloves garlic, chopped
½ medium onion, chopped
3 tablespoons tomato purée
100ml water or dry white wine, or more as needed
Salt and freshly ground black pepper
6 tablespoons chopped flat-leaf parsley
2 anchovy fillets in oil, chopped
Grated zest of 1 lemon
Risotto alla Milanese (page 90)

Roll the veal in flour, shaking off any excess. Melt the butter with the oil in a large flameproof casserole. Add the veal and brown all over. Add the garlic and onion and sauté until translucent, about 5 minutes. Add the tomato purée, water or wine, and salt and pepper to taste and bring to a boil. Reduce the heat, cover, and simmer until the veal is fork-tender, about 1½ hours. Check as it cooks and add more liquid, if necessary. The sauce should be very thick. Just before serving, combine the parsley, anchovies and lemon zest. Stir into the cooking juice and serve immediately, accompanied by the risotto. *Serves 4–6.*

Osso buco with risotto alla Milanese (page 90) ▶

Veal chops Milanese

Veal chops, bone and all, done this way look splendid, but you can use escalopes as well.

4 veal chops or cutlets, 5mm thick
2 large eggs
Salt and freshly ground black pepper
115g plain flour
115g dried breadcrumbs
Olive oil for pan frying
4 lemon wedges

Put the veal chops between pieces of greaseprof paper or clingfilm. Flatten each chop with a meat mallet or rolling pin, leaving the bone attached, until 3–5mm thick; set aside. Break the eggs into a shallow bowl and season with salt and pepper to taste. Place the flour on a plate and the breadcrumbs on another plate. Working with one veal chop at a time, dip it in the flour, shaking off any excess, then in the eggs, letting the excess drip back into the bowl, and finally into the breadcrumbs, patting them on all over. Heat the oil in a large frying pan over medium heat. Working with one or two veal chops at a time, depending on the size of your pan, fry until golden brown, but not dry, 2–3 minutes on each side. Drain on paper towels. Keep warm in a low (140°C, gas mark 1) oven until all the veal is fried. Serve with wedges of lemon for squeezing over. *Serves 4.*

Saltimbocca

450g (8–12) veal escalopes

12 sage leaves

6 thin slices prosciutto, cut to fit the escalopes

50g butter

Freshly ground black pepper

100ml dry white wine (optional)

Put the veal escalopes between pieces of greaseproof paper or clingfilm and pound with a meat mallet or rolling pin until 3–5mm thick. Lay each slice of veal flat, place a leaf of sage on top and a slice of prosciutto on top of that. Using a cocktail stick like a pin, thread it through the lot to secure them together. Melt the butter in a large frying pan over medium heat. Add as many veal escalopes as will fit in a single layer, and fry until cooked through, 2–3 minutes on each side. Sprinkle with pepper, then remove from the pan and keep warm in a low (140°C, gas mark 1) oven until all the veal is cooked. Add the wine, if using, to the empty frying pan and boil until reduced by half. Pour over the veal and serve. If you are not using the wine, pour any remaining butter and juice over the veal. Return all the escalopes to the pan just to warm through. *Serves 4.*

What's in a name?
SALTIMBOCCA
The literal meaning is "jump in the mouth." This dish is made of delicate, extremely thin, tender slices of veal, which are topped with aromatic sage leaves and paper-thin slices of prosciutto.

Veal roast

2 tablespoons olive oil

25g prosciutto in one piece, chopped

900g boneless veal roast, such as shoulder, rolled and tied

225ml dry white wine

2 sprigs fresh rosemary

Salt and freshly ground black pepper

4 medium potatoes, peeled and sliced

Preheat the oven to 180°C, gas mark 4. Heat the oil in a flameproof casserole over medium heat. Add the prosciutto and sauté until soft, about 5 minutes. Add the veal and sauté until golden all over. Stir in the wine, rosemary and salt and pepper to taste. Bring to a boil, cover, and remove from the heat.

Transfer the casserole to the oven and cook for 25 minutes. Stir in the potatoes, cover, and continue cooking for about 40 minutes, stirring occasionally, until the veal and potatoes are both fork-tender. Remove and discard the rosemary sprigs. Taste and adjust the seasoning, if necessary. Remove the string and slice the veal. Serve the veal slices on a bed of the potatoes with the pan juices spooned around. *Serves 4.*

PORK

ITALIAN SAUSAGES

The most common Italian cooking sausage outside of Italy is generally the southern Italian sausage known as *finochiona,* which includes fennel seeds among its spices. In reality, there is a huge variety of sausages, varying in flavourings, textures, shapes, and sizes. The finochiona variety will do very well for these recipes. In Britain, you will probably have to go to an Italian deli or food store for Italian sausages, but they will be well worth the search.

Sausages with peppers

2 tablespoons olive oil

450g Italian sausages

450g (2–3) green peppers, deseeded and sliced

2 medium onions, thinly sliced

Salt and freshly ground black pepper

Heat the oil in a large frying pan over medium-high heat. Add the sausages and brown all over. Reduce the heat to medium, add the peppers and onions, and sauté until the sausages are cooked through and the vegetables are soft, about 20 minutes. Season to taste with salt and pepper. *Serves 4.*

Sausages in wine

2 tablespoons olive oil

450g Italian sausages, pierced all over

1 clove garlic, chopped

325ml dry red wine

Salt and freshly ground black pepper

Heat the oil in a large lidded frying pan or sauté pan over medium-high heat. Add the sausages and garlic and brown the sausages all over. Reduce the heat to medium, add the wine and salt and pepper to taste, cover, and simmer until the sausages are cooked through, about 30 minutes. *Serves 4.*

Pork in milk

Pork in milk may sound odd, but it makes a very elegant dish. Trust me.

- 5 tablespoons olive oil
- 1 sprig fresh rosemary
- 1 small clove garlic, left whole
- 900g boned loin of pork, tied
- Salt
- 600ml whole milk

In a casserole that will hold the pork snugly, heat the oil over medium heat. Stir in the rosemary and garlic. Add the pork, sprinkle with salt, and brown the meat all over; discard the rosemary and garlic. Pour in the milk, cover tightly, and simmer until the pork is cooked through, fork-tender, and the milk is thick, about 1½ hours. Transfer the meat to a warm serving dish, cover loosely with foil, and leave to stand for 10 minutes before slicing.

Meanwhile, bring the pan juices to a quick boil. Taste and adjust the seasoning, if necessary. Slice the pork and serve with the pan juices spooned over. *Serves 4–6.*

VARIATION

Roasted Preheat the oven to 180°C, gas mark 4. Put the covered casserole in the oven and roast for 1½ hours, until the pork is cooked through and fork-tender. Continue with the recipe as above.

Mock veal cutlets Milanese

- 350g pork tenderloin, trimmed of fat and skin, cut into 1cm thick medallions, or 4–6 pork chops
- Salt and freshly ground black pepper
- 2 large eggs
- Plain flour
- 115g dried bread crumbs
- Sunflower oil
- 4 lemon wedges

Put the pork slices between pieces of greaseproof paper or clingfilm and pound with a meat mallet or rolling pin until 3–5mm thick. If you are using pork chops, put them on a chopping board. Flatten each chop with a meat mallet or rolling pin, leaving the bone attached, until 3–5mm thick. Season to taste with salt and pepper. Beat the eggs in a shallow bowl. Season with salt and pepper to taste. Place the flour on a plate and the breadcrumbs on another plate. One by one, dip each piece of pork in the flour, shaking off the excess, then into the eggs, letting the excess drip back into the bowl, and finally into the breadcrumbs. Completely cover with breadcrumbs; set aside. Heat 100ml oil in a large frying pan over medium heat. Add as many pieces of pork as will fit in a single layer and fry until cooked through and tender, turning over once, about 5 minutes. Drain on paper towels and keep warm in a low (140°C, gas mark 1) oven until all the pork pieces are fried. Serve with lemon wedges. *Serves 4.*

Pork chops with apples

2 tablespoons sunflower oil
4 pork loin chops, 1.5cm thick (about 175g each)
1 medium onion, sliced
Salt and freshly ground black pepper
4 medium apples, peeled, cored, and sliced
225ml single cream

Heat the oil in a large frying pan over medium-high heat. Add the chops in a single layer and fry until lightly brown, about 2 minutes each side. Reduce the heat to low and continue frying the chops until they are cooked through and tender, 8–10 minutes on each side, turning them over repeatedly. Remove and keep warm in a low (140°C, gas mark 1) oven. Reduce the heat to low, add the onion and salt and pepper to taste and fry until the onion is soft, about 10 minutes. Add the apples and continue frying until soft, about 5 minutes. Stir in the cream and heat through. Return the chops to the pan and heat through. *Serves 4.*

"Well, what can we say about pork chops? They are humble and ubiquitous, but they do make terrific quick dishes. The secret to cooking pork chops is to sauté both sides quickly to a golden brown, no more than 2–3 minutes per side. Then use a low flame to finish cooking, turning the chops frequently."

Pork chops with peppers

2 tablespoons sunflower oil
4 pork loin chops, 1.5cm thick (about 175g each)
4 medium peppers, in a mixture of colours, deseeded and sliced
1 medium onion, sliced
Salt and freshly ground black pepper

Heat the oil in a large frying pan over medium-high heat. Add the chops in a single layer and fry until lightly brown, about 2 minutes each side. Reduce the heat to low and continue frying the chops until they are cooked through and tender, 8–10 minutes on each side, turning them over repeatedly. Remove from the frying pan and keep warm in a low (140°C, gas mark 1) oven. Increase the heat to medium. Add the peppers and onion to the frying pan and sauté until soft, about 10 minutes. Season to taste with salt and pepper. Return the chops to the pan and heat through. *Serves 4.*

Roast pork

A pork roast can be dressed up in many ways. There are plenty of recipes with spinach, prunes, and who knows what else, but sometimes a simple roast is what you want. If you need a basting liquid, use dry white wine.

1 pork loin with the ribs, or 1 boneless pork shoulder, tied, 1.8–2.7kg
Salt and freshly ground black pepper
225ml dry white wine

Preheat the oven to 170°C, gas mark 3. Weigh the pork and calculate the roasting time at 20–25 minutes per 450g for the bone-in roast; 23–33 minutes per 450g for the boneless roast. Season the pork with salt and pepper to taste. Put the pork in a roasting pan and pour the wine into the pan. Roast, basting occasionally with the wine, until the pork is tender and the internal temperature reaches 70°C for medium and 75°C for well done on a meat thermometer. Transfer the pork to a serving dish, cover loosely with foil, and leave to rest for 15 minutes before carving. Pour the pan juices over the carved roast or make a gravy (page 117). *Serves 6–8.*

VARIATIONS
Leg of Pork Roast a 2.2-3.5kg leg of pork as above, allowing 25 minutes per 450g, about 2¼–3½ hours.

Pork Flavourings Add to the roasting pan a sliced onion, or 2 bay leaves, or 4 fresh sage leaves, or 1 teaspoon dried sage.

TONY'S TIP:
testing for doneness
A meat thermometer, which gives you a quick reading when inserted into cooked food, makes short work of checking whether meat is properly cooked. You need to pull the meat out of the oven far enough to insert the stem about 5cm into the thickest part of the food, avoiding any bones. The temperature should register in about 15 seconds. Although pork chops are done when they just lose their pink colour, pork roasts may still be pale pink inside, but as long as the thermometer measures 70°C, they will be safe to eat.

Gina's roast pork with mushrooms and Marsala

While her sister wows her friends with meatloaf (page 125), my older daughter does it with this recipe.

3 cloves garlic, chopped

1 bone-in pork loin, about 1.6kg

Salt and freshly ground black pepper

Rosemary sprigs

FOR THE SAUCE

30g butter

450g oyster mushrooms, wiped clean

1 large onion, chopped

2 cloves garlic, chopped

2 tablespoons chopped flat-leaf parsley

2 tablespoons chopped fresh oregano, or 1 teaspoon dried

2 tablespoons plain flour

50ml dry Marsala

900ml chicken stock

Preheat the oven to 170°C, gas mark 3. Rub the garlic all over the pork and season with salt and pepper to taste. Put the pork in a roasting pan and roast until the internal temperature reaches 70°C on a meat thermometer, about 1¼ hours. Transfer the pork to a serving dish, cover loosely with foil; set aside the roasting pan.

To make the sauce Melt the butter in a medium, heavy-bottomed saucepan over low heat. Add the mushrooms, onion and garlic, and sauté, stirring occasionally, until the mushrooms brown and the liquid evaporates, about 20 minutes. Remove the saucepan from the heat and stir in the parsley and oregano; set aside. Put the flour in a small bowl and stir in the Marsala. Put the roasting pan over medium heat and stir in the stock, scraping any cooked pieces on the bottom. Raise the heat to high and whisk in the Marsala mixture. Bring to a boil, whisking, then reduce the heat and simmer until thick. Stir in the mushrooms and any juices that have accumulated on the serving dish. Taste and adjust the seasoning, if necessary.

Serve the pork in slices with the mushroom sauce spooned over and garnished with rosemary. *Serves 8.*

TONY'S TIP:
tasty side dishes
This pork dish is even more delicious if you serve it with **Chilli Mash** (page 198) and **Glazed Carrots** (page 205).

Roast stuffed pork
Porchetta

In Rome an entire pig is stuffed and roasted in this way and, believe me, it was a startling sight to see a whole golden brown pig, including its head, sitting on a stall in a Roman street. The vendor would cut a few slices from the back and serve them in a hard roll—a wonderful treat in the open air! But you needn't roast an entire animal to get approximately the same taste.

1 leg of pork, 1.8–2.2kg, boned
Salt and freshly ground black pepper
350g coarsely minced pork
5 tablespoons grated Parmesan cheese
1 tablespoon black peppercorns, lightly crushed
5 slices pancetta or cured (not smoked) bacon, chopped
3 cloves garlic, minced
6 fresh sage leaves, chopped
4 bay leaves
3 sprigs fresh rosemary, leaves chopped

PEPPERCORNS

Besides salt, pepper is the most commonly used spice. The most common is black pepper, which should be kept in whole peppercorns to preserve the flavour, and ground only when needed. For a milder pepper flavour, use white pepper.

Preheat the oven to 170°C, gas mark 3. Open the pork and season with salt and pepper to taste. Combine the minced pork, cheese, peppercorns, pancetta, garlic, sage, bay leaves, rosemary and salt and pepper to taste in a large bowl. Place this on the pork, then roll up and tie securely—you should have a neat cylinder. Weigh and calculate the roasting time at 25–30 minutes per 450g. Roast until the pork is tender and the internal temperature reaches 70°C on a meat thermometer, about 2 hours. Transfer the pork to a serving dish, cover loosely with foil, and leave to rest for 15 minutes before carving. Remove the bay leaves as you slice and serve hot or cold. *Serves 6–8.*

Fried breaded lamb chops

2 large eggs
Plain flour
Dried breadcrumbs
8 lamb loin chops, 2.5cm thick (about 115g each)
100ml olive oil
Salt and freshly ground black pepper
100g butter
Lemon wedges

Beat the eggs in a shallow bowl. Place the flour on a plate and the breadcrumbs on another plate. One by one, brush each chop with oil and season to taste with salt and pepper. Roll each chop in the flour, then dip it in the egg, letting the excess drain back into the bowl. Cover completely with the breadcrumbs; set aside for at least 15 minutes. To cook, melt the butter with the remaining oil in a large frying pan let over medium heat. Working in batches, if necessary, to avoid overcrowding the pan, fry the chops until brown and tender, about 4½–5 minutes per side for rare and 5½–6 minutes per side for medium. Drain on paper towels. Serve with lemon wedges. *Serves 4.*

LAMB

"It is a true art to pick a good restaurant, and often I'm unsuccessful. My Uncle Geppino's method may have been unorthodox, but it was successful. Upon my return to Naples after an absence of more than twenty years, we visited Mount Vesuvius. As it happened to be lunchtime, we were on the lookout for a restaurant. I suggested my trusted methods: (1) Is the restaurant full? (2) Do most of the cars display local license plates? (3) Do they accept credit cards? My uncle would have none of that. He went straight to a restaurant that enticed diners into its premises by displaying a lamb's carcass hanging by the front door. Needless to say—he was right."

Grilled lamb chops

I am ashamed to list this as a recipe because it is so easy. Let's just say it is a reminder that lamb chops fixed this way are good and easy.

**12 lamb loin chops or best end of neck
  cutlets, 2.5cm thick
Salt and freshly ground black pepper
Lemon wedges**

Preheat the grill to high. Rub both sides of each lamb chop with salt and pepper. Place the chops on a rack in the grill pan, 10cm from the heat. Grill for 5 minutes. Turn the chops over and continue grilling until tender and done as desired, about 4 minutes longer for rare and 5 minutes for medium. Serve with the lemon wedges for squeezing juice over. *Serves 4–6.*

VARIATION
With Vegetables Brush 2 small tomatoes, 4 small flat mushrooms and 1 cougette (sliced lengthwise), with 3 tablespoons olive oil and grill for about 10 minutes, turning them over once. Remove and keep warm. Grill the chops as above and serve with the vegetables.

TONY'S TIP:
cooking lamb
How well do you like your lamb cooked? In France it's pink, in Italy they like it well done. Indeed, the Roman's grilled lamb is literally called "burns your fingers." If you have good lamb, then opt for pink. If your lamb is more like mutton, then by all means cook it to death. Let me recommend that you get a meat thermometer for surer results and that you start checking for doneness in the last 30 minutes of cooking time.

Rack of lamb

One of the most elegant ways to serve lamb is as a rack; that is, a number of chops stuck together. You will get praise in excess of the time that it takes to prepare this dish.

**2 cloves garlic, chopped
2 tablespoons Dijon mustard
3 tablespoons chopped flat-leaf parsley
2 tablespoons olive oil
1 rack of lamb, about 1.1kg
Salt and freshly ground black pepper**

Preheat the oven to 190°C, gas mark 5. Combine the garlic, mustard, parsley and oil in a bowl and stir until a paste forms. Season the rack of lamb with salt and pepper to taste. Spread the paste all over the meat side of the lamb. Weigh the lamb and calculate the roasting time at 20 minutes per 450g for medium-rare and 25 minutes per 450g for medium. Place the lamb on a rack in a roasting pan, meat-side up, and roast until fork-tender and the internal temperature reaches 55°C for medium-rare and 65°C for medium on a meat thermometer. (The internal temperature will rise to 60°C or 70°C on standing.) Transfer the rack of lamb to a serving dish, cover loosely with foil, and leave to rest 5 minutes before carving into individual chops. *Serves 4.*

Rack of lamb with parsley crust

1 tablespoon olive oil

1 rack of lamb, about 1.1kg

1 clove garlic, chopped

3 tablespoons chopped flat-leaf parsley

2 tablespoons dried breadcrumbs

Salt and freshly ground black pepper

1 tablespoon butter

Preheat the oven to 190°C, gas mark 5. Weigh the lamb and calculate the roasting time at 20 minutes per 450g for medium-rare and 25 minutes per 450g for medium. Heat the oil in a large frying pan over high heat. Add the lamb and brown all over. Place the rack of lamb on a rack in a roasting pan. Roast for 15 minutes. Meanwhile, combine the garlic, parsley, breadcrumbs and salt and pepper to taste in a small bowl and stir until a paste forms. Spread the paste all over the fat side of the rack of lamb. Return the lamb to the oven and roast until tender and the internal temperature reaches 55°C for medium-rare and 65°C for medium on a meat thermometer. (The internal temperature will rise to 60°C or 70°C on standing.) Transfer the rack of lamb to a serving dish, cover loosely with foil, and leave to rest for 5 minutes before carving into individual chops. *Serves 4.*

Roast lamb

Roast leg of lamb is a traditional Sunday roast or for company on special occasions. This is how Grandma Simone prepared roast leg of lamb for the family.

1 leg of lamb, bone-in, 2.2–4kg

3 cloves garlic, chopped

3 tablespoons grated Parmesan cheese

3 tablespoons chopped flat-leaf parsley

1 teaspoon salt

1 teaspoon freshly ground black pepper

225ml dry red wine

Preheat the oven to 170°C, gas mark 3. Cut deep incisions all over the lamb. Combine the garlic, Parmesan, parsley, salt and pepper in a small bowl and stir together. Using your fingers, work the mixture into the slits. Weigh the lamb and calculate the roasting time at 20 minutes per 450g for medium-rare and 25 minutes per 450g for medium.

Place the lamb in a roasting pan, pour in the wine and roast, basting occasionally with the wine, until tender and the internal temperature reaches 55°C for medium-rare and 65°C for medium on a meat thermometer. (The internal temperature will rise to 60°C or 70°C on standing.) Transfer the leg of lamb to a serving dish, cover loosely with foil, and leave to rest for 15 minutes before carving. Spoon over the pan juices. *Serves 6–8.*

"If you don't want to look silly carving at the table, remove the bone before roasting or, better yet, get that friendly butcher to do it for you."

Roast leg of lamb Puglia style

4 thin slices of pancetta or cured (not smoked) bacon, cut into 1cm strips
2 tablespoons chopped fresh rosemary
25g dried breadcrumbs
2 cloves garlic, thinly sliced
1 leg of lamb, bone-in, 2.2–4kg
2 tablespoons olive oil
Salt and freshly ground black pepper
125ml red wine vinegar

Preheat the oven to 200°C, gas mark 6. Sauté the bacon in a medium frying pan over medium heat until translucent, about 7 minutes. Add the rosemary, breadcrumbs and garlic. Cut deep slits in the lamb all over and stuff with this mixture. Rub all over with the oil and season to taste with salt and pepper. Weigh the lamb and calculate the roasting time at 18 minutes per 450g for medium-rare and 23 minutes per 450g for medium.

Place the lamb in a roasting pan and roast for 10 minutes. Pour the vinegar into the pan. Turn the oven down to 170°C, gas mark 3, and continue roasting and basting occasionally with the vinegar, until the meat is tender and the internal temperature reaches 55°C for medium-rare and 65°C for medium on a meat thermometer. (The internal temperature will rise to 60°C or 70°C on standing.) Transfer the leg of lamb to a serving dish, cover loosely with foil, and leave to rest for 15 minutes before carving. Spoon over the pan juices. *Serves 6–8.*

"These are my aunts visiting old neighbours in the village where I was born. Here, it is most likely Easter time, as my aunt is holding olive branches, which churches give out on Palm Sunday in lieu of palm fronds. It always puzzled me as a child that it was named Palm Sunday and not Olive Sunday. Another Easter tradition was lamb for the Sunday meal, usually baked, served with fresh peas and new potatoes, which are at their peak at the same time."

Lamb Abruzzi style

1 leg of lamb, bone-in, 2.2–4kg
2 cloves garlic, chopped
2 sprigs fresh marjoram, chopped
3 sprigs flat-leaf parsley, chopped
25g grated Parmesan cheese
2 sprigs fresh rosemary, leaves chopped
25g dried breadcrumbs
115g prosciutto, pancetta or cured
  (not smoked) bacon slices, cut into
  strips about 5cm long
Salt and freshly ground black pepper
25g butter
225ml dry white wine

Preheat the oven to 170°C, gas mark 3. Cut deep incisions all over the lamb. Combine the garlic, marjoram, parsley, Parmesan, rosemary and breadcrumbs in a small bowl and stir together. Place a bit of the herb mixture on each prosciutto or bacon strip, roll it up, and, using your fingers, work the rolls into the incisions. Rub the remaining herb mixture over the lamb and season to taste with salt and pepper. Weigh the lamb and calculate the roasting time at 18 minutes per 450g for medium-rare; 23 minutes per 450g for medium. Melt the butter in a roasting pan. Place the lamb in the roasting pan and brown all over, about 10 minutes. Pour the wine into the pan and transfer to the oven. Roast, basting occasionally with the wine, until the meat is tender and the internal temperature reaches 55°C for medium-rare and 65°C for medium on a meat thermometer. (The internal temperature can rise to 60°C or 70°C on standing.) Transfer the leg of lamb to a serving dish, cover loosely with foil, and leave to rest for 15 minutes before carving. Spoon over the pan juices. *Serves 6–8.*

Barbecued leg of lamb

Barbecue the lamb until almost burnt on the outside but still pink inside. Lamb done this way will have a remarkable flavour—somewhere between beef and lamb.

FOR THE MARINADE
50ml olive oil
Juice of 1 lemon
3 bay leaves, crushed, or 3 sprigs fresh thyme
1 clove garlic, chopped
Freshly ground black pepper

1 leg of lamb, boned, 2.2–4kg
Salt
Olive oil

To make the marinade Combine the olive oil, lemon juice, bay leaves or thyme, garlic and plenty of pepper in a large, non-metallic bowl. Add the lamb and rub it all over with the marinade. Set aside and leave to marinate for 1 hour.

When you are ready to cook, light a barbecue and leave until the coals are glowing. Season the lamb with salt. Open the lamb like a book and place it flat on the barbecue and grill until done as desired, about 20 minutes for medium-rare and 25 minutes for medium. (For medium-rare the internal temperature should be about 55°C and for medium about 65°C on a meat thermometer—these temperatures can rise to 60°C and 70°C on standing.) Leave to rest for 15 minutes before carving. *Serves 4–6.*

4 COURSES FROM THE SEA

Fish is a popular dish in my family,
and here is a selection of my favourites.
You will find these recipes quick and
easy to prepare. Remember, though, that
the secret to cooking fish is to use the
freshest fish available, to keep the recipe
simple, and to avoid rich ingredients.

FISH

Trout with almonds

Trout is easily available all year round. Make sure it stares at you with a clear eye when you buy it as this means it's really fresh. This is a very quick and easy no-fuss supper.

225ml milk

115g plain flour, seasoned with salt and pepper

4 medium trout, gutted and cleaned

100g butter

100ml olive oil

6 tablespoons slivered blanched almonds

Juice of 1 lemon

2 tablespoons chopped flat-leaf parsley

Pour the milk into a shallow bowl and place the flour on a plate. One by one, roll the trout in the milk, then the flour, shaking off the excess. Melt half the butter with the olive oil in a large frying pan over medium heat. Working in batches, if necessary, to avoid overcrowding the pan, fry the trout until golden on both sides and the flesh flakes easily and is opaque, 6–7 minutes on each side. Transfer the trout to a warm dish and keep warm while the remaining fish are fried, if necessary. Discard the fat in the pan. Wipe the pan with crumpled paper towels. Melt the remaining butter over medium heat. Add the almonds and sauté and stir until golden, about 5 minutes—watch carefully because they burn quickly. Stir in the lemon juice and parsley; pour over the trout. *Serves 4.*

"The port of Naples is normally the stage for drama and tragedy, as families bid goodbye to their departing loved ones. Often a goodbye was forever. For us, this visit to the port was a happy event—the return of my father from his first trip to America. All the generations were present: Grandma, Mother, Aunt, right down to my baby sister in arms."

Oven-baked trout

4 medium trout, gutted and cleaned

Bunch dill or fennel fronds

2 tablespoons sunflower oil

Salt and freshly ground black pepper

4 lemon wedges

Preheat the oven to 180°C, gas mark 4. Stuff each trout cavity with a
frond of dill or fennel. Brush the trout with the oil and season with
salt and pepper to taste, inside and out. Place in a baking dish or
roasting pan large enough to hold them in a single layer. Bake for
12–15 minutes, until the flesh flakes easily and is opaque. Serve with
the lemon wedges to squeeze over. *Serves 4.*

VARIATION

Sage Instead of the dill or fennel, use 8 fresh sage leaves, placing
two in the cavity of each trout.

Fish fillets with mint

Pesce a scapece

This fish will keep for several days—sometimes I treat leftover fish this way.

115g plain flour
675g firm fish fillets, such as swordfish or tuna
Salt
50ml sunflower oil
1 shallot, thinly sliced
Bunch fresh mint leaves, chopped
Freshly ground black pepper
6 tablespoons white wine vinegar

Place the flour on a plate. One by one, season the fillets with salt and coat each fillet in the flour, shaking off any excess. Heat the oil in a large frying pan over medium heat. Add the fillets to the pan in a single layer and fry until golden, 5–6 minutes. Turn over and fry until the skin is golden and the flesh flakes easily and is opaque, 5–6 minutes. Drain on paper towels. Transfer the fish to a serving dish. Cover with the onion, mint and a good grinding of pepper. Sprinkle the vinegar over. Leave to cool completely. This can be chilled in the fridge before serving and, indeed, it can be kept for 2 days. *Serves 4.*

TONY'S TIP:
easy flouring
For a good, even coating, put a small amount of flour in a plastic bag. Add the fish, seal the top, and shake.

Cold poached fish

Pesce in bianco

In Naples, pesce in bianco is served to convalescents, but why get sick just to have it? Traditionally we have used whole whitings and cleaned them after cooking by removing heads, skin, and bones and arranging them in their original shapes on the plate. You can use skinned fillets as an alternative.

1 whole white fish, such as cod, hake,
    haddock, or similar meaty white fish,
    about 675g

FOR THE DRESSING
6 tablespoons olive oil
1 garlic clove, chopped
Juice of 1 lemon
Salt and freshly ground black pepper
Bunch flat-leaf parsley, chopped

Bring a large frying pan or sauté pan of salted water to a simmer. Add the fish and poach until the flesh flakes easily and is opaque, about 10 minutes. Remove from the poaching liquid and set aside to cool completely. Meanwhile, combine the olive oil, garlic, lemon juice and salt and pepper to taste in a small, non-metallic bowl. Pour the dressing over the fish and sprinkle with the parsley. Serve at room temperature; the dish can be prepared ahead and kept covered in the refrigerator. It should be taken out an hour before serving. *Serves 4.*

"This is my aunt, Zia Antonietta, in the fish market in Naples, where the fish virtually jump into your arms. My wife's first visit to this market was memorable. An octopus crawled up the arm of its captor, and an eel tried to make its escape by slithering down the street. Another surprise was getting squirted with jets of seawater as we walked past the shallow tubs filled with live clams. Don't know if they were scaring us off or attracting our attention."

Grandma Flo's fried fish

2 eggs
115g plain flour
225–350g dried breadcrumbs
675g white fish fillets, such as cod, hake or plaice
100ml sunflower oil
Salt
1 lemon, cut into wedges
275ml Mom's Tartar Sauce (below)

Beat the eggs in a small, shallow bowl. Put the flour on a plate and the
bread crumbs on another plate. One by one, roll each fish fillet in the
flour, shaking off the excess. Dip in the eggs, then coat with
breadcrumbs. Heat the oil in a large frying pan over medium heat.
Working in batches, if necessary, to avoid overcrowding the pan, add
the fillets to the pan in a single layer and fry until golden, 5–6 minutes.
Turn over and fry until golden and the flesh flakes easily and is
opaque, 5–6 minutes longer. Drain on paper towels. Season with salt
to taste and serve with the lemon wedges and tartar sauce. *Serves 4.*

Mom's tartar sauce

225ml mayonnaise
2 tablespoons grated onion
2 tablespoons chopped flat-leaf parsley
2 tablespoons chopped olives stuffed with pimientos

Combine all the ingredients in a bowl. Cover and chill until required.
Serve with any fried fish. *Makes 225ml.*

"Grandma Flo Simone
is looking out for
sweetheart Ted who
has gone fishing on
the Hudson River.
The fishing was only
for fun—the fish for
cooking came from
a market that trucked
its fish freshly caught
from New England."

◄ *Grandma Flo's fried fish*

Grilled snapper with fennel

Red snappers are quite voracious and can grow to a metre. If you are able to get four small fish, one per serving, this recipe works even better.

1 whole red snapper, about 675g, gutted and cleaned
50ml olive oil
Salt and freshly ground black pepper
25g chopped fresh fennel
50ml pernod or arrack

Preheat the grill to high. Brush the red snapper with the olive oil and season with salt and pepper to taste, inside and out. Grill the fish 10cm from the heat until the flesh flakes easily and is opaque, 7–8 minutes each side. Transfer the fish to a heatproof serving dish and cover with the fennel fronds. Pour the spirit into a ladle, ignite, and when the flames die down, pour over the fish. *Serves 4.*

RED SNAPPER

Called snapper because its jaws can snap vigorously, this bright pink-red fish is rated one of the very best to eat. The moist, white flesh has a delicate sweet flavour and can be grilled, baked, steamed, poached, fried or grilled.

Fish bake

Pesce a l'isolana

This is a popular dish in fish restaurants in La Spezia where sea bass is king. Slice the potatoes thinly or you will have a cooked fish, but raw potatoes.

1 sea bass, sea bream or salmon, about 675g, gutted and cleaned
50ml olive oil
3 medium tomatoes, sliced
2 medium potatoes, peeled and sliced very thinly
Handful black pitted olives
1 teaspoon dried oregano
Salt and freshly ground black pepper
50ml water

Preheat the oven to 170°C, gas mark 3. Rub the fish all over with 2 tablespoons of the oil. Place in a large baking dish and arrange half the tomato slices on top of the fish. Scatter the remaining tomato slices and the potato slices around the fish. Sprinkle with the olives, the remaining oil, the oregano, and salt and pepper to taste. Pour in the water. Partially cover the dish with a sheet of foil. Bake for 20–25 minutes, until the flesh flakes easily and is opaque. *Serves 4.*

Salmon in a crust

30g butter

3 spring onions, chopped

115g sliced white mushrooms

Juice of ½ lemon

Salt and freshly ground black pepper

280g puff pastry

115g cooked brown rice

350g cooked salmon, boned and skinned, in pieces

2 hard-boiled eggs, shelled and roughly chopped

1 tablespoon chopped fresh dill

2 tablespoons chopped flat-leaf parsley

4 tablespoons single cream

1 egg yolk, beaten

In a frying pan, melt the butter and sauté the spring onions until soft, about 4 minutes. Add the mushrooms, lemon juice and salt and pepper to taste and cook until the mushrooms soften, about 10 minutes; set aside and let cool.

Preheat the oven to 220°C, gas mark 7. Roll out the puff pastry and cut two rectangles, each about 30x18cm. Place one piece on a greased baking sheet. Spoon on half the rice, taking care to leave a border of pastry free. Add a layer of half the mushrooms, then the salmon, followed by the chopped egg. Sprinkle with the herbs. Add another layer of the remaining mushrooms, the remaining rice, and finally the cream. Wet the edges of the pastry and put the second sheet on top, sealing the edges together. Brush the pastry with the beaten egg. Bake for about 30 minutes, until golden. Let cool for 5 minutes before cutting into slices. Can be served warm or at room temperature.
Serves 4.

TONY'S TIPS:
cooking with fish

Buying fish The essence of fish is freshness. The fundamental rule when buying fish is that it should not smell. If you can sniff it, and if it smells "fishy," don't buy it. A second rule is that the flesh should be firm. If it looks mushy, pass it by. Last, if you are one of those brave souls who buy fish with the head on, look deep into its eyes. If the eyes are dull and lacklustre, leave it on the shelf.

Refreshing fish If your fish has been resting in the refrigerator for a day, give it a bath before cooking it. First rinse it in cold water and pat dry. Then let it bathe in cold milk for 30 minutes, and pat dry before cooking.

Frying fish The oil must be hot, but not smoking. Test the temperature by adding a cube of bread to the oil and see if the oil fizzes around it and the cube browns in 30 seconds. Attempting to fry before the oil is hot enough will result in soggy fish.

"Please don't laugh because people will be laughing at your beach photos 70 years from now. But this was haute couture in Connecticut, and Aunt Thelma obviously enjoyed her ice cream."

Salmon with vegetables

Salmon has gone from being one of the most expensive fish to one of the most economical. It is easy to prepare, so pick up a steak or fillet on your way home from work. It will be ready before you have changed your clothes.

50ml olive oil
2 medium carrots, cut into matchsticks
2 medium stalks celery, cut into matchsticks
1 onion, sliced
4 salmon steaks, about 175g each
225ml fish stock or water
Salt and freshly ground black pepper
1 tablespoon chopped flat-leaf parsley

Heat the oil in a large frying pan or sauté pan with a tight-fitting lid over medium heat. Add the carrots, celery and onion, and sauté until the vegetables are tender, about 10 minutes. Add the salmon steaks in a single layer, the stock or water, and salt and pepper to taste. Reduce the heat to low and simmer, covered, until the flesh flakes easily and is opaque, 12–15 minutes depending on the thickness of the fish. Sprinkle with the parsley. Serve the salmon with a few vegetables and a tablespoon or two of the sauce poured over. *Serves 4.*

Gina's salmon parcels

Now here's a recipe so simple anyone can make it and achieve good results. The recipe offers no frills, only good taste.

4 salmon steaks or fillets, about 175g each
Butter
Salt and freshly ground black pepper

Preheat the oven to 180°C, gas mark 4. Cut 4 bits of foil large enough to wrap around the fish. Place each piece on a bit of foil. Add a large knob of butter to each and salt and pepper to taste. Wrap up the salmon pieces, with the foil puffed but tightly sealed at the seams so the bundles are leakproof. Place on a baking sheet and bake for about 15 minutes until the flesh is firm. Remove from the foil and serve. *Serves 4.*

VARIATION
Dill or Lemon Add a teaspoon chopped fresh dill or a thin slice of lemon on top of the butter.

Salmon steaks with garlic and chilli

100ml sunflower oil
115g plain flour
4 salmon steaks, about 175g each
75g butter
4 garlic cloves, chopped
½ teaspoon crushed chilli flakes
1 tablespoon chopped flat-leaf parsley

Heat the oil in a large frying pan over medium heat. Place the flour on a plate. One by one, coat the salmon steaks in the flour, shaking off any excess. Add the fillets to the skillet in a single layer and fry until golden, 6–7 minutes. Turn over and fry until golden, and the flesh flakes easily and is opaque, 6–7 minutes longer. Drain on paper towels and transfer to a warm serving dish.

Meanwhile, melt the butter in a medium frying pan over medium heat. Add the garlic and chilli flakes and sauté until the garlic is golden, 2–3 minutes. Pour over the fish and sprinkle with parsley. *Serves 4.*

"Restaurants in Italy must, by law, advise you if any of the fish they serve has been previously frozen. They do this by putting a little asterisk next to the item on the menu, and below they explain that this means *congelato*. When my wife, Carol, was learning Italian, she saw this and remarked, 'How awful, fish with ice cream!' I'll explain: *Congelato* means 'frozen,' you see, but if you write two words, *con gelato*, it means 'with ice cream!'"

LUXURY ITALIAN FISH STEW

Italian fish stews are hearty main dishes. Many versions are found around the coast, and each village seems to have a version using the fish that is caught locally. Some flexibility in fish selection is admissible in order to use what is available at the time.

Elegant Livorno fish stew
Cacciucco alla Livornese

900g assorted fish, such as sea bass and red snapper,
   scaled and gutted
Assorted raw, cleaned shellfish, such as squid (2 medium),
   octopus (1 small), prawns in the shells (about 12),
   clams (about 12), and mussels (about 12)
4 tablespoons olive oil
1 stalk celery, finely diced
1 carrot, finely diced
1 small onion, thinly sliced
1 garlic clove, left whole
1 small fresh chilli, deseeded
1 bay leaf
2 tablespoons chopped flat-leaf parsley
Salt
225ml dry red wine
450g ripe tomatoes, chopped, plus 50ml water,
   or 400g can whole tomatoes, chopped, with their juice
1 lobster, about 450g, cooked, shelled, and broken into pieces
4 Italian bread slices

Remove the heads from the fish and set side. Cut the fish into 2.5cm slices and return to the refrigerator until required. Discard any open clams and mussels that do not close when sharply tapped, and return the remainder to the refrigerator until required.

Heat the oil in a large saucepan or stockpot over medium-low heat. Add the celery, carrot, onion, garlic, chilli, bay leaf, 1 tablespoon parsley, the fish heads and salt to taste, and sauté until all the vegetables

are tender, about 20 minutes. Stir in the wine and simmer, uncovered, about 5 minutes. Stir in the fresh tomatoes with the water, or the canned tomatoes with their juice, and continue simmering, stirring occasionally, about 20 minutes.

Remove the fish heads, garlic and bay leaf; discard. Add the fish slices and simmer 5 minutes. Gently stir in the shellfish and lobster meat. Continue simmering until the clams and mussels open, about 10 minutes; discard any that remain closed.

Meanwhile, toast the bread slices. Sprinkle the soup with the remaining 1 tablespoon parsley and serve with the hot bread slices. *Serves 6–8.*

SALT COD

TONY'S TIP:
soaking baccalà

Dried salt cod is a holdover
from the days before there
was refrigeration and efficient
transportation, when bountiful
catches were preserved by
salting and then drying in the
sun. This resulted in a very
stiff, dry "plank" of fish with a
strong smell. Soaking is
required to reconstitute the
texture and remove excessive
saltiness. In Naples, fish shops
will soak the baccalà for you,
and in other places, you can
sometimes buy reconstituted
salt cod, but more often than
not, these instructions are for
you. Try to pick a piece that is
less skin and bones and more
meat, like the part in the
middle of the fish. Using a
serrated knife, cut the fish
into pieces no bigger than
7.5cm square. Put the
pieces in a large bowl and
cover with cold water. Leave
for 24 hours, rinsing and
covering with fresh water two
or three times. Drain and
rinse; the salt cod should now
be ready to use.

Fried salt cod

Baccalà fritto

675g dried salt cod pieces, soaked, rinsed, drained
  and patted dry
115g plain flour
100ml olive oil
Lemon slices (optional)

Put the salt cod pieces in a plastic bag with the flour and shake.
Remove the fish, shaking off any excess flour; set aside. Heat the oil
in a large frying pan over medium heat. Add the cod and fry until
golden brown, 5–6 minutes. Turn over and fry the other side,
5–6 minutes longer. Squeeze lemon juice over it before serving.
Serves 4.

VARIATION

Garlic Mayonnaise Mash ½ clove garlic in a garlic press and
stir into 100ml mayonnaise. Serve with the fish instead of the
lemon juice.

Salt cod salad

675g dried salt cod pieces, soaked, rinsed and drained
100ml olive oil
1 garlic clove, chopped
2 tablespoons chopped flat-leaf parsley
Juice of 1 lemon
Freshly ground black pepper

To cook the salt cod, bring a heavy-bottomed medium saucepan of
water to a boil over high heat. Add the salt cod, reduce the heat to
low, and simmer until tender, 20–25 minutes. Drain well and set aside
to cool completely. Meanwhile, combine the oil, garlic, half the parsley,
the lemon juice and pepper to taste in a screwtop jar. Secure the lid
and shake until blended; set aside. Remove the skin and any bones
from the salt cod, then flake the fish into a bowl or onto a dish.
Reshake the dressing and pour over the fish. Sprinkle with the
remaining parsley. *Serves 4.*

Salt cod, Naples style

3 tablespoons olive oil

1 garlic clove

400g can chopped tomatoes

3 tablespoons pitted and chopped kalamata olives

1 tablespoon capers, rinsed

Salt and freshly ground black pepper

Fried Salt Cod (page 156)

1 tablespoon chopped flat-leaf parsley

Heat the oil in a large frying pan over medium heat. Add the garlic and sauté until golden, 2–3 minutes. Add the tomatoes, olives, capers and salt and pepper to taste, but remember that the cod is salty. Reduce the heat to low, and simmer 20 minutes. Add the Fried Salt Cod and the parsley. Simmer 5 minutes, turn the cod over, and simmer 5 minutes longer. *Serves 4.*

"The Piazza Garibaldi in Naples in 1958. Summer evenings called for a walk around the city. Even though it was after supper, there were still lots of temptations in sidewalk stalls, including shellfish, for which Naples is the undisputed capital of the Mediterranean."

PRAWNS

"Natale, the very patriotic man who named my father-in-law Theodore Roosevelt Simone. The sailor suit was prophetic, as Grandpa Simone likes to prepare seafood dishes, while leaving the meats and poultry to Grandma Flo."

Grandpa Simone's fried prawns

675g large prawns, peeled and deveined
2 eggs
115g plain flour
115g dried breadcrumbs
225ml sunflower oil
Salt
1 lemon, cut into wedges
275ml Mom's Tartar Sauce (page 149) or
  Cocktail Sauce (below)

With a sharp knife, cut along the back of the prawns the whole length but not all the way through, as if you were going to butterfly them. Beat the eggs in a small, shallow bowl. Put the flour on a plate and the breadcrumbs on another plate. One by one, roll each prawn in the flour, shaking off the excess. Dip in the eggs, letting the excess drain back into the bowl, then coat with breadcrumbs.

Heat the oil in a frying pan over high heat until the temperature reaches 180°C, or a 1cm cube of bread browns in 30 seconds. When hot, add the prawns a few at a time to the frying pan and deep-fry, about 2 minutes per side. The prawns will curl up nicely. Drain on paper towels.

Season with salt to taste and serve with lemon wedges and Mom's tartar sauce or cocktail sauce. *Serves 4.*

Cocktail sauce

225ml ready-made chilli sauce
1 tablespoon creamed horseradish
Juice of ½ lemon

Combine all the ingredients in a bowl. Cover and refrigerate until required. *Makes 275ml.*

Prawn scampi

400g long-grain rice
25g butter
2 tablespoons olive oil
2 garlic cloves, chopped
900g raw medium or large prawns, peeled and deveined
50ml dry sherry
Salt and freshly ground black pepper
2 tablespoons chopped flat-leaf parsley
2 tablespoons chopped fresh basil

Bring a large, heavy-bottomed saucepan with about a litre of salted water to a rolling boil over high heat. Add the rice and continue boiling until almost tender, about 15 minutes, or according to the package directions. Drain well and keep warm.

Meanwhile, melt the butter with the oil in a large frying pan over medium heat. Add the garlic and sauté until golden, 2–3 minutes. Increase the heat to high, add the prawns and sauté 3–5 minutes. Remove the prawns; set aside. Add the sherry and salt and pepper to taste and continue cooking until one-third of the sherry evaporates, about 10 minutes longer. Return the prawns to the pan. Taste and adjust the seasoning, if necessary. Sprinkle with the parsley and basil and serve over the hot rice. *Serves 4–6.*

"In 1959 my mother, with five children, braved the North Atlantic to join our father who was already in America. For us children it was an incredible adventure— before this our sea trips had consisted of taking the *vaporetto* to Capri or Ischia. The first landfall was Gibraltar, where Mom took the opportunity of writing to Dad that we had at least reached that far. I don't know who reached Buffalo first— the postcard, or us."

Aunt Chickie's rice and prawns

400g long-grain rice
100g butter
1 green pepper, deseeded and chopped
1 red pepper, deseeded and chopped
4 garlic cloves, chopped
900g medium or large prawns,
   peeled and deveined
Salt and freshly ground black pepper
6 tablespoons chopped flat-leaf parsley

Bring a large, heavy-bottomed saucepan with about a litre salted water to a rolling boil over high heat. Add the rice and continue boiling until almost tender, about 15 minutes, or according to the package directions. Drain well and keep warm.

Meanwhile, melt the butter in a large frying pan over medium heat. Add the green and red peppers and sauté until soft, about 3 minutes. Stir in the garlic. Increase the heat to high, add the prawns, and sauté just until they turn pink and curl, 3–5 minutes. Taste and adjust the seasoning, if necessary. Sprinkle with the parsley and serve over the hot rice. *Serves 4–6.*

"Aunt Chickie and Grandma Flo made the boys' hearts beat fast. Fortunately, they still found time to learn cooking and enjoy eating so that they were able to pass their skills on to us."

Mussels in wine

Be sure to serve these with bread—and lots of it! French fries are also a good accompaniment, together with cold, crisp white wine, such as Greco di tufo or Orvieto.

30g butter, at room temperature

4 shallots or 1 small onion, chopped

275ml dry white wine

3 tablespoons chopped flat-leaf parsley

2 sprigs fresh thyme

1 bay leaf

Freshly ground black pepper

1.8kg mussels, washed and debearded

1 tablespoon plain flour

Italian bread or baguette, sliced

Melt 10g butter in a large, heavy-bottomed saucepan over medium heat. Add the shallots or onion and sauté until soft, about 5 minutes. Stir in the wine, 2 tablespoons of the parsley, the thyme, bay leaf and pepper to taste and bring to a boil. Reduce the heat and simmer 10 minutes. Discard any open mussels that do not close when tapped. Add the remaining mussels to the pot, cover, and continue simmering, shaking the pot frequently, until the mussels open, 6–8 minutes. Discard any mussels that are not open. Using a slotted spoon, transfer the mussels to a large bowl and keep warm. Return the pot to the heat, increase the heat to high, and boil until the pan juices are reduced by half. Meanwhile, in a small bowl, stir the remaining butter into the flour until a smooth paste forms. Add this to the pan juices a little at a time, and stir until the sauce thickens. Stir the remaining parsley into the sauce, then pour the sauce over the mussels. Remove the bay leaf before serving with bread to mop up the juices. *Serves 4.*

TONY'S TIPS:
preparing mussels

Choosing One bad mussel can spoil a whole dish. To make sure that they're OK, I smell each and every one. There's no mistaking a rotten one.

Cleaning After buying mussels, store them in the refrigerator until needed. Scrub the outside with a brush. It will have a "beard" dangling from its shell. Pull this out and discard as much of the beard as you can.

Cooking Mussels can be steamed, sautéed, baked, fried or eaten raw. The herbs that go well with them are thyme, parsley, oregano and garlic.

"Sometimes you may crunch on something hard while eating mussels. Take a look, it just may be a pearl."

TONY'S TIP:
the right time

Although mussels are available most of the year, there is an old rule of eating them only when the month has an "r" in it. Mussels reproduce during the summer and become worn out. If you are very observant, you might notice that mussels tend to be small in September, gradually getting bigger as the year wears on.

Baked Mussels

Unlike the previous recipe, here the mussels are cooked for a short period—just long enough for them to open. The rest of the cooking happens in the oven. Also, to make it worthwhile, make this dish with large mussels.

1.8kg large mussels, washed and debearded
100ml olive oil
2 garlic cloves, chopped
50ml white wine vinegar
3 tablespoons dried oregano
Freshly ground black pepper

Preheat the oven to 200°C, gas mark 6. Discard any open mussels that do not close when tapped. Place the mussels in a large, heavy-bottomed saucepan over medium heat. Cover and cook, shaking the pot frequently, until the mussels just open, about 5 minutes. Set aside until the mussels are cool, then discard any that are not open. Remove and discard the top shell of each mussel. Arrange the mussels in a single layer on a baking sheet. Strain half of the pan juices into a bowl and stir in the oil, garlic, vinegar and oregano, with pepper to taste. Pour a tablespoon or two of the sauce on each mussel. Bake for 7–10 minutes until the mussels are golden. *Serves 4.*

VARIATION

Oil and Lemon Prepare the mussels as above, but omit the vinegar, oregano and pepper. Instead, stir the juice of 1 lemon, 2 chopped garlic cloves, and 3 tablespoons chopped flat-leaf parsley into the pan juices. Bake as above.

Fried squid

Calamari fritti

Usually to get tender food, we select small and young things. When frying squid, however, we want the biggest ones we can find. The larger squid will be tastier and remain tenderer through the rigors of frying than small ones. Also do not overcook the squid—long cooking will toughen it. Be very careful when frying the squid because the hot oil may splatter. Stay well away from the pan and use long-handled utensils.

> 115g plain flour
> 900g squid, cleaned, bodies cut into rings, and
>   tentacles cut into bite-size pieces
> Sunflower oil
> Salt
> 1 lemon, cut into wedges

Put the flour on a plate. Roll the squid in the flour, shaking off the excess; set aside. Heat the oil in a large frying pan over high heat until it reaches 180°C, or until a 1cm cube of bread browns in 30 seconds.

Working in batches, to avoid overcrowding the pan, add the squid and fry until golden, about 2 minutes. (Squid cooks very quickly and should be removed from the oil as soon as it is golden. Continued cooking will toughen it.) Using a slotted spoon, remove the squid from the oil and drain on paper towels. Sprinkle with salt and keep warm while you fry the remaining squid. Serve with the lemon wedges. *Serves 4.*

SQUID AND OCTOPUS

TONY'S TIP:
cleaning squid

Place the squid lengthwise on a chopping board. Gently pull the head from the body with the tentacles attached, and set aside. This will also bring out most of the innards, so you are left with a "cone" of flesh. Reach inside and pull out the squid's "backbone," which looks like a long, transparent feather. It will come out easily. Remove any remaining guts. Using your fingers, or a small knife, peel off the thin, grey-brown skin. Rinse the flesh inside and out. The cavity can now be sliced into rings, chopped, or left whole for stuffing. Returning to the head, use kitchen scissors to cut out the eyes and the beak. The eyes are easy to find, and the beak is in the middle of the tentacles. Rinse the head well, and cut into two or three sections, so everyone can get a bit of the crunchy tentacles.

Octopus salad

Polpo alla Luciana

1–1.3kg octopus, cleaned

FOR THE DRESSING
50ml olive oil, plus a little extra for drizzling
2 tablespoons chopped flat-leaf parsley
1 garlic clove, sliced
Salt and freshly ground black pepper
Juice of 1 lemon, reserving 1 tablespoon for drizzling

Bring a large, heavy-bottomed saucepan of water to a boil over high heat. Add the octopus and reduce the heat to low. Simmer, covered, until tender, 20–45 minutes, depending on the size. Meanwhile, to make the dressing, combine the oil, parsley, garlic, salt and pepper to taste, and all except 1 tablespoon lemon juice in a large non-metallic bowl; set aside. Drain the octopus and cut into bite-size pieces. Add the octopus to the dressing and stir well. Leave to cool completely, then serve at room temperature or cover and chill. Refresh with extra olive oil and the remaining lemon juice just before serving. *Serves 4.*

TONY'S TIP:
cleaning octopus
Octopus has no backbone and the tentacles are firmly attached to the head. Clean them the same way as you would squid (page 163), or, if you like, skin them after cooking and remove the suckers.

Octopus in tomato sauce

This dish can be an appetiser on its own, or served with Italian bread. Or, for a main dish, serve it with cooked spaghetti or linguine.

50ml olive oil
1 garlic clove, chopped
1–1.3kg octopus, cleaned and chopped
400g can chopped tomatoes
2 tablespoons chopped flat-leaf parsley
Salt and freshly ground black pepper
Water (optional)

Heat the oil in a large, heavy-bottomed frying pan over medium heat. Add the garlic and sauté until soft, 2–3 minutes. Reduce the heat, stir in the octopus, tomatoes, parsley and salt and pepper to taste, and simmer, covered, stirring frequently and adding water if the sauce looks dry, until tender, 35–45 minutes, depending on the size of the pieces. *Serves 4.*

TONY'S TIP:
easy-squeeze lemon
Prior to cutting, roll the lemon on a flat surface, pressing down with the palm of your hand. Cut in half and squeeze the halves. You will find that the juice flows easier.

◄ *Octopus salad*

5 VEGETABLES

These vegetable recipes are very versatile; they can be served as appetisers, main dishes or as accompaniments. For the best results, buy your vegetables in season and use them when they are really, really fresh.

COURGETTES AND SQUASH

COURGETTES

Among the most useful and economical vegetables of summer, courgettes are popular with supermarkets because they have a long shelf life. However, the more they sit, the more tasteless they becomes. The Italians sell courgettes with the flower still attached. This is nature's "sell by" date. Since the flower doesn't last very long, the price of a flowerless courgette drops dramatically.

Grandma Casillo's courgettes

4 medium courgettes, sliced crosswise
2 garlic cloves, chopped
6 tablespoons chopped flat-leaf parsley
6 tablespoons chopped fresh mint
50ml olive oil
Salt

Combine the courgettes, garlic, parsley, mint, olive oil and salt to taste in a large, heavy-bottomed saucepan over medium heat. Cook, covered until tender, about 10 minutes. *Serves 4.*

"Grandma Casillo, my mother, has granddaughters ranging in age from three to 32. Each one in her turn has come to appreciate their grandmother's cooking and the care and attention that go into each preparation. Here the youngest is learning to prepare courgette flowers for the pot but has been distracted by the photographer."

Sautéed courgettes

50ml olive oil

4 medium courgettes, sliced crosswise

2 medium onions, chopped or sliced

Salt and freshly ground black pepper

Heat the oil in a large frying pan over medium heat. Add the courgettes and onions and sauté until tender, about 10 minutes. Season with salt and pepper to taste. *Serves 4.*

Sautéed courgette flowers

For this recipe, you will need the smaller, not yet matured, closed flowers. Since these may be more difficult to obtain, you can add baby courgettes and the end stems of the vine with the tiny leaves. Sautéed flowers are good as a side dish or in a sandwich in Italian bread, or all on their own.

50ml olive oil

2 garlic cloves, chopped

**675g young courgette flowers and baby courgettes,
   rinsed and drained**

Salt and freshly ground black pepper

Heat the oil in a large heavy-based saucepan over medium heat and fry the garlic until golden, about 3 minutes. Add the courgette flowers and baby courgettes. Sauté until tender, about 10 minutes. Add salt and pepper to taste. *Serves 4–6.*

TONY'S TIP:
cleaning flowers

You needn't fear hurting the plant by harvesting a few flowers. The female flower at the end of the fruit has performed its job and can be picked. Male flowers are the ones on the long stems. There is a profusion of them, so picking a few will not really reduce the chances of reproduction. Look inside for any creatures. The stem on the male flowers is fuzzy, so if you have any of those, peel off the fuzz, starting from the cut end. Next, tear off the small green spikes at the base of the flower. Finally, let the flowers soak in a bath of cold water in which a tablespoon of salt has been dissolved. This will encourage any passengers remaining in the flower to depart.

Courgettes with mint

Zucchini a scapece

50ml sunflower oil

4 medium courgettes, sliced lengthwise

2 garlic cloves, chopped

75ml white wine vinegar

Small bunch fresh mint leaves, chopped

Salt and freshly ground black pepper

Heat the oil in a large frying pan over medium heat. Add the courgettes and fry, turning once, until golden brown and tender, about 10 minutes. Transfer to a serving dish. Combine the garlic, vinegar, mint and salt and pepper to taste. Pour this mixture over the courgettes, then set aside to cool completely. Cover and let stand for at least 1 hour; chill if it is not to be served until later. Serve at room temperature or chilled, refreshing the seasoning if necessary. *Serves 4.*

What's in a name?
SCAPECE

The practice of preparing and preserving vegetables or fish (see page 146) in a vinegar-based sauce is widely used throughout Italy. The preparation and flavouring varies from region to region. *Scapece* is the Campanian version, using mint and vinegar sprinkled on fried foods.

Coated fried courgettes

2 large eggs

Salt and freshly ground black pepper

115g plain flour

115g dried breadcrumbs

4 medium courgettes, sliced crosswise

100ml sunflower oil

Break the eggs into a shallow bowl, beat, and season with salt and pepper to taste. Place the flour on a plate and the breadcrumbs on another plate. Working with one courgette slice at a time, dip it in the flour, shaking off the excess, then in the eggs, letting the excess drain back into the bowl, and finally in the breadcrumbs, patting them all over. Heat the oil in a large frying pan over medium heat. When hot, add the courgettes, several slices at a time, depending on the size of your frying pan, and fry until golden brown, about 3 minutes on each side. Drain on paper towels. Keep warm in a low (140°C, gas mark 1) oven until all the courgette slices are fried. *Serves 4.*

VARIATION

Coated Fried Aubergine Use 2 medium aubergines, sliced crosswise, instead of the courgettes.

◄ *Courgettes with mint*

Roasted squash

2 medium butternut or acorn squash, cut in half, seeds and
fibres scooped out
20g butter
4 teaspoons light brown sugar
Salt and freshly ground black pepper

Preheat the oven to 180°C, gas mark 4. Place each squash half on a
piece of aluminum foil large enough to wrap around it. Put a quarter
of the butter, 1 teaspoon sugar and salt and pepper to taste in each
cavity. Wrap each squash half and seal. Place on a baking sheet. Roast
until the squash is fork-tender, about 40 minutes. *Serves 4.*

BUTTERNUT SQUASH
One of the winter squashes,
butternuts have a firm, deep
orange flesh that is moist and
sweet, seeds, and a hard, thick
skin. Unless you are baking the
squash whole, remove the skin
before cooking.

Pumpkin, Sicilian style

50ml sunflower oil
900g pumpkin, cut into slices about 1cm thick,
rinds removed
Salt and freshly ground black pepper
3 tablespoons chopped fresh mint
2 garlic cloves, thinly sliced
55g sugar
50ml white wine vinegar

Heat the oil in a large frying pan over medium heat. Dust the
pumpkin slices with salt and pepper. Working in batches, if necessary,
to avoid overcrowding, fry the pumpkin slices, turning them once,
until golden brown, about 10 minutes each side. Remove and arrange
on a serving dish. Sprinkle with the chopped mint. To the remaining
oil in the frying pan, add the garlic, sugar and vinegar. Cook over high
heat to reduce by a half, 3–5 minutes; pour over the pumpkin. *Serves 4.*

Fried aubergine

50ml sunflower oil

2 small aubergines, cut lengthwise into 5mm-thick slices

3 tablespoons chopped flat-leaf parsley

2 garlic cloves, chopped

Salt and freshly ground black pepper

Heat the oil in a large frying pan over medium heat. Working in batches, if necessary, to avoid overcrowding, add the aubergine slices and fry, turning over once, until golden brown on both sides, 5–7 minutes. Drain well on paper towels. Keep warm and continue until all the slices are fried. Arrange the aubergine slices on a serving dish. Sprinkle with the parsley, garlic and salt and pepper to taste. *Serves 4.*

Aubergine Neapolitan

This is a great dish which Hassan, an old family friend, discovered. In fact, the first time he made it, he thanked me for introducing him to the dish, not realising he had made it first. And now every time he makes it, he still thanks me.

115g plain flour

3 small aubergines, peeled and cut into 4cm cubes

100ml olive oil

3 anchovy fillets in oil, rinsed

1 tablespoon white wine vinegar

2 tablespoons chopped flat-leaf parsley

1 garlic clove, chopped

Salt and freshly ground black pepper

Place the flour on a plate. Roll the aubergine cubes in the flour, shaking off the excess. Heat 6 tablespoons of the oil in a large frying pan over medium heat. Add the aubegine cubes and sauté, turning the cubes occasionally, until golden, 10–12 minutes. Drain on paper towels. Transfer to a serving bowl and keep warm.

Meanwhile, heat the remaining oil in another small saucepan over medium heat. Add the anchovies and mash and stir until they dissolve. Stir in the vinegar and simmer 2 minutes. Pour the sauce over the aubergine. Sprinkle over the parsley, garlic and salt and pepper to taste. *Serves 4.*

TONY'S TIP:
choosing oils
There are lots of oils, but for cooking, you need only two—sunflower and olive oil. For general cooking purposes, especially for frying and high-temperature cooking, use sunflower oil. For lightly cooked or sautéed dishes or where there's a chance of tasting the oil, as in salads, use olive oil. And which olive oil? Choose one by tasting. I like extra virgin with lots of green residual olive colour, thick and tasty.

FRYING AUBERGINE

This yeast batter seals in the flavour of the vegetable and provides a delectable coating. If you like a thicker batter, use more flour. If, like me, you prefer a thinner batter similar to tempura, add more water.

Batter-dipped aubergines
Melanzane fritte

1 sachet (7g) easy-blend dried yeast
225ml warm (40–45°c) water
55g plain flour
½ teaspoon freshly ground black pepper
Salt
100ml sunflower oil, or more if necessary
2 medium aubergines, sliced crosswise

Stir the yeast into the water; set aside until foamy, about 10 minutes. Meanwhile, combine the flour, pepper and salt to taste in a large bowl and make a well in the middle. Pour in the yeast liquid and stir the flour into it, gradually working in all the flour, until a batter forms.

Heat the oil in a large frying pan over medium heat. Working in batches, if necessary, to avoid overcrowding the pan, dip the aubergine slices in the batter so they are coated all over, and fry, turning the slices once until crisp and golden, about 5 minutes per side. Drain on paper towels and sprinkle with salt. *Serves 4.*

VARIATIONS
Batter-Dipped Courgette Flowers Use 12–16 large courgette flowers almost in full bloom. Clean the flowers in water (see page 169), drain well, and pat each one completely dry before coating.

Batter-Dipped Courgettes Replace the aubergine with 4 medium courgettes, sliced lengthwise.

Stuffed aubergine

2 small aubergine

75ml olive oil

1 small onion, chopped

55g small dried bread cubes or dried breadcrumbs

225g fresh mozzarella cheese, drained and shredded

1 medium tomato, deseeded and chopped

1 tablespoon chopped fresh basil or flat-leaf parsley

Salt and freshly ground black pepper

1 medium tomato, sliced (optional)

Fresh basil sprigs

Preheat the oven to 170°C, gas mark 3. Cut each aubergine in half lengthwise. Scoop out the middles to make four shells; chop the removed flesh and reserve. Brush inside and out with a little oil; set aside. Heat the remaining oil in a large frying pan over medium heat. Add the onion and sauté until soft, about 5 minutes. Add the reserved aubergine flesh and continue sautéing until soft, about 10 minutes. Stir in most of the bread cubes or crumbs, the cheese, tomato, basil or parsley, and salt and pepper to taste. Spoon this mixture into each aubergine shell and place a tomato slice on top, if using. Crumble the remaining cubes of bread and sprinkle over the top. Bake for about 40 minutes, until the aubergine shells are tender. Top each with a sprig of basil. *Serves 4.*

VARIATIONS

Mushroom Stuffing You can add 3 or 4 chopped mushrooms to the stuffing. Sauté with the onion and aubergine flesh.

Oregano Flavouring You can replace the parsley or basil with 1 teaspoon dried oregano.

AUBERGINES
Buy fresh, firm, lustrous fruit without any scarring, bruising, or dull surfaces. If the aubergine is sufficiently fresh, I don't bother with salting and draining it before frying. And if the aubergine is not fresh, I don't bother either, because I throw them away.

Aubergine Parmesan

Melanzana alla parmigiana

There are some heavy-duty versions of this main dish with breaded aubergine. But aubergines are really nothing more than sponges for oil. Try it this way—it is much lighter.

2 large eggs
Salt and freshly ground black pepper
25g plain flour
2 medium aubergines, thinly sliced lengthwise
50ml sunflower oil
Double batch Tomato Passata Sauce (page 58)
55g grated Parmesan cheese
Bunch fresh basil, with a few leaves reserved for serving
175g fresh mozzarella cheese, drained and shredded
Italian bread slices

Preheat the oven to 170°C, gas mark 3. Beat the eggs in a shallow bowl and season with salt and pepper. Put the flour on a plate. Dredge the aubergine slices in the flour, shaking off the excess. Dip in the egg and let the excess drip back into the bowl. Heat the oil in a large frying pan over medium heat. Working in batches, if necessary, to avoid overcrowding, fry the aubergine slices, turning them over once, until golden, about 5 minutes per side. Drain on paper towels. Continue until all the aubergine slices are fried.

Arrange layers of tomato sauce, aubergine slices, Parmesan, basil leaves, and mozzarella in a shallow baking dish. Continue layering until all the ingredients are used, finishing with cheeses and tomato sauce. Season with salt and pepper to taste. Bake for about 30 minutes, until the sauce is bubbling and the cheese has melted. Top with sprigs of basil leaves and serve hot or at room temperature with plenty of bread. *Serves 4.*

GRATED PARMESAN
Always buy a block of cheese and only grate what you need. Don't be tempted to buy ready grated Parmesan. Who knows what's really in it.

Aubergine timbale

Timballo di melanzana

This is a very simple dish, but when you bring it to the table it looks like a million dollars.

Sunflower oil for frying, about 450ml

3 large aubergines, thinly sliced lengthwise

2 garlic cloves, chopped

3x400g cans chopped tomatoes

Salt and freshly ground black pepper

Large handful fresh basil, chopped

250g tube pasta, such as penne or rigatoni

225g ricotta cheese

35g grated Parmesan cheese

300g fresh mozzarella cheese, drained and shredded

Heat a shallow layer of oil in a large frying pan over medium heat. Once the oil is hot, add the aubergine slices in a single layer and fry until golden, 1–2 minutes on each side. Remove and drain on paper towels. Set aside. Continue until all the aubergine slices are fried. Heat 50ml sunflower oil in the washed and dried frying pan over medium heat. Add the garlic and fry until golden, 2–3 minutes. Add the tomatoes and salt and pepper to taste and simmer, for 15 minutes, uncovered. Stir in the basil.

Meanwhile, bring a large saucepan of salted water to a boil. Add the pasta, stir, and continue boiling until the pasta is only half cooked, 5–6 minutes. In a large bowl, combine the ricotta cheese with a few tablespoons of the tomato sauce and beat until it has the consistency of thick cream. Drain the pasta, shaking off the liquid. Add the pasta and Parmesan and mozzarella cheeses to the bowl with the ricotta mixture. Reserve 225ml of the tomato sauce and stir the rest into the bowl with the pasta. Season to taste with salt and pepper.

Preheat the oven to 200°C, gas mark 6. Lightly grease a 25cm ring mould (or, if you don't have a ring mould, a 2.5 litre ovenproof bowl). Line the mould with the aubergine slices, overlapping them slightly. Fill the mould with the pasta mixture. Cover the top with foil and press down lightly. Bake for 25 minutes. Remove the foil. Loosen the aubergine lining from the mould with a thin knife. Place a serving dish, top side down, over the top of the mould, then, using oven gloves, invert the timbale onto the dish, giving a firm shake halfway over. Slice or scoop out the filling and serve with the reserved sauce. *Serves 6.*

TONY'S TIP:
the perfect timbale

Make sure the bowl is wet with sauce before lining it with aubergine, or the aubergine may burn, spoiling the look of the timbale when turned out.

Make sure there is enough sauce in the pasta, or it may dry out.

It is a good idea to have a little extra sauce at the table, just in case the timbale turns out a little dry from overcooking.

If you save the end parts of the aubergine—you know, the slices with one purple side— arrange them on top like flower petals, using a slice of tomato as the centre and big leaves of basil in between the "petals," after turning the timbale over.

TOMATOES AND PEPPERS

TONY'S TIP:
fresh herbs

Dried herbs are a great help and their concentrated flavour gives dishes a particular zing when needed. However, one of the great secrets of good cooking is using fresh herbs. Fresh parsley and basil are now almost universally available in the supermarkets. It's easy to grow your own herbs in pots or in a little patch of ground, and let me urge you to do so. Once they become established, rosemary, sage, thyme, mint and chives will thrive for years, except in the harshest climes. Pick only the amount of herb you need and wash and dry it. One trick is to add a little extra herb just before serving to give the dish that extra lift

Baked tomatoes

Butter, for greasing
4 medium tomatoes, cut in half horizontally
½ teaspoon Dijon mustard
Salt and freshly ground black pepper
75g dried breadcrumbs
1½ tablespoons finely chopped flat-leaf parsley
2 teaspoons olive oil

Preheat the oven to 170°C, gas mark 3. Use the butter to grease a baking dish that will hold the tomato halves upright snugly. Arrange the tomato halves in the dish, cut sides up. Spread the tops with the mustard and season with salt and pepper to taste. Combine the breadcrumbs with the parsley, then sprinkle over the tomato tops. Drizzle a little oil over each. Bake for about 20 minutes, until the crumbs are golden. *Serves 4.*

Tomato-potato roast

This traditional accompaniment to roasts, such as lamb, is often cooked together with the meat.

4 medium waxy potatoes, sliced
2 onions, sliced
Salt and freshly ground black pepper
6 tablespoons olive oil
3 medium tomatoes, sliced
1 teaspoon dried oregano

Preheat the oven to 190°C, gas mark 5. Combine the potatoes and onions in a bowl. Season with salt and pepper and add 3 tablespoons of the oil. Stir the potatoes and onions around to coat them thoroughly. Grease a 3 litre baking dish with 1 tablespoon of the remaining oil. Arrange alternate layers of potatoes and onions, and tomatoes, finishing with tomatoes. Drizzle the remaining oil on top and sprinkle with the oregano. Bake until the potatoes are soft, about 45 minutes. Cut into squares and serve hot. *Serves 4.*

Baked grilled peppers

Carol, my wife, says she never uses the capers in this recipe. But shouldn't you have the original recipe before you customise it? Don't even think about leaving out the anchovies; you must use them. No fish taste, I promise. We like this as a side dish and in sandwiches.

1–1.3kg medium yellow and red peppers

4–5 anchovy fillets in oil, chopped

75g kalamata olives, pitted and halved

2 tablespoons capers, rinsed

1 garlic clove, chopped

115g dried breadcrumbs

100ml olive oil

Preheat the grill to high. Grill the peppers 10cm from the heat until they are black and blistered all over. Place in a bowl and set aside until cool. Peel off the skins, then cut each pepper in half and remove the core and seeds. Tear the peppers into long strips; set aside.

Meanwhile, preheat the oven to 180°C, gas mark 4. Grease the bottom of a 2 litre baking dish. Build layers of pepper strips, anchovies, olives, capers, garlic, and a dusting of breadcrumbs. Drizzle with oil and continue layering until all the ingredients are used, ending with breadcrumbs and a drizzle of oil. Bake until bubbling, about 30 minutes. Serve hot or at room temperature. *Serves 4.*

PEPPERS

Most supermarket peppers seem to come in standard sizes today, but in Mediterranean countries, peppers come in all shapes and sizes. And the colours! There is green changing into yellow and yellow with some green to remind you of its past. There are bashful green peppers with red cheeks and envious red peppers with green faces. Why don't we see these on the supermarket shelves?

Stuffed peppers
Peperoni imbottiti

I have never seen this recipe outside our home, but it frequently appeared on my grandfather's Sunday table in Naples.

4 red or yellow peppers
3 tablespoons dried breadcrumbs

FOR THE STUFFING
3 tablespoons olive oil, plus a little extra for drizzling on top
1 medium aubergine, cut into 1cm cubes
50g cubed stale Italian bread (5mm cubes)
225g fresh mozzarella cheese, drained and cut into
    1cm cubes
2 anchovy fillets in oil, chopped
3 tablespoons pitted and chopped kalamata olives
2 tablespoons chopped fresh basil
1 tablespoon rinsed and chopped capers
Salt and freshly ground black pepper

TONY'S TIP:
adding anchovies
Anchovies are one of the great secrets of cooking. When called for in a recipe, use them, even if you don't like them. They dissolve in cooking, adding body to the dish—you wouldn't believe that there was fish in it!

Preheat the grill to high. Grill the peppers 10cm from the heat until they are black and blistered all over. Place in a bowl and set aside until cool. Peel off the skins, leaving the peppers whole so they can be stuffed. Slice off the tops and use a teaspoon to scoop out the cores and seeds, taking care not to tear the flesh; set aside. Meanwhile, preheat the oven to 180°C, gas mark 4.

To make the stuffing, heat the oil in a large frying pan over medium heat. Add the aubergine and sauté until tender, 10–12 minutes. Transfer the aubergine to a bowl. If necessary, add a little more oil to the pan and fry the bread cubes until golden, about 5 minutes. Drain and add to the bowl of aubergine and gently stir in the cheese, anchovies, olives, basil, capers and salt and pepper to taste. Equally divide this stuffing among the peppers, again taking care not to tear the flesh.

Lightly oil a baking dish that will hold the peppers in a single layer and sprinkle with 1 tablespoon of the breadcrumbs. Arrange the peppers in the dish and drizzle with oil and the remaining 2 tablespoons breadcrumbs. Bake for about 35 minutes, until the cheese melts and the flavours mix. Serve hot or at room temperature. *Serves 4.*

BRASSICAS AND GREENS

TONY'S TIP:
stop the smell
When boiling broccoli, cauliflower and cabbage, add a bay leaf to improve the odour—but remember to remove it before serving.

Grandma Flo's broccoli

1 large head broccoli, cut into florets
50ml olive oil
1 teaspoon crushed chilli flakes
2 garlic cloves, finely chopped
25g dried breadcrumbs

Bring a large, heavy-bottomed saucepan of salted water to a boil. Add the broccoli and boil until crisp-tender, about 5–7 minutes. Drain well and transfer to a flameproof serving dish. Meanwhile, preheat the grill to high. In a small frying pan, heat the oil with the chilli flakes and chopped garlic. When the garlic is golden, remove from the heat and drizzle over the broccoli. Dust the broccoli with breadcrumbs. Grill 10cm from the heat until the bread crumbs are golden, about 5 minutes. *Serves 4.*

VARIATION
Broccoli with Lemon Cook the broccoli as above until crisp-tender. Drain well and transfer to a serving dish. In a bowl, combine 2 tablespoons olive oil and the juice of 1 lemon. Spoon over the broccoli, season with salt to taste. Serve warm or chilled.

Sautéed broccoli rabe

Known as rapini *or* broccoli di rape *(*rapa *means turnip in Italian), this is a form of turnip green. Two more exotic greens,* friarelli *and* cicoria, *which are frequently found in Italian specialty stores, can be cooked the same way.*

50ml olive oil
2 garlic cloves, chopped
Small piece fresh red chilli (wear gloves when handling)
900g broccoli rabe, trimmed and coarsely chopped
Salt

Heat the oil in a large, deep, heavy-bottomed frying pan over medium heat. Add the garlic and chilli and sauté until the garlic is golden, 2–3 minutes. In a large saucepan with rapidly boiling water, blanch the broccoli rabe for 2 minutes. Drain well and add to the onion and garlic with salt to taste; continue sautéing until tender, about 4 minutes. Remove the chilli before serving. *Serves 4.*

Fried cauliflower

1 medium head cauliflower, broken into florets
2 large eggs
50ml milk
Salt and freshly ground black pepper
115g plain flour
50ml sunflower oil

Bring a large, heavy-bottomed saucepan of salted water to a boil. Add the cauliflower and boil until crisp-tender, about 5 minutes—do not overcook. Drain well. Meanwhile, break the eggs into a large bowl and beat in the milk and a pinch of salt and pepper to taste. Put the flour on a plate. Heat the oil in a large frying pan over medium heat. One by one, roll each floret in the flour, shaking off the excess. Then dip in the egg mixture, letting the excess drip back into the bowl.

As the florets are coated, add them to the pan and fry until golden all over, about 4 minutes. Use a slotted spoon to remove them from the pan and drain well on paper towels. Serve hot. *Serves 4.*

VARIATION

Garlic Fried Cauliflower Boil and drain the cauliflower as above. Add 2 garlic cloves to the oil and sauté until golden-brown, 2–3 minutes. Remove the garlic, then fry the cauliflower as above.

Cauliflower with ham and egg

1 large head cauliflower, left whole
100g butter
25g dried breadcrumbs
3 tablespoons chopped fresh parsley
3 tablespoons chopped cooked ham
1 hard-boiled egg, shelled and chopped
Juice of ½ lemon
Salt and freshly ground black pepper

Bring a large, heavy-bottomed saucepan of salted water to a boil. Add the cauliflower and boil until fork-tender, 10–15 minutes—do not overcook. Drain well and transfer to a serving dish; keep warm.

Meanwhile, melt the butter in a medium, heavy-bottomed saucepan over medium heat. Add the breadcrumbs and sauté until golden, about 6 minutes. Stir in the parsley, ham, egg, lemon juice and salt and pepper to taste. Pour over the cauliflower and serve, cut into wedges. *Serves 4.*

VARIATION

Cauliflower with Cheese Boil and drain the cauliflower as above. Melt the butter, stir in 25g plain flour and continue stirring for 2 minutes. Slowly stir in 450ml warm milk, a little at a time. Increase the heat and bring to a boil, stirring until the sauce is smooth and thick. Season with salt and pepper to taste. Remove the sauce from the heat and stir in 25g grated Parmesan cheese until it melts. Pour over the cauliflower, then serve, cut into wedges.

Christina's red cabbage

My daughter serves this cabbage with her famous **Meatloaf** *(page 125). It works equally well with most plain roasts.*

35g butter
1 medium onion, sliced
1 teaspoon caraway seeds
1 medium apple, cored and sliced
2 tablespoons light brown sugar
1 large head red cabbage, cored and shredded
275ml dry white wine, cider, or chicken stock
2 tablespoons white wine vinegar
Salt

Melt the butter in a large, heavy-bottomed saucepan over medium heat. Add the onion and caraway seeds and sauté until the onions are soft, about 5 minutes. Add the apple and sugar and continue sautéing for 5 minutes longer. Stir in the cabbage, wine (or cider or stock), vinegar, and salt to taste and bring to a boil. Reduce the heat, cover, and simmer until the cabbage is tender, about 30 minutes. *Serves 4.*

Grandma Koch's Swiss chard

I never met Grandma Koch; her granddaughter, Emily, was a co-worker of mine over 30 years ago. However, I'd still like to thank her for this wonderful dish.

50ml olive oil
1 large onion, chopped
4 slices pancetta or cured (not smoked) bacon, chopped
900g Swiss chard, coarsely chopped
2 tablespoons rolled oats

Heat the oil in a deep casserole over medium heat. Stir in the onion and pancetta and sauté until soft, 6–8 minutes. Add the chard and cook until soft, about 15 minutes. If it gets dry, add a little water. When cooked, move the greens to one side of the pan to free the juices and add the oats to the liquid. Stir and cook 5 minutes, then mix in the chard so it is coated all over. *Serves 4.*

SWISS CHARD
Not so long ago, there were just two varieties Swiss chard, both equally delicious. Large, coarse green leaves sat atop long, flat, celery-like stalks that were white or red. Today you can find chard with stems of many colours, including gold, pink, orange, purple, red and white. But the flavour remains the same—very similar to spinach.

Sautéed spinach
Spinaci in padella

900g fresh spinach leaves, trimmed and rinsed
35g butter
Salt and freshly ground black pepper

Melt the butter in a large saucepan; add the spinach and salt and
pepper to taste and cover. Sauté, stirring occasionally until tender,
about 7 minutes. *Serves 4.*

VARIATION
Spinach Genovese When sautéing, add 1 tablespoon pine nuts
and 1 tablespoon raisins to the spinach and continue as above.

Lemony spinach
Spinaci contorno

900g fresh spinach leaves, trimmed and rinsed
1 tablespoon olive oil
Fresh juice of ½ lemon
Salt and freshly ground black pepper

Bring a large, heavy-bottomed saucepan with 1cm of salted water to a
boil. Add the spinach and cook covered until tender, about 7 minutes.
Drain well. Transfer to a serving dishter. Meanwhile, combine the oil,
lemon juice and salt and pepper to taste in a small bowl. Pour over the
hot spinach. *Serves 4.*

VARIATION
Lemony Kale Substitute kale for spinach in the above recipe. It
has a sweet, distinctive flavour. It can also be cooked as the spinach
in the **Sautéed Spinach** recipe (top). Boil kale until tender, but
not mushy: 6–8 minutes for thin leaves, 18–25 minutes for thick,
densely curled leaves.

"Zia Antonietta led a
very busy life. She
worked 10 to 12 hours
in a shop, found time
to buy fresh food for
dinner, then commuted
home to cook a meal
before finding her bed
well after midnight.
I can't believe someone
managed to catch her
in a relaxed pose."

"My Uncle Nunzio and me in San Giuseppe Vesuviano in 1948. The land all around us was volcanic soil, black and very friable and fertile. A wide variety of vegetables were grown, and artichokes, escarole and fennel were among the most popular, along with tomatoes."

Sautéed escarole

50ml olive oil
2 garlic cloves, chopped
2 anchovy fillets in oil
900g escarole, trimmed and coarsely chopped
35g kalamata olives, coarsely chopped
Salt

Heat the oil in a large, deep heavy-bottomed frying pan over medium heat. Add the garlic and anchovies, and sauté until the garlic is golden, and the anchovies begin to dissolve, 2–3 minutes. Add the escarole, olives, and salt to taste and continue sautéing until the escarole is tender, about 15 minutes. *Serves 4.*

Fennel Parmesan

4 medium bulbs fennel
Butter, for greasing
225ml single cream
35g grated Parmesan cheese

Prepare the fennel by cutting off and discarding a 5mm slice off the bottom; discard the two or three outer leaves, and cut off and discard any green part of the tops. Cut into quarters. Cook in boiling salted water until just tender, 10–15 minutes. Drain immediately. Preheat the oven to 190°C, gas mark 5. Butter a shallow baking dish that will just hold the fennel. Cover with the cream and Parmesan. Bake until the cheese turns golden, about 20 minutes. *Serves 4.*

Sautéed artichokes

4 medium or 8 small artichokes, or 675g baby artichokes
100ml olive oil
2 garlic cloves, chopped
2 tablespoons chopped flat-leaf parsley
Salt and freshly ground black pepper
1 tablespoon capers
35g kalamata olives
Water (optional)

Clean the artichokes as described on page 190. Baby artichokes can be left whole; others should be cut into pieces and the choke removed. Heat the oil in a large frying pan over medium heat. Add the garlic and sauté until golden, 2–3 minutes. Drain the artichoke pieces from their bath of acidulated water and add them to the pan. Add half the parsley and salt and pepper to taste. Continue sautéing until the artichokes are tender, about 35 minutes, adding the capers and olives halfway through the cooking time. If the artichokes look dry and start to crisp at the edges, add some water. Sprinkle with the remaining parsley and serve warm or at room temperature. *Serves 4.*

Fried artichokes

4 medium or 8 small artichokes or 675g baby artichokes
2 large eggs
Salt
25g plain flour
100ml sunflower oil

Clean the artichokes as described on page 190. Baby artichokes can be left whole, larger artichokes should be cut into pieces and the choke removed. Bring a large, heavy-bottomed saucepan of lightly salted water to a boil. Add the artichokes and parboil until almost tender, about 15 minutes. Drain well, cool, and pat dry with paper towels. Meanwhile, beat the eggs in a shallow bowl with a pinch of salt. Place the flour on a plate. One by one, roll the baby artichokes or artichoke pieces in the flour, shaking off the excess. Dip in the eggs, letting the excess dip back into the bowl. Heat the oil in a large frying pan or sauté pan over medium heat. Add the artichokes and fry until golden, turning them once, about 5 minutes. Drain on paper towels. Sprinkle with more salt, if desired. *Serves 4.*

PREPARING ARTICHOKES

Fresh artichokes are in season from late autumn to early spring. For the best flavour, select compact plump globes with clinging green leaves that yield slightly to pressure. Be warned that cut raw artichokes will stain your fingers. Unless you want a serious case of smoker's tan, you may want to wear gloves.

Cleaning artichokes

Before sautéing or frying artichokes, you need to get rid of the inedible parts:

+ The skin, leaves, and spines around the stalk
+ The coarse outer petals
+ The top part of the inner petals
+ The choke

So the cleaning theory is to get rid of all the inedible bits while trying to retain the tender flesh.

+ Cut off all but 2.4-5cm of the stalk and peel the remainder as you would a carrot.
+ Discard outer petals: Put your thumb at the base of each petal and pull it back against your thumb by grasping the petal at the tip with the other hand. The tender bottom part should remain attached, and the top is discarded. As you proceed to the inner leaves, there should be more of the tender part on each leaf, so you can keep moving your thumb up. Eventually the whole petal is soft so just cut the top 5-10mm with a knife. If you're preparing baby artichokes, these are now ready to be cooked whole.

+ For small, medium, and large artichokes, cut the now-cleaned artichoke into quarters or eighths. Remove the fuzzy part, which is the choke.
+ When you cut an artichoke, it will quickly turn black, so as soon as they are cut, drop the pieces into a bowl of water into which you have squeezed the juice of a lemon. Leave them there until needed.

To keep artichokes

Store in a plastic bag in the refrigerator for up to 4 days. For year-round use, parboil cleaned artichokes for 15 minutes. Drain, cool, bag and freeze.

Eating whole artichokes

When cooked whole, artichokes are eaten one leaf at a time. Put the leaf in your mouth, grasp it gently between your teeth and pull it out of your mouth scraping the tender flesh off. It's a good idea to have an extra bowl on the table for the discarded leaves. When you finish all the leaves, the prize is the bottom. Cut away the choke and eat the bottom.

Artichokes, Roman style

Carciofi alla Romana

4 garlic cloves, chopped
2 bunches flat-leaf parsley, chopped
Salt and freshly ground black pepper
4 large artichokes
100ml olive oil, plus extra for drizzling

Combine the garlic, parsley and salt and pepper to taste in a small bowl; set aside. In this recipe, the choke is not removed as described opposite, but the whole artichoke is cooked. Take up each artichoke by the stem and bring its point smartly down on a flat surface. This should make the artichoke open up like a rose. Cut away all but 2.5cm of the artichoke stalk. Spoon a quarter of the parsley mixture inside each cavity and try to close up the leaves again. Arrange the artichokes, tops up, in a heavy-bottomed saucepan that holds them upright snugly. Pour over the oil and add enough water to cover. Bring to a simmer, cover, and simmer until tender, 15–20 minutes. Test by inserting a fork in the end of the artichoke bottom; it should go in easily. Using long tongs, remove from the cooking liquid and drain. Serve with extra oil drizzled over, if you like. *Serves 4.*

Peas and bacon

Piselli e pancetta

- 2 tablespoons olive oil
- 2 slices pancetta or cured (not smoked) bacon, chopped
- 3 tablespoons chopped onion
- 450g shelled peas, thawed if frozen
- 50ml water
- 1 teaspoon fresh thyme, or ¼ teaspoon dried
- Salt and freshly ground black pepper

Heat the olive oil in a large frying pan over medium heat. Add the pancetta and onion and sauté until the bacon is translucent, about 5 minutes. Stir in the peas, water, thyme, and salt and pepper to taste and bring to a boil. Reduce the heat and simmer until the peas are tender, 5–8 minutes for fresh peas, 3–5 minutes for thawed peas. *Serves 4.*

Peas stracciatella

The egg cooks in strips, or rags, hence the name.

- 3 tablespoons olive oil
- 1 small onion, chopped
- 450g shelled peas, fresh or frozen
- 50ml water
- 2 large eggs
- 2 tablespoons grated Parmesan cheese
- Salt and freshly ground black pepper

Heat the oil in a saucepan over medium heat. Add the onion and sauté until soft, about 5 minutes. Add the peas and water, cover and bring to a boil. Reduce the heat and simmer until the peas are tender, 5–8 minutes for fresh peas, 3–5 minutes for frozen peas. In a small bowl beat the eggs with the cheese, salt and pepper. Add to the peas and cook, stirring, for 2 minutes, until the eggs are set. *Serves 4.*

Green beans with almonds

- 450g green beans, topped and tailed
- 50g butter
- 25g slivered almonds
- Fresh juice of 1 lemon
- Salt and freshly ground black pepper

Bring a medium pan of salted water to a boil over high heat. Add the green beans, lower the heat, and simmer, uncovered, until the beans are fork-tender, about 7 minutes. Drain well. Meanwhile, melt the butter in a large frying pan over medium heat. Add the almonds and sauté until golden, about 6 minutes—take care not to overcook, or they will burn. Stir in the lemon juice and salt and pepper to taste. Add the beans and stir until beans are coated. *Serves 4.*

VARIATIONS

Green Beans with Hazelnuts

Substitute 35g toasted and skinned hazelnuts for almonds and cook in butter only until butter begins to brown, about 3 minutes. Continue with the rest of the recipe.

Green Beans with Pine Nuts

Cook the green beans as above only until crisp-tender, about 5 minutes. In a large frying pan, cook 55g chopped pancetta or cured (not smoked) bacon until golden, 2–3 minutes. Remove to paper towels to drain. Add 1 tablespoon olive oil to the pan, add the green beans and salt to taste and cook, stirring frequently, until the beans are lightly browned and tender, about 5 minutes. Remove the beans to a serving dish and top with pancetta and 25g toasted pine nuts.

◄ *Peas and bacon*

MUSHROOMS

MUSHROOMS

Mushrooms, along with *pinoli* (pine nuts), are two of the greatest Italian food passions, perhaps because they both can be had for free with a bit of effort. It was my misfortune to have city slickers from Naples on one side (the closest) of the family, so I never had the chance to learn the lore of mushroom hunting. However, in the autumn, people in certain parts of Italy go mad. Porcini mushrooms suddenly pop up in the forests and a fever akin to the California gold rush grips the citizens. A "gold vein" of porcini mushrooms can make a tidy sum and the pickers go to great lengths not to reveal the mother lode. For me, I am just happy I can buy them.

TONY'S TIP:
cleaning mushrooms
Mushrooms are full of water to begin with; I hate to add more by washing them. Therefore, I wipe each mushroom with a cloth, and cut off a bit of the stem.

Baked mushrooms

50ml sunflower oil
½ teaspoon crushed chilli flakes
1 garlic clove, chopped
450g white mushrooms, wiped clean and sliced
Salt
1 tablespoon chopped flat-leaf parsley
25g dried breadcrumbs

In a large frying pan, heat the oil over medium heat and add the chilli flakes and garlic. When the garlic is golden, add the mushrooms and sauté for about 10 minutes. Salt to taste. Meanwhile, preheat the oven to 180°C, gas mark 4. Transfer the mushrooms to a baking dish that is suitable to serve from. The dish should be just large enough to hold the mushrooms in a single layer. Sprinkle with the parsley and dust with breadcrumbs. Bake for 20 minutes. *Serves 4.*

Mushrooms in wine

50ml olive oil
1 garlic clove, chopped
450g white mushrooms, wiped clean
1 bay leaf
375ml dry white wine
Salt and freshly ground black pepper

Heat the olive oil in a large frying pan over medium heat. Add the garlic and sauté until golden, 2–3 minutes. Add the mushrooms, bay leaf, wine and salt and pepper to taste and simmer until one-quarter of the wine has evaporated. Taste and adjust the seasoning, if necessary. Remove the bay leaf before serving. *Serves 4.*

VARIATION
Mushrooms in Red Wine Follow the above recipe, adding 2 chopped garlic cloves to the oil. Replace the bay leaf and white wine with 4 teaspoons crumbled dried oregano and 225ml dry red wine. Add salt and pepper to taste and simmer until most of the wine evaporates and a sauce forms.

Sautéed mushrooms

50ml olive oil

1 garlic clove, chopped

450g white mushrooms, wiped clean
   and sliced

A few sprigs of thyme

Salt and freshly ground black pepper

Heat the oil in a large saucepan over medium heat.
Add the garlic and sauté until golden, 2–3 minutes.
Stir in the mushrooms, thyme and salt and pepper
to taste and continue sautéing until the mushrooms
are lightly brown and still juicy, about 10 minutes,
or until the liquid has evaporated, about
12 minutes. *Serves 4.*

VARIATIONS

Spicy Mushrooms Add ½ teaspoon crushed
chilli flakes to the oil with the garlic.

Simulated Wild Mushrooms Use a mixture of
cultivated mushrooms, such as large flat mushrooms
(portobello) cut into wedges, and different sizes of
button, oyster, chestnut and shiitake mushrooms.

Porcini Mushrooms Place 15g dried porcini
mushrooms in a small heatproof bowl and pour
over enough boiling water to cover. Leave
to soften for 20 minutes. Place a sieve lined with
muslin or paper towels over a bowl and strain the
mushrooms; set aside both the mushrooms and
soaking liquid. Meanwhile, follow the recipe above,
adding the porcini mushrooms and their soaking
liquid to the white mushrooms, along with 1 sprig
fresh rosemary and 1 fresh sage leaf.

◄ *Sautéed simulated wild mushrooms*   195

"Nonno Carmine Andeloro was truly the don of the family. His children, grandchildren, acquaintances and friends treated him with utmost respect. A greeting was not a kiss on the cheek, but a kiss on the right hand. And he was very particular about his food. A dish had to be done exactly right, or thunderclouds gathered over Mt. Vesuvius."

Grilled mushrooms

As well as making a great side dish, these are terrific in a sandwich made with Italian bread and topped with a slice of melted mozzarella.

> 4 large open-cup mushrooms, such as portobello, wiped clean and stems removed
> 50ml olive oil
> 1 tablespoon chopped flat-leaf parsley
> 1 garlic clove, chopped
> Salt and freshly ground pepper

Preheat the grill to high. Brush the mushrooms with the oil. Arrange the mushrooms, cup sides down, on the rack in the grill pan and grill 10cm from the heat for 5 minutes. Turn the mushrooms over, return to the grill, and continue grilling until fork-tender, about 4 minutes. Transfer the mushrooms to a serving dish and sprinkle the parsley, garlic and salt and pepper to taste over. *Serves 4.*

Cheese-stuffed mushrooms

> 50g butter
> 24 white mushrooms (about 5cm in diameter), wiped clean and stems removed
> 225g fresh mozzarella cheese, drained and sliced
> 2 tablespoons dried breadcrumbs
> 1 tablespoon chopped flat-leaf parsley
> Salt and freshly ground black pepper
> 12 black olives, pitted and cut in half

Preheat the oven to 170°C, gas mark 3. Melt the butter in a large frying pan. Add the mushroom caps and sauté for about 5 minutes. Meanwhile, combine the cheese, breadcrumbs, parsley and salt and pepper to taste in a small bowl. Stuff the mushroom caps with the cheese mixture. Put one olive half on top of each mushroom. Place on a baking sheet or baking dish. Bake until the stuffing is golden and crisp, 10–15 minutes. *Serves 4.*

Potato croquettes

Panzarotti

In Naples, nearly every street corner has a frying shop. Among the many fried delicacies are fried courgette flowers, aubergines, courgettes, doughnuts, and anchovies. A very popular selection are these golden little potato sausages. I bet you can't have just one.

- **675g all-purpose potatoes, peeled and cubed**
- **2 large eggs, beaten**
- **6 tablespoons grated Parmesan cheese**
- **2 tablespoons chopped flat-leaf parsley**
- **Salt and freshly ground black pepper**
- **115g dried breadcrumbs**
- **50ml sunflower oil**

Bring a large, heavy-bottomed saucepan of salted water to a boil. Add the potatoes and boil until fork-tender, 20–25 minutes. Drain immediately and set aside to cool. Mash the potatoes in a large bowl. Beat in the eggs, cheese, parsley and salt pepper to taste. Shape the potato mixture into croquettes, each 4cm long and 2cm thick. Wetting your hands may prevent sticking. Place the breadcrumbs on a plate. Roll the croquettes in the breadcrumbs until they are coated. Heat the oil in a large frying pan over medium heat. Working in batches, if necessary, to avoid overcrowding, fry the croquettes until golden all over, 6–7 minutes. Drain on paper towels. Transfer to a serving plate and keep warm. Continue until all the croquettes are fried. *Serves 4.*

VARIATION
Mozzarella Potato Croquettes Slip a sliver of mozzarella cheese in the middle of each croquette as you shape them. For the above quantity, you will need about 115g mozzarella cheese.

POTATOES
When deciding what potatoes to use, bear in mind there are three types. Waxy potatoes have a high water, low starch content, and floury types have a low water, high starch content. The former, which includes Charlotte, Jersey Royals and pink fir apple, keep their shapes better when cooked, so are ideal for boiling and using in salads. The latter, including King Edward and Maris Piper, fall apart and become fluffy when boiled, so are best baked or mashed. A third type with moderate moisture and starch is also available. They are considered all-purpose potatoes. For alternatives, read the labels at the supermarket shelf; they can be helpful.

Carol's mashed potatoes

*Although my wife, Carol, thinks everyone knows how to make mashed
potatoes, her version is world-class and deserves inclusion.*

900g floury potatoes, peeled and cubed
100g butter, diced
225ml milk
Salt

Bring a large, heavy-bottomed saucepan of salted water to a boil. Add
the potatoes and boil until tender, 20–25 minutes. Drain immediately,
transfer to a large bowl, and beat with an electric mixer.

Meanwhile, melt the butter in the milk in a small saucepan over
medium heat. Gradually pour the milk and butter into the potatoes,
beating until smooth. Taste and adjust the seasoning, if necessary.
Serves 4.

TONY'S TIP:
potato sizes
Try to get potatoes of
approximately the same
size so they all cook to the
same degree. If you have
a mix of large and small
potatoes, cut the large ones
into pieces approximating
the smaller potatoes.

VARIATIONS

Garlic Mashed Potatoes While you are beating the potatoes,
add ¼, ½, or 1 crushed garlic clove, to taste. Continue as above.

Olive Oil Mashed Potatoes When you are beating the
potatoes, beat in 50ml olive oil and 25g grated Parmesan cheese.
Continue with the recipe as above.

Mashed Potatoes with Parsnips Boil 2 peeled and cubed
parsnips with the potatoes. Continue with the recipe as above.

Chilli Mash Preheat the grill to high. Roast 2–4 chilli peppers,
10cm from the heat until charred. Peel and remove the stem and
seeds, then chop. Add to the potatoes while beating. Continue with
the recipe as above.

Annette's garlic potatoes

Annette is our dear friend, an incurable romantic who seeks exotic places and traditional dishes.

900g floury potatoes, peeled and sliced

4 cloves garlic, chopped

Salt and freshly ground black pepper

225ml double cream

225ml milk

50g butter

Preheat the oven to 180°C, gas mark 4. Butter a 2 litre baking dish that is suitable to serve from. Arrange an overlapping layer of potatoes in the baking dish, seasoning with the garlic and salt and pepper to taste. Continue layering until all the potatoes are used, then pour the cream and milk over. Dot with the butter. Bake until golden and cooked through, about 1 hour. *Serves 4–6.*

TONY'S TIP:
storing potatoes

Always store potatoes in a cool, dark place—but not the refrigerator. They should keep for 2–4 weeks.

Pecorino and Parmesan potato bake

225g pecorino cheese, grated

115g Parmesan cheese, grated

900g floury potatoes, peeled and thinly sliced

275ml double cream

Salt and freshly ground white pepper

100g butter

Preheat the oven to 180°C, gas mark 4. Butter a 2 litre baking dish. Combine the two cheeses in a small bowl. Arrange an overlapping layer of potatoes in the dish; cover with one-quarter of the cream, and 2 tablespoons of the cheese mixture. Season with salt and pepper to taste and dot with butter. Continue layering until all the ingredients are used, finishing with cheese and butter. Bake for about 1 hour, until the sauce is bubbling and the top is golden and crusty. *Serves 6–8.*

What's in a name? PECORINO

Pecorino is a sheep's cheese (*pecora* is Italian for sheep). Many regions vie for market supremacy. When pecorino is young and fresh, it is very sweet, becoming gradually saltier and harder as it ages. Most of us are familiar with *romano pecorino,* the hard, pungent grating version from Lazio, which can be used on pasta. If you have no experience using pecorino, start by selecting a medium-aged cheese.

Baked potatoes with rosemary

75ml olive oil

675g new or small potatoes

2 tablespoons rosemary leaves

Salt and freshly ground black pepper

Preheat the oven to 190°C, gas mark 5. Pour the oil into a baking dish large enough to hold the potatoes without overlapping. Add the potatoes and rosemary. Sprinkle with salt and pepper. Stir the potatoes around to coat them thoroughly. Bake in the oven, stirring frequently, for about 30 minutes until the potatoes are golden brown but not dry. *Serves 4–6.*

Scalloped potatoes

8 medium all-purpose potatoes, peeled and thinly sliced

100g butter

450ml milk

Salt and freshly ground black pepper

Combine the potatoes, butter and milk in a large, heavy-bottomed saucepan over medium heat and bring to a boil. Reduce the heat and simmer, covered, until the potatoes are fork-tender, 20–25 minutes. The milk should be absorbed, leaving a thick sauce. Season with salt and pepper to taste. *Serves 4.*

◀ *Baked potatoes with rosemary*

Brown sugar potatoes

I have been making brown sugar potatoes ever since I was a little fellow. Wish I could remember where I got the recipe.

900g waxy potatoes, peeled and sliced
100g butter
225g brown sugar
225ml water
Salt and freshly ground black pepper

Combine the potatoes, butter, sugar, water and salt and pepper to taste in a large, heavy-bottomed saucepan. Cook over medium heat, covered but stirring frequently, until the potatoes are soft, about 30 minutes. *Serves 4–6.*

Uncle Ted's sweet potatoes

10g butter
2 large sweet potatoes, scrubbed, but unpeeled
225ml soured cream
2 large egg yolks, beaten
1 teaspoon salt
½ teaspoon ground mace or allspice
80g miniature marshmallows

Preheat the oven to 180°C, gas mark 4. Butter a 2 litre baking dish that is suitable to serve from.

Bring a large, heavy-bottomed saucepan of salted water to a boil. Add the sweet potatoes and boil until tender, 15–20 minutes. Drain, and when cool enough to handle, peel and coarsely chop. Transfer to a large bowl and beat with an electric mixer. Beat in the soued cream, egg yolks, salt and mace or allspice. Taste and adjust the seasoning, if necessary. Spoon the sweet potato mixture into the baking dish and smooth the top. Arrange the marshmallows on top. Bake until the marshmallows are golden brown, 20–25 minutes. *Serves 4.*

"My early pride and joy was this bicycle with a fire-engine red sidecar, in which I would wheel around my baby brother so that Mother could prepare dinner."

Gattò

In Naples, Easter Monday is traditionally celebrated with a picnic in the country. Almost certainly, the picnic will include this dish.

900g floury potatoes, peeled and cubed
2 large eggs, beaten
6 tablespoons grated Parmesan cheese
50g butter, diced
Salt and freshly ground black pepper
55g salami, diced
25g dried breadcrumbs

Bring a large, heavy-bottomed saucepan of salted water to a boil. Add the potatoes and boil until tender, 20–25 minutes. Drain immediately, transfer to a large bowl, and beat with an electric mixer. Beat in the eggs, cheese, butter and salt and pepper to taste. Stir in the salami.

Meanwhile, preheat the oven to 180°C, gas mark 4. Butter a 2 litre baking dish and dust with some of the breadcrumbs. Spoon in the potato mixture and smooth the surface. Using the tines of a fork, press all around the edges for decoration. Sprinkle with the remaining breadcrumbs. Bake for about 30 minutes, until the top is golden and the cake begins to pull away from the side of the dish. Remove from the oven, and let it sit for 10 minutes. Cut individual slices to serve. Gattò is great served at room temperature, and keeps well in the refrigerator for several days. *Serves 4–6.*

What's in a name?
GATTÒ

Gattò is the Italian spelling of *gateau*, French for cake. In this instance, it's a potato cake. When I was a boy, I just couldn't figure out why this dish was named after a cat, as *gattò* in Italian means cat.

Green bean and potato salad

This is a great summer salad for barbecues. Serve it either hot or cold.

> 450g waxy potatoes, peeled and sliced
> 450g green beans, topped and tailed
> 50ml olive oil
> 3 tablespoons white wine vinegar
> 2 tablespoons chopped flat-leaf parsley or
>   fresh mint
> 1 garlic clove, chopped
> Salt and freshly ground black pepper

Bring a large, heavy-bottomed saucepan of salted water to a boil. Add the potatoes and boil until fork-tender, about 15 minutes. Drain well and transfer to a large bowl. In a second saucepan, cook the beans in salted water until crisp-tender, 3–7 minutes. Drain them and refresh in cold water to stop the cooking and also to retain their colour. Meanwhile, combine the oil, vinegar, parsley or mint, garlic and salt and pepper to taste in a jar with a screw-top lid, secure the lid, and shake until blended. Pour over the potatoes and green beans and gently toss together. Leave to cool completely, then cover and chill until you are ready to serve. Taste and adjust the seasoning, if necessary, before serving. *Serves 4.*

Carol's gold medal potato salad

Nobody makes potato salad like my wife, Carol; the empty bowl is licked all the way to the sink. She tastes and adjusts the flavoring to get it just right so that half the batch is always eaten in preparation and little is left for the table.

> 900g waxy potatoes, scrubbed,
>   but left unpeeled
> 1 small onion, grated
> 1 medium celery stalk, chopped
> 225ml mayonnaise
> Juice of ½ lemon
> 1 teaspoon sugar
> Salt and freshly ground black pepper
> 2 tablespoons chopped flat-leaf parsley
> Pinch paprika
> 6 green olives stuffed with pimentos, halved

Bring a large, heavy-bottomed saucepan of salted water to a boil. Add the potatoes and boil until fork-tender, 20–25 minutes. Drain immediately and when cool enough to handle, peel and cut into bite-size pieces. Transfer to a large bowl and let cool completely. Add the onion, celery, mayonnaise, lemon juice, sugar and salt and pepper to taste and gently stir until combined. Transfer to a serving bowl and sprinkle the top with the parsley and paprika and decorate with the olive halves. Refrigerate if you are not serving immediately. *Serves 4–6.*

Glazed carrots

450g carrots, peeled and sliced
100g butter, chopped
50g packed light brown sugar
Juice of 1 medium orange
Salt and freshly ground black pepper
Water (optional)

Combine the carrots, butter, sugar, orange juice and salt and pepper to taste in a large, heavy-bottomed saucepan over medium heat. Cover and simmer 15 minutes. Uncover and continue simmering, stirring occasionally, until the liquid has evaporated and a thick glaze forms, about 10 minutes. If the liquid evaporates before the carrots are fork-tender, stir in a little water. *Serves 4.*

Vinegar carrots

450g carrots, peeled and sliced
50ml olive oil
3 tablespoons white wine vinegar
1 tablespoon chopped flat-leaf parsley
½ garlic clove, chopped
Salt and freshly ground black pepper

Bring a large, heavy-bottomed saucepan of salted water to a boil over high heat. Add the carrots and boil until fork-tender, 8–10 minutes. Drain well and transfer to a large bowl. Meanwhile, to make the dressing, combine the oil, vinegar, parsley, garlic and salt and pepper to taste in a jar with a screw-top lid, secure the lid, and shake until blended. Pour over the hot carrots, stirring so they are coated. Serve hot or cold. *Serves 4.*

ROOT VEGETABLES

CARROTS
Carrots taste good and add a bit of colour to the dinner plate. One of the principal uses of carrots is as a basic flavouring (together with celery and onions) for sauces. Many Italian recipes for meat, fish, sauces and soups begin with a *soffritto* of these ingredients made by sautéing a finely minced blend of these ingredients.

Carrot and parsnip mash

450g carrots, peeled and chopped
4 medium parsnips, about 225g,
  peeled and chopped
25g butter
100ml milk
100ml single cream
Freshly grated nutmeg
Salt and freshly ground black pepper

Bring a large, heavy-bottomed saucepan of salted water to a boil over high heat. Add the carrots and parsnips and boil until tender, about 25 minutes. Drain immediately, transfer to a large bowl, and beat with an electric mixer. Meanwhile, melt the butter in the milk in a small saucepan over medium heat. Gradually pour the butter, milk, and cream into the carrots and parsnips, beating until smooth. Taste and add nutmeg and salt and pepper. *Serves 4.*

Roasted vegetables

900g root vegetables, such as carrots,
  parsnips, sweet potatoes and turnips, peeled
  and coarsely chopped
50ml olive oil
8 pickling onions, peeled and left whole
4 garlic cloves, unpeeled and left whole
2 sprigs fresh rosemary or thyme
Salt and freshly ground black pepper

Bring a large, heavy-bottomed saucepan of salted water to a boil over high heat. Add the root vegetables and parboil 10 minutes. Drain well. Meanwhile, preheat the oven to 200°C, gas mark 6. Heat the oil in a heavy-bottomed roasting pan over medium heat on the hob. Add the vegetables, onions, garlic, herbs and salt and pepper to taste. Stir to coat all the ingredients. Roast, stirring once or twice, until the vegetables are fork-tender, about 45 minutes. Remove the herb sprigs before serving. *Serves 4.*

TO SERVE
Horseradish Sauce Mix together 225ml crème fraîche, 1 tablespoon creamed horseradish, 3 tablespoons chopped fresh chives, 1 tablespoon lemon juice and salt and black pepper to taste. Chill the sauce until you are ready to serve. *Makes 225ml.*

VARIATION
Sweet Roasted Vegetables Parboil 1 large peeled and chopped potato, 1 small peeled and chopped swede, and 1 medium carrot. Combine the drained vegetables with 2 small roughly chopped red onions, and 1 medium peeled and chopped butternut squash in a roasting pan and drizzle with 2 tablespoons olive oil. Stir to coat. Roast for 25 minutes, then sprinkle with 3 tablespoons brown sugar. Continue roasting until the vegetables are fork-tender, 10–15 minutes longer.

Pickled aubergine

Use this pickled aubergine in sandwiches or to balance rich meats, such as pork chops.

500ml cider vinegar

500ml water

About 100ml olive oil

4 medium aubergines, sliced crosswise

1 garlic clove, finely chopped

2 tablespoons dried oregano, crumbled

Combine the vinegar and water in a large, heavy-bottomed saucepan and bring to a boil over high heat. Add the aubergine and boil until soft, about 10 minutes. Drain well and set aside to cool completely. Pour 1 tablespoon oil into each of two 500ml sterilised jars. Add a layer of aubergine, then sprinkle with garlic and oregano. Drizzle with oil and continue layering until all the aubergine has been used. Finish with oil. Cover and store in the refrigerator for at least a day before use. Keeps for up to 2 weeks stored in the refrigerator. *Makes 1 litre.*

"*Scugnizzi* is what street urchins are called in Naples, and my grandmother, uncle and aunt seem to have collected a fair bunch of them. However, the girl in the middle is the future Grandma Casillo, my mother, so watch what you say."

TONY'S TIPS:
sterilising jars
Use airtight jars with proper seals. Wash the jars thoroughly and then dry them off in a 140°C, gas mark 1, oven. Allow the jars to cool and then fill and seal.

Pickled vegetables

Giardiniera

Make a big batch of giardiniera *and use it as an accompaniment or as a salad. It keeps for a while. You can even show it off in clear glass jars.*

- **1 litre cider vinegar**
- **1 litre water**
- **1 medium cauliflower, broken into florets**
- **1 medium red pepper, cored and sliced**
- **1 medium green pepper, cored and sliced**
- **1 medium yellow pepper, cored and sliced**
- **4 stalks celery chopped**
- **12 pickling onions, peeled and left whole**

Combine the vinegar and water in a large, heavy-bottomed saucepan and bring to a boil over high heat. Add the cauliflower and parboil until crisp-tender, about 5 minutes. Do not overcook—err on the side of undercooked, as the florets will soften as they cool. Remove with a slotted spoon and set aside in a colander to cool completely. Continue to individually parboil each type of pepper, the celery, and the onions, about 5 minutes, removing them from the liquid and adding them to the colander. When all the vegetables are parboiled, remove the saucepan from the heat and leave the liquid to cool completely. Store these vegetables in the vinegar liquid in a large covered jar or bowl in a refrigerator or cool dark place. They will keep for several weeks. *Makes 1 litre.*

Preserved vegetable salad

Insalata di rinforza

This salad is based on **Pickled Vegetables** *(left). I get asked to prepare it every Christmas. Perhaps it is a counterbalance to the rich, fatty dishes of the season. Whenever you feel like it, you can make smaller batches of the salad.*

- **Pickled Vegetables (left)**
- **50ml olive oil**
- **40g black olives, pitted and chopped**
- **6 anchovy fillets in oil**
- **1 garlic clove, sliced**
- **2 tablespoons capers, rinsed**
- **1 tablespoon dried oregano, crumbled**
- **2 tablespoons chopped flat-leaf parsley**
- **Salt and freshly ground black pepper**

Place the pickled vegetables into a large bowl. Stir in the oil, olives, anchovies, garlic, capers, oregano, parsley and salt and pepper to taste. Leave to stand for a couple hours for the flavours to blend, or cover and chill for up to 2 days. *Serves 4–6.*

"In the olden days before mass food distribution, fresh vegetables were unavailable in winter, thus pickled vegetables were the winter substitutes. The tradition has continued and today *giardiniera* is still a great favorite and available from supermakets. In tradition-bound Naples, great big tubs of pickled vegetables appear in the shops at Christmas time to be used as a base for *insalata rinforza*."

6 DESSERTS AND COFFEE

Desserts are often the favourite part of

a meal, so tempt your tastebuds with

this wonderful selection of hot and

cold desserts. You'll be sure to find a

recipe that's just right for a famliy

meal or for that special occasion.

NUTS

One way to describe an elaborate meal is to say it was "from soup to nuts." Any meal can be turned into such a feast with the addition of a basket of nuts served before dessert or even as the dessert itself. Munching on nuts while sipping wine is a companionable way to pass the time, savouring the dishes just consumed and anticipating the sweet dishes to come. Select from a wide variety of available nuts in the shell and don't forget to provide the nutcrackers.

Storing fresh nuts
Nuts in their shells can be kept for several months at room temperature, but shelled nuts should be stored in a plastic bag in the freezer. Sweet chestnuts have a shorter shelf life than other nuts—they only keep for a few weeks. Beyond that, boil them (opposite) and freeze them for use in recipes.

Roasting nuts in their shells
Some nuts are improved in flavour by toasting or roasting. Some are not. Walnuts, hazelnuts, almonds, pecans and chestnuts benefit from toasting; Brazil nuts do not. Peanuts, cashews, and pistachios are good either way.
+ Preheat the oven to 170°C, gas mark 3. Place the nuts in a single layer on a baking tray and roast 20–30 minutes, until the nuts are fragrant, shaking the tray frequently. Different nuts require different roasting times. Pecans, for example, will roast faster than hazelnuts. Keep watching the nuts to prevent burning.

Toasting shelled nuts
Small quantities of shelled nuts, or seeds, can be toasted in a non-stick ungreased frying pan over medium heat. Keep shaking the pan until the nuts start turning colour. Remove them from the pan immediately.

Roasting and grilling sweet chestnuts
While the other nuts are available year-round, sweet chestnuts come to us in late autumn. They

are a wonderful treat to eat either roasted or boiled. It is important to slit the nuts first, otherwise the nuts will explode in the oven. The slit should be horizontal on the flat face of the nut. It must puncture through the brown shell and be as long as possible. This also makes the peeling easier later.

◆ To roast chestnuts: Preheat the oven to 220°C, gas mark 7. Put the chestnuts in a shallow roasting tin and roast 20–30 minutes, until tender when squeezed and easy to peel. Immediately remove them from the pan and leave to cool.

◆ To grill chestnuts: Preheat the grill to high. Grill the chestnuts 10cm from the heat, turning them frequently, until they are tender when squeezed and easy to peel, about 20 minutes.

Boiled sweet chestnuts

◆ Remove the shell from each nut, using a sharp paring knife. To speed up the operation, blanch the chestnuts in boiling water for 4 minutes, drain and cool. The shells should peel easier.

◆ Combine the peeled chestnuts with enough water to cover in a large, heavy-bottomed saucepan over medium heat. Add a pinch of salt, a pinch of fennel seeds and a bay leaf. Bring to a boil and simmer until soft, about 15 minutes. Drain well and leave until cool enough to handle, then peel off the inner brown husk. Serve warm or at room temperature.

◆ You can also purée boiled chestnuts with 2 tablespoons of double cream, and serve in a glass, with sweetened double cream as a topping.

Ricotta and honey

Most Mediterranean countries have a tradition of mixing honey with a milk product. It is kind of an emergency dessert because ricotta and honey are readily available in Italy.

450g ricotta cheese
100ml clear honey
25g toasted pine nuts

Press the ricotta cheese through a sieve into a bowl. Divide the cheese among four serving glasses. Pour the honey on top and sprinkle with the toasted pine nuts. *Serves 4.*

Orange caramel

This is a very refreshing dessert when you're serving a rich main course.

4 large oranges
225g caster sugar
100ml water

Using a thin-bladed vegetable peeler, carefully remove the zest from 2 oranges. Cut the orange zest into very thin matchstick strips. Bring the water to a boil in a small, heavy-bottomed saucepan over high heat. Add the orange zest and continue boiling until tender, about 5 minutes; drain and set aside. Meanwhile, peel the remaining oranges and remove the white pith from all 4 oranges; set aside.

In a large, heavy-bottomed saucepan over medium heat, stir the sugar into the water and bring to a boil. Lower the heat to medium and swirl once or twice so the syrup colours evenly; do not stir. When the syrup turns golden, about 10 minutes, reduce the heat to low, and add the blanched orange zest to the syrup. Simmer until the zest just starts to caramelise, about 5 minutes. Add the oranges and let them gently simmer in the caramel, basting and turning them frequently, about 5 minutes. Transfer the oranges to a heatproof serving bowl; spoon the zest and syrup on top of the oranges. Leave to cool completely, then cover and chill, at least 1–2 hours. *Serves 4.*

Zabaglione

As children we were given zabaglione to build up our thin little bodies. It was a much more agreeable tonic than pills.

6 egg yolks
75g caster sugar
100ml Marsala

In a medium bowl, beat the egg yolks with the sugar until fluffy and lemon coloured, about 7 minutes. Add the Marsala and transfer to a double boiler or place the bowl over a pan of simmering water. Heat gently and stir while the zabaglione is thickening, about 10 minutes. Do not boil. The zabaglione should have the consistency of a thin custard. Remove from the heat and serve warm. If you prefer to serve the dessert at room temperature or cold, continue stirring while the zabaglione cools to room temperature. Serve, or keep it in the refrigerator until you are ready to serve. *Serves 4.*

VARIATION

Baked Ice Cream Zabaglione An hour before serving, place four scoops of vanilla ice cream in a freezer container, being careful not to let the scoops touch each other. Refreeze until solid. Preheat the grill. Into four small ramekins or flameproof serving dishes, place one ice-cream scoop and a quarter of the zabaglione. Sprinkle ½ tablespoon pine nuts on top of each scoop. Place the dishes on a rack, 10cm from the heat, and grill until the zabaglione starts bubbling, about 5 minutes. Serve immediately. *Serves 4.*

TONY'S TIP:
leftover egg whites

When you have leftover egg whites, why not make almond meringues? Take 100g blanched almonds and toast under a grill 10cm from the heat until golden, about 4 minutes. In a large bowl, with a mixer at high speed, beat 6 egg whites with ½ teaspoon cream of tartar. Sprinkle in 170g sugar, 2 tablespoons at a time, beating until the sugar dissolves and the egg whites are glossy and stiff. Fold in the almonds. Drop tablespoonfuls onto a large baking sheet lined with foil and bake at 140°C, gas mark 1 for about 45 minutes, until dry. Allow to cool on a wire rack.

Panna Cotta

Cooked cream and milk are part of the cuisine of most Mediterranean countries. The Italian version is called panna cotta *(cooked cream). It is extremely easy to make and delicious to eat. Panna cotta tastes good on its own or you can fancy it up for company, by serving it in a fruit purée.*

2 tablespoons water

½ sachet (5g) unflavoured gelatine

275ml double cream

2 tablespoons caster sugar

1 teaspoon vanilla extract

TONY'S TIP:

using gelatine

If you use too little gelatine, the cream won't set. If you use too much, it becomes rubbery. If you don't get it just right the first time, don't worry—it is so quick to make that you can do another batch in the twinkle of an eye, until you are satisfied. And the little secret is that it's not so bad to get rid of the evidence by eating it.

Pour the water into a small heatproof bowl, sprinkle the gelatine over, and leave to stand until the gelatine softens and becomes spongy, 3–5 minutes. Bring a few inches of water to a boil in a medium saucepan and remove from the heat. Set the bowl of gelatine in the saucepan and leave until the gelatine dissolves. Lightly oil four small ramekins or cups; set aside. Meanwhile, combine the cream and sugar in another medium saucepan over medium heat. Bring to a simmer, stirring, and continue simmering until the sugar dissolves, about 5 minutes. Turn off the heat and stir in the vanilla, then pour in the gelatine in a slow, steady stream, beating until it is incorporated. Strain the vanilla-flavoured cream into the prepared ramekins and leave to cool completely. Cover with clingfilm and chill at least 3 hours, until set. To serve, quickly dip the bottom of the ramekins in a sink or bowl of hot water. Place a serving plate on top of each ramekin and invert both, giving a shake half way over. Lift and remove the ramekins. *Serves 4.*

VARIATIONS

Panna Cotta with Mango, Strawberry, or Raspberry Purée
Blend about 150g of fruit and 1–2 tablespoons caster sugar in a blender or food processor, and pass through a sieve to remove the seeds. Spoon the purée around each panna cotta to serve.

Panna Cotta with Chocolate Sauce Melt 85g dark chocolate with 50ml milk in a small, heavy-bottomed saucepan over low heat. Spoon, hot or cold, around each panna cotta.

Panna Cotta with Liqueur Topping Spoon 1½ teaspoons orange- or coffee-flavoured liqueur over the top of each.

Panna cotta with raspberry purée ▶

"All the children in our family have learned to appreciate home cooking by participating in the preparation. Here our niece Allison is helping Carol make her yellow cake."

What's in a name?
ZUCCOTTO

Zucca means "pumpkin" and *zucchino* "little pumpkin." It is believed that *zuccotto* derives from the Tuscan word *zucchetto*, which is a clerical hat that has the same shape as this dessert, or half a pumpkin. So we could say that this Florentine speciality means "dear little pumpkin" in Italian. You can buy special pumpkin-shaped molds in which to make it.

Florentine cream and cake dessert
Zuccotto

This dessert can be made days in advance and frozen, but defrost it in the refrigerator for at least an hour before serving.

> Yellow Cake (page 230)
> 450ml double or whipping cream
> 60g icing sugar
> 35g blanched and toasted almonds, coarsely chopped
> 35g blanched and toasted hazelnuts, coarsely chopped
> 55g dark chocolate, shaved
> 2 tablespoons brandy
> 2 tablespoons maraschino liqueur
> 3 tablespoons cocoa powder

Prepare the yellow cake. In a medium bowl, whip the cream with half the icing sugar until very stiff. Mix in the almonds, hazelnuts and chocolate. Cut the cake into 1cm thick slices and cut each slice diagonally in half to make two triangles. Line a 1.5 litre bowl with clingfilm and then arrange the cake triangles to cover the sides and bottom of the bowl. Mix the brandy and maraschino liqueur and sprinkle it over the cake lining. Fill the cake-lined bowl with the whipped cream and cover the top with more cake triangles.

If you are serving the same day, refrigerate the dessert for 2 hours. When you are ready to serve, turn the bowl over onto a chilled serving dish; discard the clingfilm. Dust with the cocoa powder and the remaining icing sugar in alternate stripes. *Serves 8.*

Trifle

Zuppa inglese

Chiffon cake (Aunt Mary's Whisky Cake, page 233)

400g can peeled apricots

100ml Marsala

240ml milk

2 tablespoons cornflour

2 tablespoons sugar

3 large egg yolks

80g crumbled amaretti

TOPPING

450ml double or whipping cream

½ teaspoon vanilla extract

60g icing sugar

Fresh raspberries, strawberries or pitted cherries

Prepare the chiffon cake. Purée the apricots in a food processor or blender. With a serrated knife, cut the cake horizontally into three layers. Spread one-third of the purée on top of one layer, cover with another layer, and spread another third of the purée on it, and then put the last layer on top. Cut crosswise into 1cm thick slices and place in a 4 litre serving bowl, stacking them in even layers. Sprinkle generously with the Marsala and spread with the remaining purée.

In a small, heavy-bottomed saucepan, heat 225ml milk over medium heat, until it just reaches simmering point. Mix the cornflour and sugar with the remaining cold milk in a small bowl until it forms a paste. Combine the paste and the hot milk in a double boiler and cook, stirring constantly, over medium heat until the milk thickens, about 5 minutes. Remove from the heat and beat in the egg yolks, one by one, until well blended. Return the custard to the double boiler, and cook over medium-low heat, stirring continuously, until the mixture thickens and coats the back of a spoon, about 10 minutes. Remove from the heat. Add the amaretti, allow them to soften and stir frequently until they are dissolved; pour over the cake. Chill for at least 2 hours.

To make the topping In a medium bowl with a mixer at medium speed, beat the cream with the vanilla and icing sugar until stiff peaks form. Spread on top of the custard and top with the fresh berries or cherries. *Serves 12.*

What's in a name? AMARETTI

Amaretti are Italian macaroons made from sweet and bitter almonds. The most well-known come from Saronno and are sold, wrapped in pairs, as *Amaretti di Saronno*. They can be eaten as they come or used as a flavouring.

FRUIT DESSERTS

"No Italian meal is complete without fruit to finish, often replacing dessert. The sight, smell and taste of ripe fresh fruit rival any concocted dessert. At our table, peeling and cutting up and serving a piece of fruit is a slow ritual to permit contemplation of the great meal that has just been consumed. On some occasions, a prepared fruit salad may make more of a statement, especially for a crowd."

Fresh fruit salad
Macedonia di frutta

Use ripe fruit with good flavour, as opposed to good-looking, unripe fruit. Try to include one or two exotic ones just to promote after-dinner conversation.

1 watermelon
Approximately 1.3kg fruit, reserving some for garnish:
  Galia or cantaloupe cubes or balls
  Peaches, peeled, pitted, halved, and cubed
  Apricots, halved, pitted, and cubed
  Plums, halved, pitted, and cubed
  Oranges, peeled, pith removed, sectioned, and halved
  Small pineapple, peeled and cored, cut into 1cm chunks
  Pears, peeled, cored, and cubed
  Cherries, pitted and halved
  Strawberries, hulled and halved
  Bananas, sliced (immediately sprinkled with lemon juice)
Juice of 1 lemon
225g caster sugar
100ml chiaretto (or Poire William or kirsch)
Sprigs of mint

Using a large, sharp knife, cut a thin slice from the bottom of the watermelon so it will sit flat as you work on it. Then slice two sections from either end to form the basket, as follows. First make a vertical cut about 2.5cm from the centre halfway through the melon. Then in the middle of the melon make a horizontal cut from the end to join the vertical cut. Repeat the operations on the other side. Using a large metal spoon, scoop out the red flesh of the melon until only the white rind is left. Do this neatly to create an even surface and a neat-looking basket. Using a sharp small knife, cut the edge of the basket into a zigzag pattern. Reserve the two large sections and the flesh and discard everything else. Using a melon baller, scoop out about 350g of melon balls from the reserved flesh. If you don't have a baller, cut it up into 1cm cubes. Place the cubes or balls in a large bowl. Add the other fruit. Sprinkle with the sugar and the remaining lemon juice, add the chiaretto, give it all a good stir, and refrigerate it for 2 hours. When you are ready to serve, ladle the fruit into the basket, and decorate the top with the reserved fruit and the mint sprigs. *Serves 12–15.*

TONY'S TIPS:
exotic fruit

Figs can be black or white, but they must be ripe and plump. To peel, hold one in one hand and pull the skin, starting from the pointy end, a section at a time. Segment to use in a fruit salad.

Kiwis are usually associated with the South Pacific, but, in fact, Italy is a major kiwi producer. The kiwi's skin needs to be removed before serving. To peel the fruit, cut the ends off, then remove the skin with a peeler or sharp paring knife.

Pomegranates are great tasting fruit, but a bit awkward to eat, as they contain a tough white pith, surrounded by lots of tiny tart-sweet ruby seeds. The fruit is prepared by cutting several deep vertical scores into it, then breaking it apart, allowing the seeds to be removed. The seeds make a nice garnish when sprinkled over a dish.

Prickly pears are yellow, orange or red, but be careful, the skin has hundreds of spines, which will give you great discomfort if they get on your skin. Always use rubber gloves when handling them. Before serving, make a lengthwise slit in the skin with a sharp knife. The skin peels back, allowing the pear to pop out. Serve cut up in a fruit salad.

Loquats are the size and shape of apricots but smooth and very orange. They have a fresh, tart taste. To prepare, remove the stem, then peel off the skin. Next, cut the fruit in half, remove the seeds, and cut off the whorl at the bottom and the inner membrane. Cut up for a fruit salad.

Persimmons have a red-orange skin and flesh, with a smooth, creamy texture and tangy-sweet flavour. Unripe persimmons are very astringent.

Pears in Marsala

6 ripe pears, peeled, halved, and cored

115g caster sugar

225ml dry Marsala or medium-dry sherry

1 teaspoon vanilla extract

225ml water

1 stick cinnamon

225ml double or whipping cream

2 tablespoons icing sugar

Preheat the oven to 150°C, gas mark 2. Place the pears in a baking dish, cut side up, and sprinkle with the sugar, Marsala or sherry, vanilla and water. Tuck in the cinnamon stick. Bake until the pears are tender, 30 minutes to 1 hour, depending on the ripeness. Check occasionally and baste if the pears are not wholly covered by the liquid. In a medium bowl with a mixer at medium speed, whip the cream, gradually adding the icing sugar, until firm peaks form. Serve the pears warm or chilled in their syrup, topped with whipped cream. *Serves 4–6.*

Stuffed baked peaches

Pesche ripiene

5 large peaches

1 large egg yolk, beaten

2 tablespoons caster sugar

25g butter, at room temperature

4 amaretti, crumbled

6 tablespoons water

Preheat the oven to 190°C, gas mark 5. Cut four of the peaches in half, remove the pits, and scoop out some flesh into a bowl to make room for the filling. Peel the fifth peach, discard the pit and place in the bowl along with the reserved flesh. Mash to a purée. Add the beaten egg yolk, sugar, half the butter and the crumbled amaretti. Mix well. Divide the mixture among the peach halves, mounding it, if necessary. Dot with the remaining butter. Place the peaches in an ovenproof dish and add the water to the dish. Bake until the peaches are tender, about 1 hour. Serve warm or at room temperature. *Serves 4.*

TONY'S TIP:
peeling peaches
Bring a small saucepan of water to a rolling boil over high heat. Add a peach and leave about 15 seconds. Remove with a slotted spoon and immediately dip into cold water. Using a paring knife, peel off the skin.

Bread and butter pudding

Butter

2 tablespoons dried currants, rinsed and dried

4 thin slices bread

3 large eggs, plus 1 extra yolk

115g caster sugar

Pinch freshly grated nutmeg

225ml milk, warmed

225ml double cream, warmed

¼ teaspoon vanilla extract

Preheat the oven to 190°C, gas mark 5. Generously butter the bottom of a 1 litre baking dish, and scatter the currants over the bottom. Generously butter each bread slice, then cut off the crusts and cut each slice in half. Put a layer of bread in the dish. Combine the eggs and extra yolk, sugar, and nutmeg in a large bowl and beat until blended. Stir in the milk, cream and vanilla. Pour the liquid over the bread slices. Bake for about 45 minutes, until a knife inserted in the middle comes out clean. Serve warm or at room temperature. *Serves 4.*

VARIATIONS

Orange Bread and Butter Pudding Spread 2 tablespoons orange marmalade on the bread slices along with the butter.

Val d'Aosta Bread and Butter Pudding Instead of currants, use 2 tablespoons chopped dried figs and 2 tablespoons chopped dates. And to the cream mixture, add 2 tablespoons dark rum. Otherwise, follow the method above.

TONY'S TIP:
nutmeg graters

I keep my nutmegs whole in a sealed jar and grate just what I need each time. I use a paring knife and just scrape the nut. But these fancy graters do a good job and are designed to hold the nuts inside. They also make a great gift for that someone who has everything.

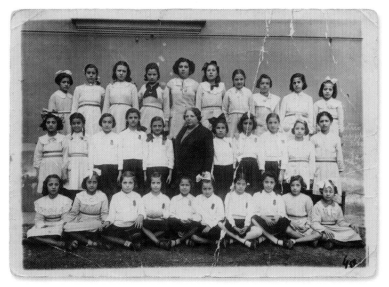

Rice pudding

175g short-grain rice
325ml milk
325ml double cream
2 large eggs
170g caster sugar
Pinch salt
Pinch ground cinammon

Cook the rice in water according to the package directions, until tender, and drain. Preheat the oven to 180°C, gas mark 4. Heat the milk and cream in a large, heavy-bottomed saucepan over medium heat until the mixture simmers. Remove from the heat and stir in the rice. Meanwhile, beat the eggs, sugar and salt in a large ovenproof bowl or baking dish. Slowly stir in the milk mixture and rice. Place the bowl in a large roasting pan. Pour in enough boiling water to come half way up the sides of the pan. Bake, stirring occasionally, for 15 minutes. Then continue baking for 15–25 minutes longer, until a knife inserted in the centre comes out clean. Sprinkle the cinnamon on top. Serve warm or cold. *Serves 4–6.*

Chocolate-almond cake

The chocolate-almond cake is very rich, so small pieces please... that way your guests can come back for seconds.

Butter
2–3 tablespoons cocoa powder
140g dark chocolate, chopped
1 teaspoon instant coffee powder
50ml water
5 large eggs, separated
340g caster sugar
125g butter, diced
55g dried breadcrumbs
225g finely ground almonds
¼ teaspoon cream of tartar
450ml double or whipping cream
30g icing sugar
Whole almonds, to decorate

TONY'S TIP:
dessert wines
With dessert, a sweet wine is obligatory. Choose from *passito di Pantelleria*, a still wine, *Asti Spumante*, a bubbly, as the name implies, or *aleatico*, a sweet red wine.

Preheat the oven to 170°C, gas mark 3. Butter a 23cm round springform cake tin and dust the bottom and side with sifted cocoa powder, tipping out the excess. Combine the chocolate, coffee powder and water in a double boiler over medium heat. Simmer, stirring, until the chocolate melts, about 5 minutes; set aside.

In a large bowl, combine the egg yolks, sugar and butter and beat together until fluffy. Beat in the chocolate mixture, breadcrumbs and ground almonds. Clean the beaters thoroughly. In another large bowl, with the mixer at high speed, beat the egg whites with the cream of tartar until stiff peaks form; set aside. Using a large metal spoon or rubber spatula, beat about 2 tablespoons of the egg whites into the cake mix to lighten it, then fold in the remainder—do not overmix. Spoon into the cake tin and smooth the top. Bake for 1–1¼ hours, until the middle of the cake feels firm and springs back when touched. Leave to cool completely in the pan on a wire rack.

In a large bowl, beat the cream with the icing sugar until stiff peaks form. Remove the cake from the pan and sift some icing sugar over. Decorate with the almonds and serve with the whipped cream. *Serves 6–8.*

Nada's cheesecake

We have many, many cheesecake recipes in our family. Uncle Ted, Carol and Gina all make wonderful cakes. But space was limited, so after much deliberation, I decided to go with my friend Nada's recipe. She shares my passion for cooking and for seeking out delectable dishes.

> 50g butter
> 15 digestive biscuits, finely crushed
> 675g cream cheese, at room temperature
> 4 medium eggs, separated
> 225g caster sugar
> 1 teaspoon vanilla extract
> 450ml soured cream

Preheat the oven to 180°C, gas mark 4. Melt the butter in a small, heavy-bottomed saucepan over medium heat. Add the biscuit crumbs and stir until blended. Press the crumbs over the bottom of a 23cm round springform tin; set aside.

Combine the cream cheese, egg yolks, 170g sugar and the vanilla in a bowl and beat until blended. In a separate bowl, beat the egg whites until stiff. Fold the egg whites into the cheese mixture. Pour the mixture into the tin and smooth the top. Bake for 45 minutes. Meanwhile, combine the soured cream and remaining sugar in a bowl and stir until blended. Pour on top of the cheesecake, smooth the top. Increase the oven temperature to 230°C, gas mark 8. Return the cheesecake to the oven and continue baking for 5 minutes longer. Leave to cool completely on a wire rack, then cover and chill at least 6 hours. *Serves 6–8.*

Note Try the cheesecake freshly made at room temperature. It is lighter than when chilled.

TONY'S TIP:
crushing biscuits
Place the biscuits in a plastic food storage bag, seal the end, place on a flat surface and roll a rolling pin back and forth until the crumbs are the desired size.

Plum tart

FOR THE PASTRY

250g plain flour

½ teaspoon salt

3 tablespoons sugar

150g unsalted butter, chilled

2 egg yolks, beaten

5 tablespoons ice-cold water

FOR THE FILLING

100g unsalted butter, at room temperature

225g caster sugar

115g finely ground blanched almonds

1 tablespoon all-purpose flour

1 egg, beaten

1 teaspoon almond extract

3 tablespoons dark rum

12 ripe but firm plums, quartered and stoned

2 tablespoons fresh lemon juice

Zest of 1 lemon

FOR THE GLAZE

140g apricot jam

50ml Grand Marnier

Sift together the flour, salt and sugar. Rub the butter into this mixture. In a small bowl, combine the egg yolks and water, then mix into the flour mixture, a tablespoon at a time. Mix until the dough begins to come together. Turn out onto a floured board and knead until smooth. Roll into a ball, cover with clingfilm, and refrigerate for at least 20 minutes. Roll out into a circle about 3mm thick and use to line a 25cm flan tin. Trim the edges, and refrigerate for 20 minutes.

Preheat the oven to 200°C, gas mark 6. Cream the butter and half the sugar until light and fluffy. Mix in the almonds, flour, egg, almond extract and rum. Spread the mixture over the pastry case. Arrange the plums vertically in the case in concentric circles. Sprinkle with the lemon juice, zest and remaining sugar. Bake for 45 minutes, until the filling is set and the pastry is golden. Leave to cool.

In a small saucepan, heat the apricot jam and Grand Marnier until runny. Brush the top of the tart with this glaze. Let the tart stand 2 hours before serving. *Serves 6.*

"My mother, Grandma Casillo, with my younger brother and me in the garden of the villa in Tavarnuzze. We were surrounded by olive trees and vineyards, the Chianti region being immediately south of us. Scattered all around were fruit orchards where, in the summer, the trees groaned with peaches, apricots, cherries and plums."

TONY'S TIP:
successful pastry
The golden rule is to keep everything cold—cold butter, cold eggs and ice-cold water. And work the dough as little as possible with warm hands.

CAKES

TONY'S TIP:
freezing
The great thing about this yellow cake recipe is that it makes two. One cake easily serves four people. So the second cake can be frozen for use at another time for a different recipe. Place each layer in a plastic freezer bag or wrap in clingfilm. Defrost at room temperature for about an hour before using.

Yellow cake

When we were children, mother would hoard eggs for weeks prior to a special occasion to make her cakes. Whether there were enough depended not on the supermarket but whether the hens were laying. The really special treat was a fluffy golden cake redolent of vanilla.

150g butter, plus extra for greasing
225g plain flour, plus extra for dusting
225g caster sugar
2 large eggs
1 tablespoon baking powder
½ teaspoon salt
225ml milk
1 teaspoon vanilla extract
Basic Cream Filling or Custard Filling (page 232)
Basic Icing or Chocolate Icing (page 232)

Preheat the oven to 170°C, gas mark 3. Grease two 20cm cake tins and dust with flour. In a large bowl, beat the butter and sugar with an electric mixer at high speed until light and fluffy, about 10 minutes. Beat in the eggs one at a time. Sift together the flour, baking powder and salt and beat into the butter and sugar, a little at a time, alternating with the milk and vanilla. Beat until smooth. Pour into the cake tins. Bake for 30 minutes, or until a skewer inserted in the middle comes out clean. Cool on wire racks for 10 minutes. Remove the cakes from the tins and continue cooling on the wire racks.

While the cakes cool, prepare the filling and icing. When the cakes are cool, slice the cakes horizontally in half to make four layers. On a serving plate, place one cake layer, and spread a third of the filling on top. Cover with another cake layer and repeat until all the cake and filling are used, finishing with a layer of cake. Cover the top and sides with icing. *Serves 12.*

YELLOW CAKE VARIATIONS

Upside-Down Fruit Cake (*Crostata di frutta*) Preheat the oven to 170°C, gas mark 3. Place 50g butter and 150g brown sugar in a 23x33cm cake tin. Over medium heat on the hob, stir until the sugar starts to melt. Remove from the heat. Arrange 225g sliced fruit, such as apples, pineapple, pears, rhubarb or plums in the pan. Top with the **Yellow Cake** mix. Bake for 30 minutes or until a skewer inserted in the middle of the cake comes out clean. Let cool in the tin for 10 minutes, then invert onto a serving dish.

Chocolate Cake (*Torta alla panna di cioccolata*) Prepare the cake and, when cool, fill with **Chocolate Cream Filling** (page 232). Pour **Chocolate Icing** (page 232) over the top of the cake and let it drip evenly down the sides. Decorate the cake with six fresh pansy flowers.

Almond Cake (*Torta alle mandorle*) Prepare the cake, and when cool, fill with **Vanilla Cream Filling** (page 232). Frost with **Almond Icing** (page 232). Toast 55g sliced almonds and sprinkle over the top.

Strawberry Cake (*Torta alle fragole*) Prepare the cake and **Vanilla Cream Filling** (page 232). Hull and slice 450g fresh strawberries, reserving six whole ones to decorate. On a serving dish, place one cake layer and spread a quarter of the filling on top. Arrange a quarter of the sliced strawberries over the filling. Cover with another layer of cake and repeat, until all the cake layers, filling, and sliced strawberries are used, ending with a layer of cream. Decorate with the reserved whole strawberries.

Orange Cake (*Torta d'aranci*) Prepare the cake and fill with **Vanilla Cream Filling** (page 232), sprinkling each cake layer with 1 tablespoon Grand Marnier before spreading on the filling. Ice with **Orange Icing** (page 232).

"One of my party pieces in 1960 was Upside-Down Fruit Cake. Here my sister, Adriana, is helping out."

TONY'S TIP:
unmoulding cake
If you have trouble unmoulding the **Upside-Down Fruit Cake**, do this: Remove the cake to a wire rack and let cool for 5 minutes. Run a knife blade between the pan and the cake all around the circumference. Place a serving dish upside down over the cake. Wearing mitts, invert the cake and plate, and lift off the pan.

"These filling and icing recipes make enough to fill and ice four layers of Yellow Cake. The basic cream filling and basic icing lend themselves to many more variations. Be creative and change the flavouring—try coffee or lemon."

Basic cream filling

450ml double or whipping cream

Icing sugar to taste, about 60g

Using an electric mixer, whip the cream, adding the sugar, a spoonful at a time, until fluffy.

VARIATIONS

Vanilla Cream Filling Combine the cream with 1 teaspoon vanilla extract before whipping.

Chocolate Cream Filling Add 1 tablespoon cocoa powder to the sugar before whipping.

Custard filling

450ml double cream

6 egg yolks

55g light brown sugar

2 tablespoons cornstarch

½ teaspoon vanilla extract

In a medium, heavy-bottomed saucepan over medium heat, heat the cream until it simmers; remove from the heat. In a bowl, beat the egg yolks with the sugar and cornstarch until fluffy. Slowly add the egg mixture to the cream, stir in the vanilla, and return the mixture to simmering, stirring until the custard thickens, about 10 minutes. Cool to room temperature, cover with clingfilm, and refrigerate until needed.

Basic icing

50g butter, at room temperature

250g icing sugar

⅛ teaspoon salt

2 tablespoons double cream, or more as needed

With an electric mixer on high speed, cream the butter. Gradually add half the sugar and the salt. Add the remaining sugar a little at a time, alternating with the cream.

VARIATIONS

Almond Icing Finally beat in 1 teaspoon almond extract. If the icing is too thick to spread, add a little more cream until you get the desired consistency.

Orange Icing Beat in 2 tablespoons orange juice, or more as needed, and 1 teaspoon of finely grated orange zest. If the icing is too thick to spread, add a little more juice until you get the desired consistency.

Chocolate icing

225g dark chocolate

225ml double cream

In a double boiler over medium heat or in a bowl set over a saucepan of simmering water, heat the chocolate and cream slowly. Stir the mixture until amalgamated. Cool slightly before spreading. If the icing is too liquid, cool some more by immersing in iced water.

Aunt Mary's whisky cake

FOR THE CHIFFON CAKE

250g plain flour, sifted

340g caster sugar

1 tablespoon baking powder

1 teaspoon salt

100ml sunflower oil

5 large egg yolks, beaten

150ml cold water

2 teaspoons vanilla extract

225ml egg whites (7–8 egg whites)

½ teaspoon cream of tartar

FOR THE FILLING AND GARNISHING

Custard filling (page 232)

225ml whisky

115g finely chopped walnuts

Preheat the oven to 170°C, gas mark 3. Stir the flour, sugar, baking powder and salt together in a large bowl. Make a well in the middle and add the oil, egg yolks, water and vanilla. Using a wooden spoon, beat the liquids into the dry ingredients until the mixture is smooth. In another large bowl, beat the egg whites with the cream of tartar until stiff peaks form. Using a large rubber spatula, gently fold the mixture into the egg whites until incorporated; do not stir. Pour the batter into an ungreased 25cm (4 litre) tube pan, at least 10cm deep. Bake for 55 minutes. Increase the temperature to 180°C, gas mark 4, and continue baking until the top of the cake springs back when lightly pressed, 10–15 minutes longer. Invert the pan onto a wire rack and leave the cake to cool completely in the pan. Run a metal spatula between the cake and pan, then lift off the pan. Meanwhile, prepare the custard filling.

Slice the chiffon cake into flat "bricks" about 2.5cm thick, not wedges, and remove any unsightly brown crust. On a round cake plate, arrange the first layer of cake slices close together to form a circle, about 30cm in diameter. Sprinkle with whisky and spoon on enough custard filing just to cover, spreading it evenly. For the next layer, overlap the cake slices of the previous layer, as bricks are laid. Continue until all the cake, custard filling and whisky are used up, finishing with custard filling on the top and the sides. Sprinkle the nuts on the top and sides. Refrigerate for at least 6 hours. *Serves 8.*

"Aunt Mary with Uncle Sam. Her cake is legendary in our family and was made for all special occasions. The combination of cake, custard, and a spirit is, for me, the quintessential Italian sweet."

TONY'S TIP:
laying bricks

Don't cut the cake into wedges or you will have a hard time stacking them. What you need are bricks, so that the cake can be built like a bricklayer builds a wall. The key, of course, is to build your cake by overlapping the bricks, so that you don't end up with a straight line of "mortar" or filling.

ITALIAN FAVOURITES

Many desserts are made only for specific occasions. Usually, they involve quite a lot of preparation so you wouldn't want to make them frequently. Panforte is one of the exceptions.

Fruit and spice cake
Panforte di Siena

Panforte di Siena *(strong bread of Siena) can be bought in Italian delicatessens, where it is sold in distinctive octagonal boxes; but panforte is also easy to make at home.*

2–3 sheets rice paper

200g blanched almonds, toasted

115g hazelnuts, toasted

75g plain flour

3 heaped tablespoons cocoa powder

1¼ teaspoons ground cinnamon

½ teaspoon ground allspice

85g candied orange peel, finely chopped

85g candied fruit (citron, cherries or similar),
   finely chopped

75g granulated sugar

100ml honey

1 teaspoon icing sugar

Preheat the oven to 180°C, gas mark 4, and line the bottom and sides of a round 20cm cake tin with the rice paper. Combine the nuts, flour, cocoa powder, cinnamon, the allspice and the candied peel and fruit in a large bowl and stir together; set aside. Dissolve the granulated sugar in the honey, stirring, in a small, heavy-bottomed saucepan over medium heat, about 10 minutes. Remove from the heat and stir into the flour mixture, until well blended.

Spoon the mixture into the cake tin: It should be about 1cm thick. Bake for 30 minutes. Remove from the oven and leave to cool completely, then turn out of the pan. Just before serving, sift the icing sugar over. *Serves 6.*

TONY'S TIP:
buying rice paper
Rice paper is an edible, translucent paper made from a dough of water combined with the pith of a Chinese shrub. Sometimes rice flour is used instead. Rice paper is often used as a base for delicate sweet confections. After baking, the confections are removed from the sheets and the flavourless paper, which sticks to the confection, can be eaten along with it. Rice paper can be bought in Asian food shops and some supermarkets. The paper is available from small to large, and can be round or square.

Christmas ring

Struffoli di Natale

CANDIED PEEL

Candied peel of lemon, orange, and citron is a quintessential ingredient of Italian desserts. Apart from *struffoli*, it is also used in Sicilian cassata and Neapolitan *pastiera*. It can be bought in whole pieces, which make attractive displays, or ready cubed, which saves time.

"*Struffoli* is a traditional southern Italian dessert, but it still surprised us when we discovered that the Casillo, Andeloro and Simone families all made it without having previously consulted with each other!"

FOR THE PASTRY
225g plain flour
Freshly grated zest of ½ lemon
Freshly grated zest of ½ orange
Dash salt
5 large eggs, beaten
25g butter, at room temperature

Sunflower oil, for frying
Hundreds and thousands, to decorate

FOR THE GLAZE
75ml honey
2 tablespoons sugar
2 tablespoons water
175g chopped candied fruit peel

Stir the flour, zests and salt together in a large bowl. Make a well in the middle, add the eggs and butter and use your hands to mix everything together . Knead thoroughly until a smooth, pliable dough forms. Cover and set aside to rest 1 hour. Roll out the dough on a lightly floured surface until about 1cm thick. Cut into 1cm strips, then cut each strip into 5mm pieces, to make a whole lot of 10x5mm "pillows."

Heat 1cm oil in a deep frying pan over medium heat until it reaches 180°C, gas mark 4, or until a 1cm cube of bread browns in 30 seconds. Working in batches to avoid overcrowding the pan, add the dough pillows and fry, stirring occasionally, until golden, about 6 minutes. Drain well on paper towels. Continue until all the dough is fried.

Meanwhile, make the glaze. Melt the honey, sugar and water in a heavy-bottomed saucepan large enough to hold all the pastries over medium heat, until the sugar dissolves. Turn off the heat and stir in the pastries and candied peel until all the pieces are coated. Pour the mixture onto a serving dish. Wet your hands and shape the mixture into a ring. Sprinkle with hundreds and thousands to decorate. Cut into serving slices as you would a cake, except make the pieces smaller, because this is a rich dessert. *Serves 6–8.*

St. Joseph's Day doughnuts
Zeppole di San Giuseppe

Certain foods are traditionally associated with feasts. Doughnuts are for St. Joseph's day. But if you go to my native town, San Giuseppe Vesuviano, to the bar across the street from the church in the main square, the chances are they will sell you these doughnuts all year-round—maybe even filled with custard and with a cherry on top. For me, the remembrance is of my aunt beating in the eggs with a wooden spoon in the second stage of preparation. She did this one egg at a time, but in this recipe I've made that step easier for you.

450g plain flour, plus extra for dusting

115g caster sugar

1 sachet (7g) fast action dried yeast

Pinch salt

325ml milk, heated to 50–55°C

2 large eggs

35g butter, melted

Freshly grated zest of 1 lemon

Sunflower oil, for frying

Icing sugar

Sift the flour, sugar, yeast, and salt into a large bowl and make a well in the middle. Gradually add the milk, stirring until a dough forms. Knead the dough on a lightly floured surface until smooth, about 10 minutes. Return it to the bowl, cover with clingfilm, and leave until double in size, which can take up to 2 hours, depending on the room temperature.

In a bowl, beat the eggs, butter and lemon zest. Knock back the risen dough and gradually beat the egg mixture into it. Knead the dough until it becomes soft and homogenous. Roll out the dough on a floured surface to a 1cm thickness. Cut into rounds with a cutter (a glass will do), 5–7cm inches in diameter. Place on a floured surface, cover, and let rise again. Naturally you can knead all the offcuts together to make more rounds.

Heat 5cm oil in a frying pan until hot but not smoking. Fry the doughnuts a few at a time until golden and puffed up, about 5 minutes. Turn over and do the other side. Drain on paper towels. Dust with icing sugar and serve. *Makes about 24.*

"My aunts, Nina and Antonietta, were indefatigable day-trippers. With them, I would visit monasteries and churches and not indiscriminately. There were visits set for a saint's festival day as well as set rituals to be followed, like making *struffoli* at Christmas and *zeppole* on the feast of San Giuseppe."

Neapolitan ricotta pie

Pastiera

Pastiera is made in Naples on festive occasions and particularly at Easter. It constitutes a labour of love as you need to start the day before. Aside from that, it really doesn't take much more time than any other pie. This recipe makes a large pie that can be refrigerated for several days.

200g wheat grain
450ml milk
½ teaspoon salt
200g icing sugar, plus extra for dusting
1 teaspoon ground cinnamon
2 lemons
450g ricotta cheese, drained
5 eggs, separated, plus 1 extra yolk
2 tablespoons orange-flower water
115g finely chopped candied peel
115g finely chopped candied fruit

SWEET PASTRY
170g all-purpose flour
150g caster sugar
125g butter, chilled
3 egg yolks

Two days before you plan to bake, combine, in a bowl, the wheat grain with water to cover, and leave to soak, changing the water once. Meanwhile, to make the sweet pastry dough, mix the flour and sugar together in a large bowl and make a well in the middle. Add the butter and egg yolks and use your fingers to work in the flour until a smooth dough forms—do not overwork. Lightly shape the dough into a ball, wrap in clingfilm, and chill until you are ready to use it.

Drain the wheat berries and combine them with the milk, salt, 1 tablespoon icing sugar and ½ teaspoon of the cinnamon in a large, heavy-bottomed saucepan over low heat. Using a swivel-bladed vegetable peeler, pare the zest from one lemon and add to the saucepan. Cover and simmer until the milk is absorbed, about 25 minutes. Remove the lemon peel and discard. Meanwhile, preheat the oven to 180°C, gas mark 4, and grease a 25cm springform cake tin. Put the cheese in another bowl and beat until smooth. Beat in the remaining

TONY'S TIP:
substitute barley
This tart can also be made with pearl barley instead of the wheat grain. The barley only has to be soaked overnight, not two days before like the wheat.

icing sugar and add the egg yolks, one by one. Grate in the zest from the remaining lemon, then stir in the orange-flower water, candied peel and fruit, the remaining cinnamon and the grain mixture. In a large bowl, beat the egg whites until stiff peaks form. Using a large metal spoon or metal spatula, beat 2 tablespoons egg whites into the grain mixture to lighten, then fold in the remainder.

Remove about one-fifth of the pastry dough; set aside. With a lightly floured rolling pin, roll out the remaining pastry on a lightly floured surface until 3mm thick. Line the bottom and side of the cake tin, leaving the excess overhanging. Spoon in the grain mixture. Roll out the remaining pastry, until about 2mm thick. Cut into twelve 28cm strips, each 2cm wide. Arrange the strips over the top of the pie in a lattice pattern, pressing them securely to the pastry round the rim; trim the excess. Bake for 45 minutes, or until the pastry is golden. Leave to cool in the tin on a wire rack. Remove from the tin, cool and dust with icing sugar. *Serves 6*.

"Weeks before Easter, the Neapolitan grocers would start selling soaked wheat for the making of this pie. Nowadays, a pie maker can buy the grain already soaked in a can."

Cassata alla siciliana

Not to be confused with the ice cream of the same name.

Yellow Cake (page 230)
Almond Icing (page 232)
675g ricotta cheese, drained

400g caster sugar

1 tablespoon water

450g candied fruit, chopped, plus a few extra
   pieces for decoration

140g dark chocolate, shaved

25g pine nuts, toasted

½ teaspoon ground cinnamon

50ml maraschino liqueur

Prepare the yellow cake, but bake it in one 33cm tin. Prepare the almond icing. Put the ricotta cheese in a large bowl and beat until smooth; set aside. Dissolve the sugar in the water, stirring, in a medium saucepan over high heat. Bring to a boil, without stirring, and continue boiling until the syrup just begins to take on a golden colour, about 10 minutes. Immediately beat the syrup into the ricotta and continue beating 10 minutes. Stir in the candied fruit, chocolate, pine nuts and cinnamon. Place a layer of cake on a cake plate, sprinkle with half the maraschino liqueur and spread with all the ricotta mixture. Top with the remaining cake layer and sprinkle with the remaining liqueur. Spread the icing over the top and side. Decorate the top with extra pieces of candied fruit. Let the cake rest for at least 3 hours before serving. *Serves 6.*

TONY'S TIP:
cutting the cake

The trick to cutting a large cake is to cut a circle inside the large cake before cutting wedges. This means you don't end up with enormous slices.

"Cassata is a cake that was always reserved for special occasions, such as here at my parents' wedding anniversary celebration. The cake was usually bought from a *pasticcierìe* that only made it in the cold winter months."

Grandma Simone's honey buns

I never start off to make honey buns from scratch. They usually get made from dough left over from pizza (page 92) or bread making.

1 sachet (7g) easy blend dried yeast

225ml warm water (40–45°C)

400g plain flour

1 teaspoon salt

2 tablespoons olive oil

1 teaspoon granulated sugar

225g butter, at room temperature

340g brown sugar

1 tablespoon ground cinammon

225ml honey

Stir the yeast into the water and set aside until foamy, about 10 minutes. Meanwhile, stir 225g flour, the salt and the granulated sugar together in a large bowl and make a well in the middle. Add the olive oil and the yeast mixture to the well and stir to mix the flour into the liquid. Gradually work in the rest of the flour until a smooth dough forms.

Turn the dough onto a lightly floured surface and knead until the dough is smooth and elastic. Place the dough in a greased bowl. Cover tightly with a towel and let stand in a warm, draft-free place until it doubles in bulk, which can take 45 minutes to several hours, depending on how warm the room is. Knock back the dough and knead lightly for about 30 seconds. Form the dough into two balls and roll each one out into a 20x30cm rectangle, about 3mm thick. Spread thinly with half the butter and sprinkle with the brown sugar and the cinnamon. Roll up into a long cylinder and cut into 2.5cm lengths.

Grease two 12.5x23cm loaf tins with butter and pour half the honey in each. Melt the remaining butter and dip each roll in it, then place them flat in the tins. Cover and let rise for 30 minutes. Heat the oven to 190°C, gas mark 5, and bake the buns until golden, about 30 minutes. Let cool and remove from pan. *Makes 24.*

HONEY
Honey was the universal sweetener prior to the arrival of granulated sugar. The flavour of honey is affected by heating— so if you are going to cook with it, you don't need to buy the most expensive honey.

TONY'S TIP:
sweet rolls
If you fancy something more interesting, roll out the dough as for the honey buns. Along with the butter, sugar and cinnamon, add one or two of the following: candied fruit peel, walnuts, hazelnuts, almonds, pecans or dates.

Chocolate chip cookies

My daugther Gina makes the best chocolate chip cookies in the whole wide world. I have often asked her to change her career. She could bake cookies, I would bag them, and we would sell them as "Mamma Gina's Chocolate Chip Cookies." I am sure she could retire rich inside of a year.

225g butter, at room temperature
175g firmly packed light brown sugar
175g granulated sugar
2 large eggs, beaten
280g plain flour, sifted
1 teaspoon bicarbonate of soda
¾ teaspoon salt
1 teaspoon vanilla extract
175g dark chocolate chips, or 175g dark chocolate, chopped
225g walnut halves, coarsely chopped

Preheat the oven to 180°C, gas mark 4. Beat the butter in a large bowl until creamy, then beat in the brown and granulated sugars until light and fluffy. Beat in the eggs one at a time and continue beating until incorporated. In another large bowl, combine the flour, bicarbonate, and salt together. Slowly stir the dry ingredients into the egg mixture and add the vanilla, beating until a soft dough forms. Stir in the chocolate and nuts. Drop tablespoonfuls onto the baking sheet, about 7.5cm apart. Bake 10–12 minutes, or until golden brown. Cool on the baking sheet for 1 minute. Transfer the cookies to wire racks to cool completely. These will keep for a week in an airtight container, or you may freeze them. *Makes about 48 cookies.*

TONY'S TIP:
baking sheets
None of these biscuits require that the baking sheet be greased. Mrs. Taylor, a friend who was a whiz at baking biscuits, used to say that it was a poor biscuit that didn't grease its own baking sheet.

Cara Lu's hazelnut crescents

Cara Lu, my friend for more than 20 years, introduced me to southern cooking. These biscuits are utterly delightful with tea or coffee. They also freeze well; just defrost at room temperature for an hour before dusting them with sugar. Make these small, so they are just bite-size.

225g unsalted butter, at room temperature

225g caster sugar

225g plain flour, sifted

225g shelled and skinned hazelnuts, finely ground

2 teaspoons vanilla extract

¼ teaspoon salt

125g sifted icing sugar

Preheat the oven to 180°C, gas mark 4. Beat the butter in a large bowl until creamy, then beat in the sugar until light and fluffy. Gradually beat in the flour, hazelnuts, vanilla and salt until blended and a soft dough forms. Lightly flour your hands and break off about a teaspoon of dough. Roll the dough between your hands until it is a "sausage" of about 2.5x1cm. Shape into a crescent, tapering it off at the ends, and place on a baking sheet. Repeat until all the dough is used, placing the crescents about 4cm apart.

Bake until golden, about 20 minutes. Cool on the baking sheet for 5 minutes. Meanwhile, place the icing sugar in a small bowl. Remove the crescents from the baking sheet, dredging them in the bowl of sugar to coat well. Transfer them to wire racks to cool completely. These will keep for a week in an airtight container, or you may freeze them. *Makes about 48 biscuits.*

VANILLA SUGAR
If you are lucky enough to live near an Italian grocery store, look for little paper envelopes labeled *zucchero velato vanigliato*. This is vanilla-flavoured icing sugar, which can be used instead of ordinary icing sugar.

Almond biscotti

Cantuccini di Prato

In the city of Prato, not far from Florence, I am told there is a shop that sells only cantuccini *and* vino santo*, and has done so for decades. The shop is tiny and the lines stretch outside on the pavement. As far as I know, the secret recipe has not gone outside the family, but you will find many attempts in cooking literature. This is as close as I have gotten to it.*

3 large eggs, plus 2 extra yolks, beaten

225g plain flour

175g caster sugar

140g unblanched almonds, roughly chopped and toasted

2 teaspoons baking powder

Freshly grated zest of 1 orange

Preheat the oven to 190°C, gas mark 5, and grease two baking sheets. Put 2 tablespoons of the beaten eggs in a separate bowl; set aside. Combine the flour, sugar, almonds, baking powder and orange zest in a large bowl and stir together. Make a well in the middle and stir in the eggs, stirring until a dough forms. Shape into a ball.

Roll the dough into two logs, about 5cm wide and 2.5cm high, and place them on the baking sheet, 7.5cm apart. Brush the tops with the reserved egg.

Bake for 25 minutes, until the middle is baked though. Remove the logs from the oven and increase the temperature to 200°C, gas mark 6. Cut the logs diagonally into 1cm slices. Return to the baking sheets, cut sides up, and bake until golden, about 15 minutes. Cool and transfer to wire racks to cool completely. Serve with a glass of *vino santo* for dipping. *Makes about 40.*

TONY'S TIP:
freezing biscotti

Freeze the biscotti after the first baking, and then complete the second baking just before serving. Your friends will be impressed with warm biscotti and will be rewarded with rich baking aromas.

Pecan biscuits

Yummy and rich…. Make these small so you can pop them into your mouth at one go since they are crumbly.

48 shelled pecan halves
225g butter, at room temperature
125g icing sugar, sifted, plus extra for dusting
1 teaspoon vanilla extract
225g plain flour, sifted

Preheat the oven to 180°C, gas mark 4. Finely chop one-quarter of the nuts; set aside. Beat the butter in a large bowl until creamy. Beat in the icing sugar and vanilla until light and fluffy. Add the chopped nuts and stir in the flour until blended and a soft dough forms. Break off about a teaspoon of dough. Roll the dough into a ball and place on a baking sheet. Continue until all the dough is used, placing the dough balls about 2.5cm apart. Press a pecan half into each dough ball. Bake for about 10 minutes, until light golden brown. Cool on the baking sheet for a minute. Transfer the biscuits to wire racks to cool completely. Sift with icing sugar just before serving. *Makes about 48 biscuits.*

Aunt Bessie's biscuits

85g desiccated coconut
25g butter, softened
225g caster sugar
2 eggs, beaten
350g chopped pitted dates
225g chopped walnuts
50g rice crispies

Place the coconut on a sheet of greaseproof paper; set aside. Combine the butter and sugar in bowl and beat until creamy. Stir in the eggs and dates until blended. Transfer to a saucepan and heat over low heat. Simmer, stirring constantly, until the dates dissolve, about 10 minutes. Remove the saucepan from the heat and stir in the nuts and cereal. When cool enough to handle, but still warm, shape the mixture into little sausages about 2.5cm long and 1cm in diameter. Roll the sausages in the coconut. These will keep for 2 weeks in an airtight container. *Makes about 36 biscuits.*

Stir and drop cookies

2 large eggs
125ml sunflower oil, plus extra for finishing
2 teaspoons vanilla extract
1 teaspoon freshly grated lemon zest
175g caster sugar, plus extra for finishing
225g plain flour
2 teaspoons baking powder
½ teaspoon salt

Preheat the oven to 200°C, gas mark 6. Beat the eggs in a large bowl with a fork until broken up. Stir in the oil, vanilla and lemon zest. Add the sugar and beat until the sugar dissolves and the mixture is thick. In a separate bowl, sift together the flour, baking powder and salt. Add the dry ingredients to the egg mixture and beat until a soft dough forms.

Drop teaspoonfuls of the dough onto the baking sheets, about 5cm apart. Pour about 2 tablespoons sunflower oil into one bowl and some extra sugar in another bowl. Dip the base of a 5cm wide glass in the oil, and then in the sugar bowl, then press it down on each mound of dough to flatten. Wipe the glass clean occasionally. Bake for 8–10 minutes, until the cookies are just golden on the edges. Transfer the cookies immediately to wire racks to cool completely. These will keep for a week in an airtight container, or you can freeze them. *Makes about 48 cookies.*

"A very old friend of the family, Sue Packer, would make these stir and drop cookies and bring them to my wife, Carol, and her brothers when they were children. No wonder they always looked forward to Sue's visits."

Rum balls

225g finely chopped walnuts

250g icing sugar

100g finely crushed vanilla wafers or all-butter biscuits

2 tablespoons cocoa powder

50ml white rum

2 tablespoons light corn syrup or golden syrup

TONY'S TIP:
teetotaller's option
If you'd like to make the rum balls and truffles without the alcohol, simply replace the rum with 3 tablespoons cream and 1 teaspoon rum extract.

Place 55g nuts and 55g icing sugar in separate small bowls; set aside. Combine the remaining nuts and icing sugar, wafers or biscuits, and cocoa powder in a large bowl and stir together. Stir in the rum and corn or golden syrup, stirring until blended. Using your hands, shape the dough into about fifty 1cm balls.

Roll half the balls in the reserved icing sugar and the other half in the reserved nuts. These balls should be stored in an airtight container for at least 3 days before serving. *Makes about 50 rum balls.*

Madam Lillaz's truffles

Gina's French teacher, Madame Lillaz, introduced the whole class to truffles. In turn, we have introduced truffles to all of our friends.

100g butter, chopped

250g dark chocolate

2 large egg yolks

95g icing sugar, sifted

50ml white rum

75ml double cream

3 tablespoons cocoa powder

TONY'S TIP:
storing truffles
These truffles can be kept for several weeks in the refrigerator. Or you can freeze them in an airtight container for up to 2 months. Remove the truffles from the freezer 5 minutes before serving.

Melt the butter and chocolate in a large, heavy-bottomed saucepan over low heat, stirring, about 5 minutes. Remove the saucepan from the heat and set aside to cool. Beat the egg yolks with the sugar in a large bowl until pale, about 5 minutes. Beat in the chocolate mixture, then stir in the rum and the cream. Cover with clingfilm and chill overnight. The next day, place the cocoa powder on a plate. Using your hands, roll the mixture into balls the size of small walnuts. Roll in the cocoa powder. Return to the refrigerator at least 8 hours and up to 5 days until you are ready to serve. *Makes about 30 truffles.*

COFFEE

There's nothing quite as satisfying as finishing a meal with a freshly brewed cup of coffee. The best coffee is made from freshly roasted beans; however, today's packaging helps to maintain the flavour of ready-ground coffee. Once the package is opened, put it in an airtight container and keep it in the refrigerator or freezer.

The science of coffee making

If you want to master coffee making, you have to be aware, in the first place, of the variables involved. These are the pot, the water and amount of it, the water temperature, the coffee and amount of it, and the time that it is allowed to brew. If you use the same pot, the same amount of water from the same tap, and boil it, we have eliminated a few variables. Let's say that we stick to the same coffee for a while, and we trust you to fill the pot to exactly the same level each time. The only variables now left are the amount of coffee and the brewing time. Let's eliminate the time by insisting that the coffee brews 5 minutes— not a minute more, not a minute less. So really, to get the taste you like, you need only vary the amount of coffee you use.

How to make good coffee every time

Select a coffee. Measure an exact amount, brew 5 minutes, and taste. If it's too strong or too weak, next time reduce or add to the amount of coffee

used by a teaspoonful. If, at the end of the package of coffee, you are still unhappy with the results, buy a different coffee and repeat the process. When you're satisfied, you should have a repeatable process with guaranteed results, and you'll never have to apologise to your guests for the flavour.

Cafetière coffee

For cafetière coffee, use a medium or dark roast.

◆ For 2-cup size: use 4 heaped teaspoons ground coffee; for 6-cup size: use 9 heaped teaspoons. Preheat the coffeepot with hot water; drain. Add the coffee and then boiling hot water; stir. Place the top assembly on the pot. After 5 minutes, push the plunger down and serve.

Espresso coffee

The best espresso comes from a full-size professional espresso maker used in bars—the gleaming one that looks like a steam locomotive or an art deco ship's engine. Until Rita, my Neapolitan cousin, showed me her foam trick

(below), I didn't bother making espresso at home. For espresso, use only dark roast.

◆ Fill the bottom half of an Italian-made stovetop espresso maker with cold water. The level should touch, or be just below, the basket bottom when inserted (in other words, just below the safety valve). Fill the basket with ground coffee. Press the grounds down and heap on some more. Screw the coffeemaker top on tightly. Put over medium heat—you'll hear hissing, then perking. When the perking stops, the coffee is ready.

Rita's foam

◆ Put 5–6 teaspoons sugar in a cup. Stand by the coffeemaker as it heats up. When the very first few concentrated, thick drops come out of the spout, add them to the sugar—the later drops won't work. Beat this sugar and coffee mixture until a thick, rich cream results, and pour a spoonful into each cup. Add the steaming espresso and stir.

Cleaning your apparatus

Make sure you disassemble and clean all the parts of your cafetière or espresso maker. It is also best to store cafetières and espresso makers unassembled.

Caffè corretto

Somehow Italians sometimes feel that coffee on its own is not quite right, and that they have to "correct" it. It's easy to guess how they do this!

◆ Pour 1 cup black coffee, sweetened to taste, and add a measure of one of grappa, kirsch, brandy, Grand Marnier, sambuca, or any of your favourite spirits or liqueurs. Mix and serve.

Iced coffee

Perfect for those hot, sunny days...

◆ Put sweetened, cold coffee in a glass and simply add ice cubes and a sprig of mint.

◆ If you prefer iced coffee slush or *granita*, freeze the cold coffee in an ice cube tray, and process the cubes in a food processor. Serve in a tall glass with a twist of lemon.

INDEX

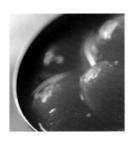

ACKNOWLEDGMENTS

Carroll and Brown Limited would like to thank the following:

Production Manager Karol Davies

Production Controller Nigel Reed

Computer Management Paul Stradling

Home Economists Lizzie Harris, Louise MacKaness

Indexer Hilary Bird

AUTHOR'S ACKNOWLEDGMENTS

I always approach acknowledgments and thanks with trepidation, afraid to forget a deserving person. In case I do forget, please forgive me.

First acknowledgments go to the dear departed who set me on the road to appreciate good food, my father, Zia Nina, Zia Antonietta, Aunt Thelma, Aunt Bessie, and Zia Maria. I am grateful to my mother, Assunta, for teaching me and my mother-in-law, Flo, for the many direct contributions and the use of the treasured photographs.

My wife, Carol, gets a big hug for sharing the passion with me and for her enormous help in testing and refining the recipes and the book. Thanks to Gina and Christina who were the *primo mobilis* for assembling this collection.

Thank you to all that directly contributed: Ted, Nada, Sue, Cara Lu, Aunt Chickie, Aunt Mary, Annette, Madame Lillaz, and Grandma Koch (wherever you are). Thanks to my sisters, Maria and Adriana, and my brothers, Al and Frank, who are all great cooks.

Thanks to Dino's, Armanda's, and the many, many restaurants that have provided inspiration and restoration.

Thank you to my friends whose encouragement and critical suggestions have pushed me along: Hassan and Cara Lu, Derrek and Jenny, Francis and Jenny.

Special thanks to Ian and Karen (and Keith) who put me in the way of Carroll and Brown, to Rachel who put the book under Amy's nose, and thanks to Amy for thinking this "quirky" book should be published.

Carla, thanks for finishing the job so many others started. Gilda, thank you for your infinite care and patience—great job! Thanks to Jules for the photography and to home economists Lizzie and Louise for their contribution. You make a great team.